THE THINGS
OUR
FATHERS SAW

VOLUME X:
OVER THE HUMP
CHINA, BURMA, INDIA

THE UNTOLD STORIES OF THE
WORLD WAR II GENERATION

Matthew A. Rozell

WOODCHUCK HOLLOW PRESS

Hartford · New York

Front Cover: Merrill's Marauders in Burma, 1944, likely U.S. Army Signal Corps, possibly photographer David Quaid. Public domain.

Back Cover: Merrill's Marauders take a rest break, somewhere in Burma. U.S. Army Special Operations, public domain.

Any additional photographs and descriptions sourced at Wikimedia Commons within terms of use, unless otherwise noted.

Publisher's Cataloging-in-Publication Data

Names: Rozell, Matthew A., 1961- author.
Title: Over the hump: China, Burma, India: the things our fathers saw : the untold stories of the World War II generation, volume X / Matthew A. Rozell.
Description: Hartford, NY : Matthew A. Rozell, 2024. | Series: The things our fathers saw, vol. 10. | Also available in audiobook format.
Identifiers: LCCN pending | ISBN 978-1-948155-52-6 (hardcover) | ISBN 978-1-948155-51-9 (paperback) | ISBN pending (ebook)
Subjects: LCSH: World War, 1939-1945--Personal narratives, American. | Civilians--United States--Biography. |
www.matthewrozellbooks.com
www.teachinghistorymatters.com
Information at matthewrozellbooks.com.

Created in the United States of America

~To the children of
The World War II Generation~

"They say the coward dies a thousand deaths, the valiant dies but once. But possibly the valiant dies a thousand deaths too, if he is cursed with imagination."

— GENERAL JOSEPH W. STILWELL

THE THINGS OUR FATHERS SAW X:

OVER THE HUMP:

CHINA, BURMA, INDIA

THE STORYTELLERS (IN ORDER OF APPEARANCE):

MORGAN VAUX

JANE HANKS

PATRICK SCARANO

NORMAN HANDELMAN

ROBERT O'BRIEN

LEONARD 'RANDY' REEVES

KENNETH W. THOMAS

SAMUEL V. WILSON

PHILIP PIAZZA

MORRIS FACTOR

HERBERT CLOFINE

ROY MATSUMOTO

ROBERT E. PASSANISI

WARNER KATZ

DAVID QUAID

KERMIT 'TONY' BUSHUR

THE THINGS OUR FATHERS SAW X:

OVER THE HUMP:

CHINA, BURMA, INDIA

TABLE OF CONTENTS

Author's Note

"All Americans, they were ready to go and ready to fight. My thing, [today], is that I would like to see them outlaw wars."

—98-year-old Russell Hamler, at a ceremony honoring him, 2022

The newspaper from New York landed on my doorstep. A long obituary graced A-9 of the Weekend *Wall Street Journal*, circulation 610,000 print and over three million digital subscribers. A slight smile, tempered with a resigned sadness, spread as I noted the headline. At least someone was paying attention.

'Last of the WWII 'Marauders' Unit Dies'

The time had finally arrived—the last Marauder had passed, signifying the end of an era, and just as I began this book that very month to remember them and the other men and women of this most forgotten arena of World War II.

"Russell Hamler was born June 24, 1924, and grew up in Mt. Lebanon, a suburb of Pittsburgh. His father, Robert Hamler, worked with teams of horses moving dirt at construction sites. Young Russell's habit of roaming the outskirts of Pittsburgh earned him the nickname of Huck, a nod to Huckleberry Finn."

"When he learned that the Army was seeking volunteers in 'a high state of physical ruggedness' for a dangerous mission in an unspecified location, he put up his hand. It was simple, he said later: 'You joined the Army to fight the war.'"

"Soon Hamler found himself among nearly 3,000 volunteers in an Army unit that became known as Merrill's Marauders, named after their leader, Brig. Gen. Frank Merrill. They fought behind Japanese lines in Burma, now known as Myanmar, in some of the most hellish conditions faced by troops during World War II."

"In February 1944, the Marauders were ordered to march into Burma, ready or not. 'It was an organization that was never given time to organize,' Charlton Ogburn Jr., a Signal Corps officer in the unit, wrote later in a memoir, The Marauders. Amid bickering among the British, Chinese and American allies over strategies, Louis Mountbatten, the top Allied commander in Southeast Asia, assigned oversight of the unit to the American Lt. Gen. Joseph 'Vinegar Joe' Stilwell."

"The hastily trained and often ragtag unit lugged packs along twisting trails over mountain passes, endured ravenous leeches and tropical diseases, chopped through bamboo thickets and won battles against highly experienced Japanese forces. The Marauders' most famous exploit was capturing the strategic Myitkyina airstrip in May 1944, an accomplishment described by Winston Churchill as 'a brilliant feat of arms.'" [1]

After the war, Russell returned home to work for Trans World Airlines in Pittsburgh, Pennsylvania. It was there, in 1968, that he met a touring Lord Louis Mountbatten at the airport, and they had the opportunity to meet and chat about the Marauders, twenty-three years after the war. Russell left us quietly at the end of December 2023 at the age of 99.

*

In the writing of this series, I have been approached by people, generally children of combatants, and sometimes in slightly indignant fashion, wanting to know 'why there is no CBI Theater' focus in my books, as if I considered these men and women who served in that arena somehow less worthy of recognition and study.

The ordinary unfortunate explanation was simply that comparatively few Americans served there, a complex and confusing pocket of activity that technically is not even classified a 'theater' of operations in the sense of, let's say, the European or Pacific Theaters. It did not have a unified combat command per se; there weren't any conventional U.S. infantry divisions slogging it out in China, Burma, or India—most of the ground fighting was done by British, Indian, and Chinese troops. Only about a percent and a half of Americans in uniform during World War II were engaged here, most in supporting roles; less than 3,000 U.S. ground troop volunteers made up legendary long-range fighting forces known as Merrill's Marauders and others, who were pushed to the brink of extinction after just five months of combat. And so, the sad fact is that the sampling of archived interviews with these veterans is comparatively small, though some interviewers working through the auspices of the Library of Congress were able to attend a Marauder reunion or two in Virginia about the time I was undertaking my oral history project with my students.

This is not to say that it has been entirely forgotten; as we have seen, with the recent passing of Merrill's Marauders Russell 'Huck' Hamler, China-Burma-India was momentarily thrust back into the spotlight. Of course, there are more authoritative tomes out there, but it was the ordinary individuals like Huck who carried out the plans of 'gods and generals' who will be the focus of this book, including the Marauders and the brave men and women carrying out harrowing mercenary and support duties and 'flying the Hump' to resupply our Chinese allies. I hope that I have done them a degree of justice.

Matthew Rozell
September 11, 2024
Washington County, NY

Merrill's Marauders take a rest break, somewhere in Burma. U.S. Army Special Operations, public domain.

Introduction

To understand the significance of the China-Burma-India area of operations during World War II, the reader has to understand that from the Allied perspective, keeping China in the war against Japanese aggression was of importance not as a priority mission but as it related to keeping Japanese forces tied down as the war in Europe was won first. Here we will venture back to the political, military, and geographic origins of the 'War in the Pacific,' beginning with the root causes of Sino-Japanese conflict. From the American perspective, it is a fascinating and complex history, the remnants of which are manifested to this day, especially as we seek to understand China's rise as a superpower in the post-World War II and 21st century landscape.

*

In 1853, when Millard Fillmore was in the White House, Commodore Matthew C. Perry steamed into Edo (now Tokyo) Bay with his seven 'Black Ships,' equipped with the latest in military firepower, and let loose with a 73-gun display of firepower and intimidation to signal that the United States was interested in opening Japanese ports to commerce and mooring stations with the West. No would not be an acceptable response, and in 1854 he returned. The Japanese acquiesced to opening six ports, with concessions of extraterritoriality, or rights for foreigners accused of a crime in Japan to be tried by their own nation's courts. After 250 years of national seclusion, Japanese leaders shrewdly decided to 'Learn from the Barbarian'—sending students abroad to acquire the latest in

Western fashion and customs, but especially in industrial and technological advances that had passed the East by as China and Japan had closed their doors to outside interference and 'corruption' to their millenniums-old cultures. Japan now saw it had to adopt these concessions to the West to survive, simply by looking at what had happened in China only a decade or so before.[1]

By the end of the eighteenth century, Imperial China, with its history of dynastic rule spanning nearly four thousand years, was having none of the similar Western demands to open its doors to barbarian outsiders. Frenzied European demand for fine silks, tea, porcelain, and other goods was met with their contempt for outside trade goods; gold and silver were the only acceptable commodities. The British East India Company found a workaround in the illegal importation of opium cultivated in their holdings in India and a ripe market as addiction took hold in some Chinese ports. The destruction of British opium by Chinese authorities in the 1830s spurred the lopsided Opium Wars and subsequent humiliating treaties in which Western military superiority forced huge indemnity payments, the rights to open ports to Western zones of interest, and extraterritorial concessions; the British also got the port of Hong Kong for the next 150 years. China descended into addiction, corruption, rebellion, and civil war that ended their dynastic system on the eve of World War I.

Japan, on the other hand, by adopting selective cultural borrowing, adapted and thrived in her stunning transformation from a feudal society to a modern industrial state. As her hunger for raw materials and 'necessary' territorial expansion grew, she looked at

---

[1] Townsend Harris (1804-1878) was appointed the first U.S. Consul General to Japan. In that capacity, he promoted U.S. interests and navigated the intrigues of Japanese court life at the end of the 'Shogun' era. I mention this because he was born a fifteen-minute walk from my high school in Hudson Falls (then Sandy Hill), New York.

her neighbor to the east—Korea, historically a tributary state of China and now one that the Chinese viewed as still a dependency of China.

By the 1880s, Japanese military leaders also came to view Korea as 'a dagger pointed at the heart of Japan'; the Russian empire also was poised just to the north by this time, coercing a lease from the Qing Chinese authorities at Port Arthur.

The First Sino-Japanese War (1894-1895) revealed the gains made by Japan over the previous twenty years' crash programs of industrialization and modernization and whetted the appetite of the Japanese for further expansion into China. Japan acquired parts of Northeast China and Taiwan at comparatively little cost with a burst of nationalistic pride and Western astonishment and mixed admiration.

Japan's 1894 victory over China. Source: Japan Punch, 1894
Public domain.

This, after all, was the golden age of imperial outreach and conquest, and the United States' interest in the Pacific region was also peaking. In 1898, the war with Spain over Cuba resulted in a sudden surge, with the annexed prizes being a host of little-known islands that would take on such tremendous name recognition as World War II in the Pacific unfolded, including the Philippine Islands, Guam, Wake Island, and Hawaii. Three-quarters of a million Filipinos died between 1898 and 1901 in the failed independence uprising that followed.[2]

Back in China, anti-foreign sentiment was coming to a head. China's loss in the First Sino-Japanese War increased the likelihood that China would be threatened with foreign partition as Britain, Italy, France, Germany, Russia, and Japan continued to advance their overseas trading and colonial interests. The United States, now with Asian interests and footholds, sought to introduce the Open Door Policy, by which all signatories would respect each other's rights to sharing markets in China. A secret anti-imperialist group, the Society of Righteous and Harmonious Fists, quasi-mystics who practiced martial arts ('Chinese boxing' to Europeans) and came to believe they were impervious to bullets, began to target Christian missionaries and their followers in North China. The movement spread to the capital, Beijing, where foreign legations were put under siege with the blessing of the elderly Qing dynasty empress dowager Cixi, who issued an imperial decree essentially declaring war on foreign influence. Eight nations, including the United States, responded with 30,000 troops to counter the rebellion and extracted more monetary concessions, revealing fully the weakness and corruptness of the old imperial regime.

Russian incursion into Manchuria in 1902 in violation of the Open Door Policy inflamed tensions, especially with Japan over conflicting spheres of influence in Korea and Manchuria, culminating in the 1904-1905 Russo-Japanese War. Japan's victory stunned and shocked the world, curbing Russia's eastern expansionist powers and encouraging Japanese militarist sentiments. Her swift surprise attack at the Russian eastern 'warm water' fleet at Port Arthur on February 9, 1904, in some ways foreshadowed her future assault on Pearl Harbor. The Russian Empire, dealing with its own nascent revolutionary uprisings and an as-yet-uncompleted Trans-Siberian Railway (troops and supplies from the west had to be unloaded and then sledged two weeks overland to be repacked and retracked to the front in the far east), ran out of time and men to stem the onslaught, contributing to the decisive Russian defeat in the Battle of Tsushima in the Sea of Japan, the first naval engagement to be fought with steel battleships and wireless technology.

"A Righteous War to Chastise the Russian Destroyer Force's Night Attack," likely the Battle of Port Arthur, Shinohara Kiyooki, 1904. Japanese block print propaganda. Public Domain.

The Treaty of Portsmouth [New Hampshire] awarded Japan her newfound spoils and netted U.S. President Teddy Roosevelt a Nobel Peace Prize, the first ever for an American recipient (even though he was not even in attendance at Portsmouth). It allowed for the Japanese colonization of Korea, culminating in the outright

Japanese annexation of Korea in 1910. The table of Japanese aggression and the reward of overseas success was being set.

China's revolutionary turmoil boiled over in the Revolution of 1911, ending the Qing dynasty and thousands of years of imperial dynastic rule. China was declared a republic in 1912 under Sun Yat-sen as the first president. The Nationalist Party Kuomintang was founded, and Dr. Sun turned over power to Yuan Shikai, who then died in 1916, after which a period of civil war between warlords once again plunged China into chaos. With the outbreak of World War I, Japan joined the Allies with the promise of acquiring German territories in Asia, landing in China's Shandong Province to attack the German settlements at Tsingtao and later their Pacific possessions in the Marianas, Carolines, and Marshall Islands.

Japan then presented the Republic of China with its Twenty-One Demands, designed to cement control over China with the intention of making it a Japanese protectorate; Japan's position was strong enough that it was awarded the Shandong Province at the Paris Peace Conference in 1919, despite U.S. misgivings at the end of the Open Door Policy and Chinese objections.

Communists and Nationalists

In 1917, the Romanov dynasty collapsed in Russia as the Bolsheviks under Lenin orchestrated the world's first Marxist revolution amidst catastrophic wartime defeats and the economic turmoil of World War I. The new 'workers' revolution' appealed to revolutionaries everywhere as a possible alternative path to power, the parliamentary path viewed by them as hopelessly corrupted by capitalist and imperialist class influences. The Communist International, or Comintern, was organized to foment the worldwide socialist revolution; only then would the true Marxist state of communism exist. In 1921, the Chinese Communist Party was founded, aligning itself with the Nationalist Party as the left wing of the Kuomintang under its emerging leadership of Mao Zedong and Zhou Enlai. Dr. Sun Yat-sen sent Chiang Kai-shek, the head of the right wing of the KMT, to Moscow to study in 1924, but Chiang returned disillusioned with the Soviet model of governing for China. When Dr. Sun died in 1925, Chiang emerged victorious in the power vacuum that ensued in the KMT. As the commander-in-chief of the National Revolutionary Army, the military arm of the KMT, in 1926 he led the Northern Campaign to put down warlord factions and solidify the Kuomintang's power and authority over China. Troubled by competing communist influences in the ranks, in 1927 Chiang turned on the CCP and began purges and massacres of communists that would end their cooperation and foment civil war until the eve of Japanese full-scale invasion ten years later; in the famous Long March of 1934-35, Mao's forces evaded Chiang's pursuit and encirclement in a 5,600-mile retreat; out of the 65,000 soldiers of the CCP's First Army, just 8,000 weary but battle-hardened troops survived, with the support of local peasantry along the way, resentful of the heavy-handed treatment by Nationalist forces and government policies. For years, the peasantry had been subjected to over forty different taxes, some levied years in advance, controlling every aspect of a miserable existence where half the population already had a life expectancy rate of just thirty years.[3] Nationalist forces responded by laying waste to entire villages and communities suspected of aiding the communists, yet the remaining communist forces emerged battle-hardened on the eve of the Second Sino-Japanese War (1937-1945) when the two armies united to confront the all-out Japanese offensives for the conquest of all China.

World War II Begins in Asia

As we have seen, the stage was set for China's World War II conflict with Japan decades before 1937. Manchuria, about the size of France and Germany combined, with its fertile land and rich coal and iron resources, was key to Japan's expansionist ambitions. Already in control of railroads in the region, in 1931 the Japanese manufactured a railroad sabotage incident in Mukden that gave the pretext for a full-scale invasion, which led to the creation of the puppet state of Manchukuo in 1932. Worldwide condemnation resulted in Japan withdrawing from the League of Nations in February 1933, which was followed in October by Nazi Germany and signaled the death knell of the concept of collective security, though it was probably doomed from the outset, as the United States never joined the League due to the Senate rejection of the Treaty of Versailles in 1919.

In July 1937, an incident at the Marco Polo Bridge outside of Beijing escalated the tensions that would begin the full-fledged war with Japan that some historians place as the true beginning of World War II (in Asia, at least). While the exact cause is unknown, it seems that the occupying Japanese forces demanded entry to search for a missing soldier; shots were exchanged and skirmishes escalated. The subsequent Battle of Shanghai lasted from August 13, 1937, to November 26, 1937, and resulted in massive destruction and the Japanese capture of the city. Chinese forces suffered over 200,000 casualties, more than twice as many as the invader, and the Japanese had no qualms about using gas attacks and instituting the commission of atrocities on a large scale, soon to be amplified in the 'Rape of Nanking' the following month, which fell on December 13. A note of horror was a beheading contest between two Japanese officers, competing to see who could behead 100 Chinese captives first; the number was upped to 150 prisoners for the subsequent round. Consensus estimates place the number of Chinese massacred at around 200,000.

Japanese Occupation of eastern and northern China, 1940. US Army, public domain.

'Vinegar Joe' Stilwell

One American became the personification of the United States' efforts to keep China engaged in World War II and its efforts in the China-Burma-India arena.

Joseph Warren 'Vinegar Joe' Stilwell was born on March 19, 1883. With deep Yankee roots, he was raised in Yonkers, New York. Young Joseph pushed back against his strict religious upbringing; though a good student, he fell in with the wrong crowd in his post-graduate studies at Yonkers High and instead of the originally planned course of college study at Yale, his father used his influence to get him accepted into the U.S. Military Academy at West Point. With an aptitude for languages and athletics, he graduated in 1904 with his commission and a lifelong pride in keeping himself in top physical condition, especially running in cross country and track, which would pay off in many ways—most notably his retreat on foot through the mountains of Burma in 1942 at the age of sixty.

Stilwell chose the Philippines for his first posting in 1904, because as a product of the recently concluded Spanish-American War, it was an area that was still actively rebellious at the time. In his early twenties, he came away with some valuable lessons in mid-tropical highland country skirmishing before being posted in 1906 to West Point as an instructor in the Department of Tactics and as a coach. Restless and feeling a bit too close to home—Yonkers was just down the Hudson—his second tour of the Philippines commenced in 1911 with his new bride in tow. He was determined to see the 'Orient' with his wife before she departed for the United States for the birth of their first child, Joe Jr. (who would in later years serve as his father's chief of staff in China). They spent time in Japan before she left, and he continued on to see China on the eve of the Revolution of 1911, marveling at a culture nearly four thousand years old boasting 400 million souls, but also confiding disgust in his journal at the extreme ignorance and poverty he encountered in a country where 70 to 80 percent of the population remained illiterate.

Stilwell returned to the United States in January 1912 just before the old Chinese regime was toppled. He rounded out his twenties and entered his thirties on duty in California and back teaching at West Point. As the Great War in Europe unfolded, Congress authorized doubling the size of the regular army and in April 1917 entered the war. This period of exponential, unprecedented growth culminated in the Selective Service Act the following month, calling for the conscription of a million more men, an army that had to be trained before taking the field, a task for which Stilwell was selected at various postings until ordered to France as a newly minted captain to the Commanding General's AEF office for intelligence duty; his command of the language was sorely needed.

After the war, he sought a distant posting and jumped when the opportunity to serve in China came up. In the interwar years, he served three tours in China, picking up the language, studying the people, and making key connections, like that of his lifelong champion, George C. Marshall, whose own posting overlapped with Stilwell's for eight months. In his third posting to China, he was the military attaché of the U.S. Legation in northern China between 1935 and 1940, where he became acquainted with Chiang Kai-shek in late 1938. In between his tours of duty in China, he also held several staff officer positions in the United States.[4] He didn't care for pomp and ceremonies and overbearing discipline of subordinates, but he was a stickler for tactics and maneuvers, dishing out criticism without reserve to those he felt were not pulling their weight in the field. One disgruntled soldier drew a caricature of his head and face emanating spectrally from a vinegar bottle; upon discovering it, a tickled Stilwell had it copied and distributed to friends and posted on the board.[5]

After the fall of France to Germany in 1940, the Japanese government ordered the British to close the Hong Kong frontier and the Burma Road, the last backchannel of supply to China from the West. The British acquiesced, not willing to risk war with Japan while in a state of war with Germany and finding no assurance of joint action with the United States, still neutral, in the event of a refusal.[6]

In September 1940, Stilwell attained the rank of major general, having been assigned to command his first division, the 7th, that

July. He loved driving the draftees and whipping them into shape, a taskmaster who often accompanied them on hikes and maneuvers, acquiring the nickname Uncle Joe or Galloping Joe in his hiking boots, sweater, and crushed hat, blending in with the 15,000 soldiers and ordinary workers at the post in California. At the ceremony put on by his staff to address the assembled soldiers to acknowledge and celebrate his promotion, he kept it brief: 'The higher a monkey climbs the pole, the more you see of his behind.'

The same month, Japan joined the Axis alliance. Shortly thereafter, President Roosevelt and his service chiefs, including George C. Marshall (sworn in as Chief of Staff of the Army on September 1, 1939) agreed in theory to follow a Germany or 'Europe First' policy in the future planning for what now looked like an inevitable eventual entry of the United States in this world war, with the prevailing notion that Europe was the seat of world power politics, whereas China should continue on the defensive, with U.S. backchannel support, buying time for the time being—which would eventually define the China-Burma-India operations in the future.[7]

*

"Roosevelt's governing idea was that China should be one of the great powers after the war to fill the vacuum left by Japan. He was not unaware of shortcomings for he once acknowledged to his son that China 'was still in the eighteenth century.' Nevertheless that great and ancient country with its 500 million enduring people, however frustrated by endless misgovernment, was a geopolitical fact. Roosevelt wanted it on America's side in the future."

-Barbara Tuchman, *Stilwell and the American Experience in China*[8]

President Roosevelt had floated to the American public a naval quarantine of aggressor nations in an October radio address. In December, the USS *Panay*, in Nanking to evacuate Americans, came under attack by Japanese aircraft. American presence in China, including business and missionary interests, had been active for decades; the president settled at the time for an official apology and indemnity settlement, though diplomats were working the back channels to get the British on board with the idea of a quarantine of Japan. As 1937 turned into 1938, Prime Minister Neville Chamberlain turned down a proposal to discuss a joint conference on the subject, formulating his appeasement policy toward Italy and Germany; why provoke the Japanese? Without support from the Royal Navy, any idea of a quarantine was doomed, so it was scuttled.[9]

The United States finally instituted an oil and scrap metal embargo on Japan in the summer of 1941. Following the September 1940 invasion by Japan of French Indochina, ostensibly to cut off Chinese access to raw materials, American supplies of rubber, one of the few precious war materials the United States could not produce on its own, were greatly endangered. By then, the war in Europe was in full swing, with Warsaw and Paris having fallen to the Germans, and ten months later, France, Norway, and the Low Countries occupied. Chiang Kai-shek sought American support through the Lend-Lease Act and began getting financial and military aid. At the invitation of Chiang, Claire Chennault arrived with the 1st American Volunteer Group, the Flying Tigers, American fighter pilots in American aircraft affixed with the Chinese flag to do battle with the Japanese in the skies over China. Three squadrons would arrive to train in Burma after April 1941.

*

On December 7, 1941, General and Mrs. Stilwell were having an open house for junior officers at their home overlooking the Pacific at Fort Ord, California, when the news arrived over the radio that Pearl Harbor had been attacked. The Japanese, underestimated once again, had struck a stinging blow over three thousand miles across the Pacific. For the next several hours and days, Stilwell rushed to bolster his Southern California coastal command, chagrined at reports of logistical bottlenecks for men and materiel to defend the territory all the way to the Mexican border that he was responsible for. Thankfully, all the panicked rumors were false.

The Japanese continued their lightning blow across the Pacific. Guam and Wake Island fell on December 23. Hong Kong surrendered on Christmas after a century of British control. Manila fell on January 2, as did the Dutch East Indies shortly after. French Indochina, controlled by the Vichy French, opened its doors, cutting off the port of Hanoi as a resupply route for China. The invaders had cut the Malay Peninsula in half and began laying siege to Singapore. Thailand was also occupied, and the Japanese had begun to make inroads into Burma.

The Pacific and CBI Theaters, 1942. U.S. Army, public domain.

The conquest of British Malaysia and her rubber plantations was complete with the fall of Singapore in mid-February 1942. Britain, with its Asian colonial empire in tatters, was immediately concerned that the fall of Burma would remove the last obstacle to a Japanese assault on British India. While the United States had little interest in defending British colonial possessions, keeping China in the war to tie down over a million Japanese troops on the mainland was critical. The Burma Road resupply route to Kunming, China, from India had to be defended and improved. Lend-Lease supplies destined for road transport into the backdoor of China were piling up on the docks at the port city of Rangoon, Burma, in the south.

*

Universally recognized by now as a top commander, Stilwell was summoned to Washington for the joint British/American Arcadia Conference just before Christmas to help formulate the war direction, which would essentially boil down to 'Europe First.' Stilwell was initially selected to plan and command the Allied invasion of North Africa. He harbored some logistical doubts, however, and events pushed the invasion back; he also was not shy in his blistering opinions and criticism of British attitudes and how its officer staff carried themselves with swagger, and consistently referred to them as 'limeys' in his journal. Marshall called him in for mild reprimand, but also to pick his brain on a military point man to work with Chiang Kai-shek in China. When their top pick did not pan out, the chief-of-staff informed him, 'Joe, you have 24 hours to think up a better candidate, otherwise it's you.' Stilwell responded, 'I'll go where I'm sent.'[10]

In February 1942 Stilwell got his third star and as lieutenant general was assigned as commander of all U.S. forces in China, Burma, and India, deputy commander of the Burma-India Theater under the British, later to be led by Vice-Admiral Louis Mountbatten, and military adviser to Chiang Kai-shek and his Chinese forces. It was a complicated balancing act that would have been difficult for a tactful commander to pull off; dealing with egos and pomp was not

Stilwell's strong suit. While Japan was the common enemy, the British and Americans had different agendas. The British primarily wanted to protect their empire, especially in India, and would be wary of strengthening China too much, lest they experience a postwar resurgence to threaten Britain's interests; the two countries already had an uneven and complicated past. The Americans would hope to keep China from being knocked out of the war and wished to use Chinese coastal fortifications as a launchpad for the eventual invasion of Japan.

Stilwell would especially resist the effort to place his U.S. soldiers under British command. His main logistical military effort would be to use Chinese and American forces to keep and improve the Burma Road, though it was clear that Rangoon would soon fall. Planners were already envisioning building the Ledo Road to the north to connect with the Burma Road to Kunming, and flying supply planes over the Himalayas, a dauntingly skilled task that would be costly in men, planes, and fuel. A land route had to be maintained.

The Ledo Road would begin in India, connect with the Burma Road to Rangoon, (when re-opened from Japanese conquest), and pivot northwest from Burma to Kunming, China. U.S. Army, public domain.

'We Got a Hell of a Beating'

Stilwell arrived in China via Cairo and India in early March to present himself to Chiang and reacquaint himself with China and her troops, sorely in need of training and discipline. On March 8, Rangoon fell to the south; it was hoped to hold the line to contain Japan's advance up the Irrawaddy. It was not to be. Stilwell was in

Burma at the former British post at Maymyo east of Mandalay, establishing his command with Chinese generals amidst poor communications and medical facilities and disease as the Japanese continued pounding Burmese towns and cities from the air as they moved northward. Monsoon season was fast approaching, which would turn any eventual withdraw to defend India a quagmire. Here he conferred with Major Frank Merrill, another West Pointer he was acquainted with, who briefed him on the situation in Burma and became a trusted adviser whom he later selected to lead the first American long-range penetration force in Burma that would become Merrill's Marauders.

Air support was then lost in another surprise Japanese bombing raid on March 22 that caught RAF and AVG (American Volunteer Group) planes on the ground. Chinese troops were slow to move on the offensive at Stilwell's commands, upset at what they perceived to be a lack of support from the British. The rail system broke down; refugees clogged the roads. Stilwell was also frustrated that Washington and London were preoccupied with the war elsewhere.

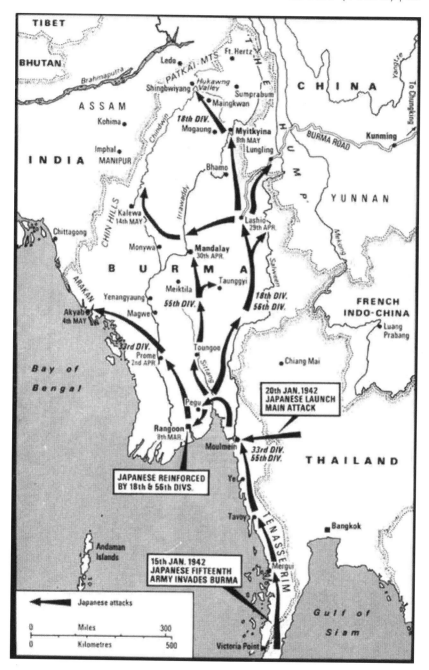

Japanese conquest of Burma, 1942. U.S. Army, public domain.

The decision was made to decamp to India with the Chinese troops before it was too late. Mandalay had fallen, the Japanese three-pronged attack now coming rapidly into wider focus. British leaders had left Burma, and Stilwell's staff was evacuated by air as Stilwell planned to move on to Myitkyina (pronounced 'Mitcheneau'), the main northern airbase, with a party of just over a hundred including Frank Merrill and other American officers, Burmese nurses, missionaries and Quakers, civilians and Chinese soldiers. Scouts reported the railway and roads heading there were hopelessly jammed. He decided they would take a rugged path on foot over the mountains and across rivers for 140 miles northwestward to Imphal in India. 'Keep moving. Don't stop for anything. By the time we get out of here, many of you will hate my guts, but I'll tell you one thing: you'll all get out.' Three-star generals command tens of thousands of men and materiel in an army corps. This one, carrying a rifle and no insignia, was leading a column of souls worn out by heat exhaustion, combat, sickness, and disease. The monsoon season began; men cursed as they slipped up and down the trails. Slowed by sickness and sunstroke, some were dragged along by others; Merrill, with a weak heart, was one of them.

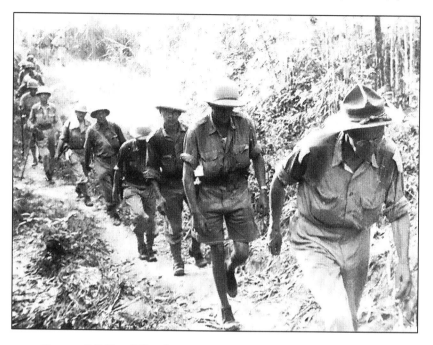

General Stilwell leads troops on foot out of Burma, 1942.
U.S. Army, public domain.

On May 20, 1942, the day the Japanese completed their conquest of Burma, the party of 114 arrived in Imphal, India. He was bewildered at messages of commendation from Marshall on behalf of the president and secretary of war, and the press noted this exploit where he had not lost one person in the confused exodus from Burma that would kill 900,000 refugees.

Stilwell flew then to Delhi, where, pressed by hounding newsmen, he gave an impromptu news conference, chaffing at British characterizations of a 'heroic, voluntary withdrawal' and a 'glorious retreat.' He ended famously with, 'In the first place, no military commander in history ever made a voluntary withdrawal. And there's no such thing as a glorious retreat. All retreats are ignominious as hell. I claim we got a hell of a licking. We got run out of

Burma, and it's humiliating as hell. I think we ought to find out what caused it, go back, and retake Burma.'

The Americans would return.[11]

P-40 Flying Tiger in China. Public domain.

PART ONE

THE FLYING TIGERS

Many Americans have heard of the Flying Tigers, but not many understand that they were the best organized American mercenaries to fight in World War II, assembled and trained in a time of neutrality.[2] Their leader, Claire Chennault, with several tours of China under his belt, had resigned from the Army in April 1937, having been recommended for a medical discharge due to poor health brought on by two decades of open cockpit flying, though it was no secret that over the years he had had his disagreements with superiors, the last straw being passed over for a promotion. Retiring as captain, now a civilian, he was recruited to inspect and advise the Chinese Air Force. His recommendations to Chiang Kai-shek would lead to the formation of the First American Volunteer Group, recruited under the authority of President Roosevelt to support the Chinese in their war against Japan. The volunteer force was made up of American veterans of the Army Air Corps, Navy, and Marine Corps, and was nicknamed the Flying Tigers. Commanded by Chennault, bestowed with the rank of colonel by Chiang, he was essentially a civilian mercenary from the American military point of view during this period. He clashed repeatedly

---

[2] *American mercenaries*-another group that comes to mind would be the young American pilots flying for the RAF in 1941 prior to Pearl Harbor.

with Army brass, most notably General Stilwell, who disagreed that Chennault's original plan for raiding Japanese bases from the air would be sustainable as a successful use of scarce resources, and would be more likely to invite Japanese counterassaults that the Allies did not need.

The Flying Tigers began to arrive in China in April 1941; trained in Burma and given delays and growing pains, they saw their first combat less than two weeks after Pearl Harbor, flying in their P-40s with the distinctive shark nose art.

Officially members of the Republic of China Air Force, AVG pilots destroyed almost three hundred Japanese aircraft, while losing only fourteen pilots in combat; they were the first Americans to engage the Japanese in open combat after Pearl Harbor and brought a much-needed antidote to the cascading news cycle of calamities brought on by the lightning Japanese advances across Asia.[12]

The American Volunteer Group ceased to exist on July 4, 1942. Many pilots drifted back to their original branches of service, some went home, and five others folded into now-Brigadier General Chennault's new Army Air Corps 23rd Fighter Group in what would become the 14th Air Force in southern China, flying air support and conducting a war of attrition for General Stilwell's ground forces. Today, their exploits are fondly recalled by the Chinese people; in 2005, pilots were given a heroes' welcome upon their return.

Morgan Vaux in China. Library of Congress.

CHAPTER ONE

The AVG Stationmaster

Morgan H. Vaux was born July 21, 1918, in Watertown, South Dakota. He graduated from Kenosha High School, Wisconsin, in 1936, serving in the Civilian Conservation Corps during the Great Depression. He enlisted in the U.S. Army Air Corps in 1939, and in 1941, upon receiving a special discharge from the Army, he joined the American Volunteer Group (AVG), the Flying Tigers, and served in Burma and China until they were dissolved. He then enlisted in the U.S. Marine Corps in late 1942 and served in the Pacific theatre until 1945. For his service, he was awarded the Bronze Star, Presidential Unit Citation, and the WWII Victory Medal.

Morgan H. Vaux

I had basic training at Chanute Air Base and Scott Field Air Base in radio operating and mechanics, aircraft specialty. A hell of a training I got. After that, it was maintaining aircraft in the 39th Pursuit Squadron, and also working field operations with field radios. That's about it until I got the contract to go to China with the American Volunteer Group; that was when I used my training to be an early warning radio station as a stationmaster in China.

'We Wrecked A Lot of Planes'

The learning curve for many of the young pilots transitioning into the P-40 fighters was steep; three pilots were killed in accidents early on. On November 3, 1941, a day that went down in their history as 'Circus Day,' no fewer than eight P-40s were damaged by accidents and mishaps.[13]

In Burma, we were there from August 1941 until August 1942. We went there mainly for training, because Chennault and his people had leased Kyedaw Airdrome at a town called Toungoo, Burma, north of Rangoon, from the British Royal Air Force. At that airbase, the pilots were trained in all kinds of things—landings and takeoffs and maneuvers. They were from the Army Air Corps, the Navy, and the Marines. The Navy and Marines had never seen the planes we had; they were all new to them. In fact, one man was a flying boat pilot; he had to go from high-flying boat pilot to a fighter plane pilot. It took a lot of practice, landings and takeoffs, at Kyedaw Airdrome. We lost a lot, and wrecked a lot of planes, too; propellers bent and smashed when they landed the nose over the plane, hit too hard, and broke the landing gear because they were used to [landing on] carriers—most of them were carrier pilots. On the carrier landings you cut your speed and just kind of drop down on the ground, maybe a couple of feet. You can't do that with another type of fighter plane. You have to grease it, more or less, on the runway. So, anyway, we lost quite a few planes to start with.

No Replacements

There were no replacements. In fact, all during our tour over there we had no replacements to talk about in terms of propellers and tires, things wearing out and blowing out. The only replacements we were able to get were by air by the China National

Aviation Corporation. They were flying over the Hump from Kunming to India, and they would ferry in spare parts for us. But they had to come all the way across from the Ivory Coast in Africa, all the way across. I think they were shipped from there by air somehow. I don't know how they got to India.

Our fellas at one time were asked to go to the Gold Coast to pick up about, I think, four or five new model P-40 aircraft. We were flying the original old 'B' model, [before] we were flying Tomahawks. The new ones were Kittyhawks.[3] They had bomb racks on them, they had much better firepower. Anyway, we used those few planes to bomb the Japanese Red Dragon Division that was coming up the Burma Road.

---

[3] 'Built by Curtiss-Wright Corporation, the Curtiss P-40 Tomahawk was a single-seat, all-metal fighter and ground attack aircraft that first flew in 1938. 13,738 were built from 1939 to 1944. It is the third most-produced American fighter, after the P-51 and P-47. The P-40 design was a modification of the previous Curtiss P-36 Hawk. The design continuation helped reduce development time and enabled a rapid entry into production and operational service. The Tomahawk was used by most Allied forces during World War II. The P-40 remained in front line service until the end of the war. The U.S. Army Air Corps named the P-40 Warhawk. The British and Soviet air forces used the name Tomahawk for the 'B' and 'C' models and Kittyhawk for the 'D' models.' Source: HISTORY OF THE P-40 TOMAHAWK, Curtiss P-40B Tomahawk, www.americanheritagemuseum.org/aircrafts/curtiss-p-40b-tomahawk.

Burma, 1942. U.S. Army, public domain.

After they had bombed out Rangoon, everybody kind of got out of there if they could—they destroyed the docks, so we moved out of there up the Burma Road. On the way we had to detour. Over there we lost some men and planes because [we were used to the fact that] the British Royal Air Force had radar at Mingaladon Airdrome at Rangoon. That's where two of our squadrons were placed to help out the RAF, because they had only one squadron there; their American Brewster Buffalos weren't very good aircraft. Anyway, they took their radar with them when they moved out, so when we moved out, we had no early warning, we had no warning of raids. That's why [after that] we lost several men and planes there, due to there being no warnings. So we moved out of there as soon as we could. We had to move to Kunming then, up the Burma Road. Of course, pilots flew in there with P-40s.

Chennault's Early Warning System

'Starting from areas in Free China, in hundreds of small villages, in lonely outposts, in hills and caves, stretching from near Canton through all Free China to the capital in Chungking and to Lanchow, far northwest, are a maze of alarm stations equipped with radios and telephones that give instant warning of the approach of Japanese planes.'
-Life Magazine, August 10, 1942.[14]

Prior to that time we had another engagement with the Japanese from Hanoi French Indochina. They came up on December 20, 1941. Ten twin-engine bombers, they were headed for Kunming; they had bombed Kunming for years at their liberty, see, they had no protection at all there. So they came in and we got word of it. See, my radio station was down in an area toward Hanoi. Chennault had also set up a telephone reporting warning system. So he had Chinese Army Signal Corps guys down near Hanoi Airport. When those planes would take off, they would phone up my station. Then the telephone guys talked through my interpreter and told me what was going on, what was coming up this way. And I called in to report to headquarters at Kunming, and they got word of it in plenty of time. And planes of two of our squadrons hit those ten bombers. Needless to say, none of them ever got to Kunming; I think all but one was shot down. That was the first engagement of our Flying Tigers with the Japanese.

The first combat mission made a big splash in the news back home, hitting back against the Japanese, but Chennault debriefed his pilots with his chagrin at the overenthusiasm of some, believing that in the excitement of first combat, they had let down their discipline; instead of coordinated dives at the bombers, they had attacked them in a free-for-all that could have resulted in the AVG shooting each other down or colliding. Three bombers were confirmed downed, any survivors turned away.[15] Chennault concluded with, 'Next time, get them all!'

Then, of course, when the Royal Air Force asked for help down in Rangoon, that's when we got into the big fleets of Japanese coming in over from Thailand, where they had bases. They'd come over in huge formations, a hundred-some at a time. Of course, the British and we didn't have any more than, say, twelve, maybe fifteen planes, to go up at a time against those. That's where Chennault's tactics paid off [utilizing] hit-and-run. You hit them, dive off, and come back again; that way we saved our men and planes. Shot down quite a few of them, too, but it didn't stop them. They were able to bomb night and day. When they started doing that, we had to move out. I think in March of `42 we had to move out again until we had to move into Kunming. They made the big record down there right after Christmas time.

The Burma Salween Gorge Mission

The Burma Road was a supply line for the Chinese at that time because the east coast docks, all the east coast harbors, were controlled by the Japanese. The Japanese had the whole east coast [of Southeast Asia] pretty well tied-up. So the only way the Chinese could get supplies, maintain their country, was through the Burma Road. And I think our biggest effort we made was when we hit what they call the Salween Gorge of the Burma Road.

The Burma Road goes across this bridge at this gorge, to get to the other side of the mountain to go on toward Kunming from Rangoon. At this time, it was in around May I think of 1942, the Japanese were coming up that road with that Red Dragon Armored Division, a whole division. They were going to sweep up into Kunming and that would be the end of Kunming, as far as World War II, the Japanese were concerned, they would stop them right there because they would have no way of getting any supplies except by air and that could easily be controlled by the Japanese. They could shoot them all down. So we had three of those late-model P-40 aircraft with the bomb racks. We loaded 500-pound Chinese bombs on those racks. I think three of our former Navy dive-bomber pilots agreed to make a run on the Japanese lines coming up the Burma Road, and at the same time bomb and destroy that river bridge so they couldn't cross the Salween River, what they called 'The Gorge,' a big opening there. So they first destroyed the bridge. Then the army column was there, so they bombed against the wall of a mountain and had the mountain come crashing down on the line of troops down below, on the Japanese. Then they would bomb the road itself and then strafe all along there. They did that for several days. The Japanese never got up to Kunming; Kunming was able to continue the war effort. Let's see—that, I think, was the crowning effort of the AVG.

Conditions

I was at that little place, [a radio station near Kunming]. I was using an Army camp cot for a bed. My arm happened to fall down off the camp cot. Boy, one of those rats got me, bit me. It was the hepatitis, I got that somehow over there. A lot of that from poor food, poor sanitary conditions. At the radio station, when I moved over there, see, I stopped at Kunming Black Dragon Pool Factory. The Black Dragon Pool Factory got a Chinese transmitter, it was about a 60-watt transmitter they said, an old receiver that looked like it had been on at the docks somewhere in Indochina. Pretty bad shape. Anyway, it worked. And I picked up an old motor generator, put that on the truck. And basically they sent me some canned goods, quite a few canned goods, to last for a while. I was eating that down there at this pagoda where we set up the station. Then the cook decided he would go to the bazaar. We'd go over there and see what they had to buy to eat. Most of it was chickens hanging from wires. We had quite a bit of chicken. Then along with the canned goods, if I ran out of canned goods, I notified the head office up there in Kunming, the base, they'd try to get more to me. But I had to pay for that stuff. I was given 30 dollars a month extra to be living out there and live with regular meals. They were getting pretty good meals up in Kunming. So I had to pay for them. There was another [radio station] down closer to Burma. I forget the name of it. Another one up there closer to Chungking on the Burma Road. Three of them on the Burma Road. Then my first station was south of Kunming, down toward Indochina. That's where I worked until the end of the tour.

I think the Japanese were able to know about it, but the stations were too far away for them to do anything about it, I think. They didn't think we could do much anyway. They didn't bomb us, though they would strafe my station. They would come and strafe my station a couple of times, trying to hit planes on the airfield at Unanei. I was up here in a hill, then right down there was a field. They'd come strafing me and then hit whatever they could get down in the airfield. Usually didn't get anything, because we didn't have anybody there anyway.

Other Missions

After that, the Japanese never came up that far. After we destroyed their planes on December 20, coming up from Hanoi, they never came back that way either. From that time on, we moved east to an airfield called Kweilin. Formosa was operating under the Japanese, so they made raids on the Japanese airfields in Formosa. Then up farther they had advanced airfields we had made northeast of Kunming and used those airfields to attack Japanese airfields farther north. Before we left we were working in the area of the northnortheast China starting with the southwest part of China. The Burma Road went northwest up to Chungking, and that was somewhat due north. We did some operations toward the east, toward the ocean, toward the seaports in that direction, large cities.

'I Went Around The World'

[So that was a one-year tour of duty with the Flying Tigers]; I went around the world on that. I left my hometown of Kenosha, Wisconsin, by rail. I went by rail to Los Angeles, about one hundred of us met there, various air bases. We took a bus to San Francisco. We got the Dutch passenger freighter at San Francisco, the *Jagersfontein*, that took us to Hawaii. From Hawaii we picked up two cruisers and escorts because the Japanese had word we were coming to aid the British in Burma. So there was a cruiser *Salt Lake City* and a cruiser *Northampton*. We got escorted to the Dutch East Indies, as far as that went. From there a Dutch cruiser took over and went as far as the Dutch East Indies somewhere. We went to Singapore. So then coming home, we had no way to get out of China by ship or India by ship; [I'll explain why in a moment]. So the China National Aviation Corporation guys would pick up a few of us at a time, we'd manage to get as far as Karachi, India. In those days Karachi was Indian. From Karachi, India, our embassy, it or the consulate, was able to get us a trip over to Bombay. We were over there for a while. Then it took about a week before we could get a ship from Bombay, an ocean-going ship. We got a ship of the United States lines called *Mariposa*. That took us to South Africa, Cape Town, and we stayed there a short time. From there, that's where I got my hepatitis, it showed up there. Up until then it was dysentery. Went from there to New York, then from New York I took a train to Kenosha. I went all the way around the world on that trip. It was all by civilian boats really, wasn't any military transport at all.

You see, when our time was coming to an end up there in China—we had until July 4, 1942, that was the end of our contract—the Army Air Corps sent quite a few people to re-enlist us back in the service. They didn't care whether you came from the Marines or Navy, they wanted them in the Army Air Corps. I had dysentery pretty bad. I said, 'I don't think I can make it.'

'We will make you a first lieutenant if you come.'

I said, 'No, I have to get back.' Hell, I left the Army as a corporal. They wouldn't give us any time off. You couldn't go home on leave, we had to either stay or leave. The head of the recruiting team was a guy named Colonel Bissell. I will never forget that guy. He would not allow any planes to take us out of China. So, hell, I wasn't about to sign up with that dingbat guy. A lot of the fellas were unhappy with him, especially, and then they wanted to get home after a year fighting out there, living pretty tough. They wanted to get home so they had very few people that re-enlisted. It took us about, I'd say about a month, to get there, and I'd say it took a month on the sea to get home. But we spent about three weeks trying to get passage out of India just because of Bissell! I remember two or three of the fellas rented camels. They rode around the embassy building there at Bombay trying to influence the consulate, whoever was there, to get us a ship, transportation out of there. They rode around there about half a day until they got a detention of people there. It worked out pretty well, in a couple of days we had something, the *Mariposa*, and we were able to get home on that. Just about all the guys came home that way. But I spent the whole time coming up from South Africa, New York in the sick bay with hepatitis. Couldn't manage anything. Pretty sick guy. Then I got a sick leave. I got home 60 days. Colonel Bissell said the draft board would be waiting, he would have the draft board draft us as privates in the Army, that's another thing that turned the guys against him. He threatened us! When I got home, the draft board gave me 60 days' sick leave before I had to re-enlist. I didn't care about that. I was going to re-enlist anyway.

The Marines

[From there, I went into the Marines.] The Marines was a move from one darn island to another. Pack everything, get on a ship, and get off. Our main objective, when we were out in the Marines, was to destroy the shipping and the air facilities at a big island base at Rabaul—they had a big navy base there, they had an air base there.[4] We had the first Marine B-25s. Marines didn't have twin-engine bombers until we got ours. PBJ because it was a patrol bomber, they said. We did night bombing of Rabaul with radar. It was a confusing situation in the Marine Corps because I was trained with Signal

---

[4] Rabaul was the principal Japanese forward operating base in the South Pacific at New Guinea, with tens of thousands of troops in reserve.

Corps Army equipment. The Navy had different equipment. The radio, we had one set of radio, what they call a command set in the fighter plane for the fighter pilots to use. With the bombers you had a long-range set of transmitter, a receiver, besides a short range for the pilots. Then they had radar. I had never been to radar school. I didn't know anything about the radar. In fact, at that time the Signal Corps didn't have radar, the Navy had started it out at Chicago. So I was promoted to head of the communications of the squadron. I was to be in charge of every part of communication on the radios, so I had pretty much to delegate.

We bombed mostly by radar at night, bombing Rabaul. Rabaul was in the Bismark archipelago, near the Admiralty Islands. You would find it by going north probably from New Guinea, in that area. It was a big Navy base at Rabaul, they had a lot of anti-aircraft equipment. We even lost the planes at night, we did all the bombing at night, we lost planes and people due to the heavy anti-aircraft they had. We did some strafing of other islands that had some Japanese installations still there, small installations. I went on some raids, strafing raids with them, to see what it was like. Then I just did enough flying to get my flight pay. Usually I would get flight pay ever since I joined the Marines. But we did mostly that one island. I guess we were pretty effective because they weren't sending out fighter planes and raiding around very much after for a while there. We were pretty effective.

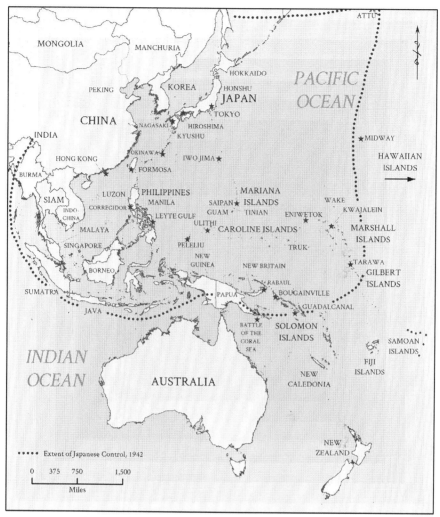

**Extent of Japanese Control in the Pacific, 1942,
Including Rabaul.
Drafted by Susan Winchell.**

We were out there in 1943. Then the war had moved up to the Philippines, up that way, so they moved my squadron north up to the Philippines. That's when they said, well, your time is up. I don't have to go to the Philippines. So I got a hop over to Admiralty Islands. I got on the troop ship, came home that way. Came home a long ways. Still other guys said their time was up. They had time overseas. I think they had Army time, Marine time.

Booze For Spare Parts

My volunteer service helped toward the experience. That's how they figured I was capable of taking care of communications of the entire squadron. There was a lot more communications [logistics] involved in that squadron, twin-engine bombers, fighter planes. I got a couple of guys who went to the warehouse, we pretty well took care of moving stuff out of the fourteen warehouses we needed to operate our squadron overseas, motor generators and stuff like that, we took along that we were going to need. Then we got over there, and we found out we didn't have any spare parts. They had mixed Army and Navy radio equipment on the planes. So we didn't have any spare parts for the Army stuff. Luckily there was a fire squadron, a P-38 squadron, over at Sterling Island when we got there. I went over there, found a bunch of parts over there I could use. They let me have them for a couple of bottles of booze. I brought booze over in my footlocker, in my tent where I was with several other guys; when we would have a birthday, I broke out a bottle of booze. I packed it in there with straw, Three Feathers; lousy booze. So I would use a bottle, go over there, the Army base, and trade it for parts for the planes.

The Slit Trench Encounter

Strange story happened when I was over there. It was on Sterling Island. We knew there was another squadron, the other side of the base, Army with P-38s. I never went over there but one time. One night we had a raid, not a raid, but Japanese search planes were running around one night. We had a blackout. I was in a slit trench there by the tent, some guy jumped in and just about jumped on me. I said, 'What the hell are you trying to do?'

Turned out to be, it's the strangest thing I ever had, thinking about it afterwards, because it was one of our guys in the Flying Tigers, a pilot, who had jumped on me in the slit trench over Sterling Island, in the Treasury group out there in the Southwest Pacific! Of all the guys you could think of, how could one guy from that one group over there in China, years ago, be jumping into my slit trench? He must have been visiting or something over in our squadron some of our guys; he was from that P-38 outfit. It turned out he was from Wisconsin. Years later I drove up to see where he was in northern Wisconsin. He was at a resort or something. I asked him about it. I said, 'Remember that time?'

He remembered it. But he didn't have much time to talk, he was busy, so we didn't talk much about it. I thought I would see him at the reunions, but the bugger never came to the reunion. All the years I am wondering if it really happened. That guy from our old Flying Tigers squadron would be in a P-38 squadron and jump in this Marine Corps slit trench years later. It was about a year after they left China. [*Laughs*]

Home

When I came back in 1945, I was 27. I enrolled on the GI Bill at 16 Lawrence College, Appleton, Wisconsin, and I graduated in 1949 with a B.S. degree. Then I went to the Civil Service Naval Electronics Supply Office at Great Lakes, until I got a transfer to the Air Force Material Command. I was stationed at Kingston Products in Kokomo as an inspector. While at Kokomo I was hired at Delco Radio, that's how come I came here, as a process and production engineer. So I was at Delco Electronics for 27 years.

Morgan H. Vaux passed away at 92 on August 3, 2010.

CHAPTER TWO

The Flying Tigers Nurse

Emma Jane Foster Petach Hanks, or Jane, as she was known, was one of only two women who joined the 120-strong American Volunteer Group, or Flying Tigers, in 1941, before Pearl Harbor and while the United States was still a neutral nation.[16] At 25 she was a registered nurse with them in Burma and China; known simply as 'Red' for her flaming red hair highlighted by her light complexion, she married a Flying Tigers pilot while there and lost him less than two weeks before they were due to leave for home. She returned to the United States a widow at age 27, but carrying the child who would become their daughter.

'About ten days before our contract was up, [Chennault] asked the fellas if they would stay over, because the army hadn't come in. He didn't have help [to train the Chinese pilots], and so some of the fellas stayed over. Pete was one of them... [pauses for a moment] ... and that's when I lost him. He got shot down bombing and strafing. I went home, and of course, my father wasn't... [trails off, then imitates father's voice, asking with incredulity] He said, 'You were a nurse, you were in the army, and you were in war, and you got pregnant?' And I never told him the truth, [which was that] I always felt [that with] Pete, we were never coming back together. And if I

was going to lose him, I wanted part of him, and that's why I deliberately had gotten pregnant. When I came back home, of course, my daughter was born.'

Jane Hanks

My maiden name is Emma Jane Foster. I was born February 14, 1916, [in Bellefonte, Pennsylvania]. As a kid, I used to say, since I was the youngest of six, I was my mother's heart because I was born on Valentine's Day. But as a kid, I was always adventuresome. And I remember they tell me when I was about a two-year-old, they found me in the outskirts of town, walking away, having a fine time because I was exploring everything. Since I was the youngest of six, I had to make my own way.

'I Felt Like Alice in Wonderland'

Ever since I remember, I was always interested in the culture in Asia. It fascinated me. I read all of Pearl Buck's books I could get my hands on, all that kind of material because Asia, especially China, intrigued me. And when I finally got to get my college education, I went to Penn State, and I found that they had an exchange student program at Lingnan University, Canton, China. Only men were going. And I thought, if men are going, no reason why women can't go. So with much—how will I put it? —'investigation,' anyway, I did get a chance. I was one of the first group of women that ever went that went to Lingnan University as an exchange student. It was the most wonderful experience of my life! I enjoyed every bit of it. I enjoyed the Chinese professors much better than the professors that I had in college because they were gentlemen. They were well educated, spoke very good English, and were very good to their students. It was such a wonderful experience for me that I always wanted to get back there somehow. But while we were there, we did a lot of traveling by bike, and I can remember going to formal occasions with my dress hanging over my arm, my formal dress. But we biked a lot through China. And during intermission from the sessions, the four of us went through the interior of China. And up there at that time, Beijing was called Peking. We went by bus and by train; there were just two girls and two boys. We stayed at the Chinese inns, and we never had any comment about that situation until we got to a missionary's house. And I was insulted that the missionaries would think anything was wrong with us!

When we got to Peking, I was fortunate enough to go to the Forbidden City. And I was there after the Dowager had left the city. There was a moat all around the city where the Chinese stayed. And I was lucky enough to go all the way through the Forbidden City. There was food still left on the beds, and the clothing was still on the beds.

I felt like Alice in Wonderland, because nobody was there but me. I went to all these little rooms and saw how they lived. I was just fascinated by the whole thing. When I came back to visit later, of course, they had taken all the furniture out of those little rooms and put them in a big room, so the Chinese really didn't believe that I had been there. But it was a fascinating experience. Chiang Kai-shek was there, and he had preserved a lot of this material, a lot of the culture, the Chinese culture. I went to the wall, the Great Wall, climbed the Great Wall, it was fascinating, and the culture was just terrific. And the Chinese were so respectful.

A 'Foreign Devil'

Of course, at that time, I was a flaming redhead, with blue eyes and light skin. So every place I went, I was surrounded by the Chinese. They called me a 'yángguǐzi,' foreign devil. The older, the more elite Chinese were embarrassed every time I told them about that. But I can see that I was taller than they were, except when I went to Beijing. And, of course, a different coloring, and they'd never seen anybody like me, so I always drew a crowd.

I took mainly political science and Chinese history while I was there. But as I said, we knew a lot of the officials because we were students and we were given special privileges, so we got around. I'll never forget the first time we were at a party for one of the officials. It was after our meal, and one of the officials burped and you could hear it all over the room. I was so embarrassed for him. I thought, 'it's a shame,' until I learned that that was a sign that they were congratulating the cook, that the food was so good. So, anyway, my experience there was just so great that I wanted to go back and help them.

Getting Back To China

I knew the best way to get back [to China] was in the medical field. But being a doctor took too long, so I went into nursing. I went to the Yale School of Nursing, got my master's degree. When I graduated, the only way I could get back to China was via the missionary field, and I wasn't exactly the missionary type, so I did visiting nursing in Minneapolis. Now, about that time, the American Volunteer Group was being organized. Chiang Kai-shek had asked Chennault to go to the States to get some help for him to fight the Japanese, and when Chennault went to Roosevelt, Roosevelt liked the idea, but the generals hated it. They said they already had their hands full in Europe, they didn't want another battle to fight, because we weren't at war with Japan. But since Roosevelt liked it, he helped set up a covert action group and the Chinese paid for us to do it. So he told us that we were there to protect the Burma Road.

Major Gentry was looking for his medical team, and when he came to Yale, he was looking for a nurse. Yale told him, 'Well, there's a girl, she's always wanted to go back. I don't know where she is, but I know she wants to go back.' So Major Gentry called my father. My father called me while I was in town doing work, and he said, 'You're going to get a call to go back to China. Go back and get it. Stay there until you get it.' He wanted to get me out of there; somebody with a master's degree shouldn't be wasting their time being in the slums! So Major Gentry called me, and within twenty-four hours, I was on my way back to China.

When I went to Shanghai, that was when I first met the AVG. I thought that they were just very young, very inexperienced, and I wasn't about to have anything to do with it. Those fellas were so immature! We were all waiting for a boat because in that time there weren't planes, and we were supposed to be the second boatload to go back to China. They took one look at two girls; said they had no room for the two girls! But we heckled and heckled, and finally we got our way, and they put us up on the top deck and they had set up cots. We used the children's facilities, and the captain did let us use his shower facilities for bathing, but it was fairly inconvenient. We also had a Victrola with really good classical music and jazz, and some of the fellas used to come up and we would dance on the top deck. I really had a good time on that boat, and that's where I met my future husband.

'These Kids, They're Going to Fight?'

My first experience with these AVGs, from the medical stand-point, we lined the fellas up to give them shots for Asia, and a couple of those big burly men took one look at that needle and landed on the deck! And I thought, 'They're going to fight?'

We landed in Hong Kong and Singapore, then we finally landed in Rangoon. We couldn't land in the other areas, really, because the Japanese controlled all the Chinese ports, and when we landed in Rangoon, they wouldn't let us disembark, because they had problems before, and the fellas were so frustrated, they threw overboard every portable thing they could find! And I thought again, 'These kids, they're going to fight?'

The next day we went by train up to Toungoo, which was north of Rangoon, and there was an old British base there and that's where we were going to stay. Now, since I had been in the Orient, I was expecting some primitive conditions, but I really didn't expect the conditions that we found in Burma. They were fat huts, really. The hospital had about ten beds and the nurses had quarters adjacent to the hospital, and other than having a sink, the facilities were all outside, so we had to go out to take care of them. And the beds were set in little cans of water, so that would keep the ants from getting up into our beds. And fortunately we did have mosquito netting over our beds, and it was very lucky really, because the rats would run around the ceilings and every so often they would fall on our mosquito netting, so we were glad that we had that mosquito netting! Another thing we had to be careful of was when you got into your shoes, you had to be very careful that there wasn't any living thing in your shoes!

In the first couple days we had a Burmese cook, and we had highly seasoned food—breakfast, dinner, and supper. That finally got a couple of the fellas, they weren't going to put up with that. They went home! Since we were under contract, we could go home. And the rest of us thought, 'Well, if they can't take it, they can go.' But then they got Chinese cooks, and they got screens at the windows, so we didn't have to fight the bugs to the food, and that food was much better.

Medically speaking, we weren't very busy, and one of the doctors was an ear, nose, and throat person and he was bored to death so he took out every pair of tonsils that he could find! I felt very comfortable because I used to help my father doing the same thing in the office, but it wasn't very long until they came down with malaria and dengue fever. And when they got dengue fever, they were really sick, so we were busy taking care of those fellas. But fortunately, we didn't lose any of them.

Spending Time With Chennault

After they got over that, we dealt with a lot of accidents, because they weren't used to those very fast planes. A lot of them had just come right off of aircraft carriers, and they hadn't experienced this real fast flying. So we worked in our days in Burma, we worked very hard during the day, and then we would get out and get down to Rangoon and party. So I had a good time in spite of it all, as I had a good time on the boat. Mister Chennault liked feminine company, so when he went to the very formal parties, he would take Josie, the other nurse, the other girl, because she was older, and when he went to the informal things, he would take me. I remember one time in particular, I was playing cribbage with a man, he was supposedly the best cribbage player in the east, and I was beating him. And Pete, whom I later married, was standing back of me; he was counting for me, because he could count much faster than I could. Well, Chennault [didn't take it well], and he said, 'Young man, that girl would do a lot better if you'd leave.' So Pete left, and I lost! And I've talked to Chennault's family since, and they said that's the way he acted with his family, he wanted to win. He was going to win! But when we'd go to parties with Chennault, sometimes when he was feeling very good, he would go to a step and try to reach the step below, and pretend like he was struggling, trying to reach this step. He [acted like] he couldn't do it, and so he'd bet his guests so much if he could make it, reach that lower step. And as soon as his guest took the bait, he reached the lower step! Another thing he used to do is, when he had guests for dinner, he loved these really hot pickles, and he'd take a big bite out of these hot pickles, and the guests would follow his lead, and they would [nearly choke]! They couldn't take that really odd stuff. [*Laughs*] In spite of working hard, we played hard, and we did have a good time in Burma.

War

Then the word came around that the Japanese had bombed Pearl Harbor. And then we knew that the United States was going to war, and now everybody wanted us. Right after, very close to that time, when we heard that we were at war with Japan, we heard that the Japanese were going to come over and bomb us. We had no air raid system, no nothing in Burma. And we dragged some of those fellas out and put them in ditches, because that was the only thing we had; they later said that they were all eaten up with ants. But fortunately, the Japanese didn't bomb us. They had heard about us, and they didn't think we were worth bothering with. And they have since said they were very sorry.

As soon as possible, the medical staff, or we nurses, were sent up into China, into Kunming. I wanted to go by the Burma Road, but they had me fly up to Kunming, and Kunming was our headquarters during the war. When we went up to Kunming, it was going to be our headquarters for the rest of the time, because we have this contract for a year. And Josie, the other girl, was Josie Stewart, from Dallas, Texas. I didn't know it at the time, but I was the only registered nurse.

The Warning System

Before the flyers got there, the Japanese came and bombed Kunming, and then we went out to the graveyards with the Chinese and stayed there until they finished bombing. The next day, our flyers came in, and the Japanese came back. They were going to bomb Kunming. But one of the most important things about General Chennault, he taught the Chinese to keep track of these Japanese planes, so they would follow the Japanese planes from their origin to where they were going. So we knew ahead of time where they were and how far away, so we could get them. And then the next time the Japanese came to bomb Kunming, Chennault's warning system worked very well. We met them outside of Kunming. They never got to Kunming and clobbered them there [before they could reach the city]. The Chinese were just so grateful that for once they weren't going to be bombed, and because of Chennault's warning system and the AVG being there, the Japanese never came back to Kunming, to bomb Kunming again. As long as we were there, they'd stay away.

Married With A Black Eye

The conditions for the living quarters in Kunming were much better than in Burma. It was a temporary building, but it was a building, and we were heated by charcoal. And we had about four beds in what was like a clinic, but when the boys were really ill, we would go down to the Chinese hospital. In the hospital, Josie and I would take one day on and one day off. They put up a cot and we'd sleep in the cot. I didn't tell you, we had three doctors. One was, as we said, eye, ear, nose, and throat. The other one was orthopedic, and the third one was a general medical person. We also had a dentist, and we had a chaplain, and we had these two girls. Chennault wanted us American girls to take care of his boys, and we were there to just take care of the AVG. We were busy with one day on and one day off, and of course, we didn't have all of the entertainment that we had before the war, but even then, I used to go on bike trips with Pete. Well, I was falling in love with him, and we wanted to get married. And it was generally understood that we [weren't supposed to] get married. And of course, at first, I didn't think I'd have anything to do with those fellas. But when we decided, we checked with Chennault, and he liked both of us, so he decided it was all right if we got married. As I said, I was falling in love with this guy, and he was doing a job trying to get me. So he would fly over our hospital and the fellas found out what he was doing, so he would fly over and wiggle his tail to make sure that I knew that he was doing it, and they got it, too, so that I could be sure that it was he that was out flying for me, letting me know. I said, 'I guess not very many women have had a courtship like that!' Bit by bit, he got me.

We were married in Kunming, in the French consulate. I only had a couple people there at our wedding. Padre Paul Frohman, who was our chaplain, was not there; he was out somewhere on the advanced post, so it was a minister in town that married us. And the night before our marriage, Chennault invited us to his apartment for dinner. I was Indian wrestling with Chennault, and if you know what Indian wrestling is, he gave me a big pull and I flew across the room, hit my eye on a corner of a table, and was married with a black eye! Then right after our honeymoon, we rode up briefly on Burma Road. After that, we stayed in my quarters, and he would run back and forth to the airfield.

'When They Came Back, They Were Men'

Later on, just about two months before our year was up, they shipped us to Kunming, Fletcher and Pete—John Petach was his real name—and the other nurse, Josie Stewart. I didn't know at the time, but I was the only really registered nurse with the crowd. But anyway, we went up to Kunming. We were there about two months before we were to leave—our time was up; our yearly contract was up. While we were there, one thing happened. It was the first time General Stilwell had asked our fellas to fly low over the Chinese airfield, and our fellas wouldn't do it, because if you fly low, that's then when a Japanese can punch in, and your survival rate would be practically nil. And they almost came to blows with Chennault.

One of the fellas says, 'We're not cowards, you know that.'

And Chennault said, 'I know. I realize that!' Well, they finally didn't have to do that.

Another experience that we had when we flew up to Kunming, General Bissell came to get us to enlist in the armed services.[5] Now, the fellas really worshiped Chennault. They would have done anything for Chennault, but they were tired. They had just about a year of just battling five-to-one, ten-to-one with the Japanese. I think talking about the experiences of the AVG in Rangoon, what they did is they would have one squadron at a time [at the main base]. One squadron was kept in Rangoon, and the rest of them were sent to advanced posts. Now, when those fellas went to Rangoon, they were fighting with two, four, six, ten, sometimes twenty Japanese airplanes after them! I remember that one of the fellas, his plane was shot down and he fortunately was able to get out of the plane and was going down by a parachute, and the Japanese were trying to get him, and he would shuffle around one side to the other [as the bullets went by], and finally he got tired and he just slumped down, and the Japanese thought they'd got him. And that boy is

---

[5] General Clayton Lawrence Bissell (1896-1972) was principal aviation officer for General Stilwell in China; in August 1942 he was named head of the 10th Air Force in India and Burma as the AVG contract with the Chinese government expired.

alive today. One of the things that was amazing, was startling to me actually, is when these fellas went to Rangoon, they were boys. When they came back, they were men. If I'd have seen that in the movies, I would have thought it was overdrawn. But they were fighting death the whole time; now they just wanted to go home and rest, and then they'd come back. But General Bissell was so nasty, and he told the fellas that, 'You will have a very difficult time to get home, and when you get home, you'll just be drafted.' But most of them went home.

'That's When I Lost Him'

About ten days before our contract was up, [Chennault] asked the fellas if they would stay over, because the army hadn't come in. He didn't have help [to train the Chinese pilots], and so some of the fellas stayed over. Pete was one of them... [*pauses for a moment*] ... and that's when I lost him. He got shot down bombing and strafing. So when I was on my way, when I was on my way home, our other commander, asked two of the fellas to escort me home, Bob Neal and Charlie Bond.[6]

Home

Well, then, when we got to Calcutta, since they weren't very fond of us, fortunately, one of those fellas, I think Charlie Bond, had gotten to Hap Arnold, and Hap Arnold gave me A-1 priority to go home.[7] So I flew home, we three flew home. I didn't have to go by

---

[6] Charles Bond is sometimes credited, along with another man, for the distinctive AVG shark face nose art.

[7] Hap Arnold- Henry Harley "Hap" Arnold (1886-1950). Major pioneer of strategic bombing theory in Europe, later head of the Twentieth Air Force command in the CBI and Pacific. He was named a five-star General of the

boat or anything. And when we landed in Miami, well, those boys were heroes, [they got a heroes' welcome]. They took those boys away and wined them and dined them. Now, I'd been very careful of them. Me, [to those in Miami], I was a camp follower, I was a prostitute. I was so embarrassed that I'd been well respected in every other country but my own, I cried for about two days, but I got over it. [*Chuckles*]

I went home, and of course, my father wasn't... [*trails off, then imitates father's voice, asking with incredulity*] He said, 'You were a nurse, you were in the army, and you were in war, and you got pregnant?' And I never told him the truth, [which was that] I always felt [that with] Pete, we were never coming back together. And if I was going to lose him, I wanted part of him, and that's why I deliberately had gotten pregnant. When I came back home, of course, my daughter was born.

I wanted to get a job in the States, but I was too well educated. They didn't want me. In those days, nurses didn't have any master's degree, but I finally did get a job. I was a health educator, and I stayed in Harrisburg, Pennsylvania. I was a health educator because I did have health information, and I was in that job for quite a couple years, and they did pay enough money that I could raise my daughter. That was another problem with some of the other opportunities I had. They didn't pay me enough so that I could raise my daughter. Then I became executive director of the Tuberculosis and Health Society, which was a voluntary organization. I was there a couple of years, and then I had the opportunity to be secretary of the Public Health Association in Harrisburg, the same place. And I really liked that job because we watched all the health legislation through the congress in the state. It was very interesting, and I liked

---

Army in 1943, placing him fourth in rank to only Marshall, MacArthur, and Eisenhower.

that. The Flying Tigers had a reunion every two years. And in those days, the China National Airway, which was the only other civilian war citizens group in World War II, they used to have reunions together with the Flying Tigers. And usually when I went to a reunion, I wanted to see my friends. I didn't pay much attention to the China National Airway, but one year, one of the fellas got my attention and.. we got together and we finally were married. I married Fletcher Hanks from Oxford, Maryland. He, of course, wanted me to come down to Oxford, Maryland, and, well, I moved, and it was a big change for me because I was used to going my own way, and I wasn't used to being adapted to somebody else. But we managed all right.

'Women Didn't Talk About Those Things'

I got involved in politics in Maryland, I enjoyed that. I was in a different environment because all the girls when they got together, talked about their children. And when I wanted to talk to the men about human events and other things, they looked at me as though there was something wrong with me. Women didn't talk about those things! But it's finally changing. But I got involved in politics and I enjoyed that for a while. I was president of the Maryland Federation of Republican Women for a couple years and I was a delegate to the convention for Ronald Reagan, whom I admired very much. The Flying Tigers have reunions every year because we're losing people so fast that we get together every year; every year I look forward to going to the Flying Tiger reunions because they're like going back to my family, since my family's all gone now and there aren't very many of us AVG left. One of the unique things about AVG was the same people who joined up were the same people who left after a year. Nobody came in between, [no replacements], so we had a closely knit group. And as I said, it's just like visiting somebody from your own family; we started out with about 350 and we're down to, I think the last count was 48. So we really look forward to that, do our reunions and see it.

[My husband and I], we both have a respect for China and admiration for the Chinese people. I should mention to you that we were never given veteran status. We were given veteran status only fifty years after we came back; we weren't recognized as a veteran until that time. We did get the Bronze Medal for our achievements in World War II.

Jane Hanks died Oct. 17, 2009, at the age of 93. Her and Pete's daughter, the only 'Flying Tiger Cub,' noted, 'To many who never knew Jane but recognized a tall, stooped, elderly lady doddering along with her American flag-bedecked walker, she was just another of Oxford, [Maryland's] elderly. What a shame they didn't know Jane, or 'Red,' the fiery Flying Tigers nurse, the dedicated public health nurse, the devoted mother, the nationally ranked cyclist, the consummate tennis player. A moment with Jane would have revealed there was no loss of acuity, no loss of wit, no loss of candor. Towards the end, Jane was frail, but her intellect never failed.'

The Curtiss C-46 Commando flying over the Hump. National Museum of the U.S. Air Force. Public domain.

PART TWO

THE HUMP

General Chennault's Flying Tigers withdrew their planes from Burma to China. In seven months of aerial combat, his volunteer force had destroyed nearly 300 Japanese aircraft. But for the next three years, the most vital use of aircraft would be getting supplies to China by flying them over the lower Himalayas in India. The Air Transport Command created to fly the treacherous 500-mile route between Assam and Kunming was nicknamed 'The Hump' by pilots flying over mountain ranges as high as 15,000 feet. They were subjected to extreme turbulence, unpredictable winds and weather conditions, and, after the fall of the airfield in Burma at Myitkyina, Japanese fighters. One peak in particular was called 'the aluminum-plated mountain' because so many cargo planes had crashed on it; over the course of that period of time, 650,000 tons were airlifted, at a cost of more than 600 planes lost and a thousand men killed.[17]

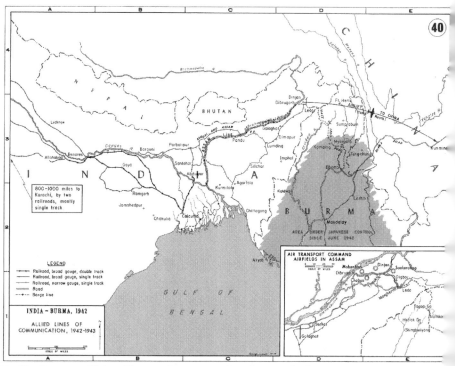

India-Burma-China lines of communication and air route over the Hump, 1942.
U.S. Army, public domain.

CHAPTER THREE

The Cargo Pilot

Patrick Scarano was born on April 14, 1915, in Cortland, New York, to Italian immigrants. He flew for Eastern Airlines in the early 1940s until he joined the U.S. Army Air Corps and wound up in the China-Burma-India Theater, flying multi-engine cargo planes over the Himalaya Mountains.

'Going back home, you are traveling westbound, into the face of the jet stream. So, it would take you longer. We'd head back to the Assam Valley, pick up a beacon, circle down to sea level as we broke out of the overcast, and land at the airport where we took off from. But here's the hazard—you'd get there early morning and there would be fog. So, you'd have to circle until the fog would lift or go to an alternate airport. If the fog did not lift and the alternate airport is too far away, you would run out of gas, then you would have to jump out of the airplane and lose the airplane. A lot of ships were lost that way.'

He sat for this interview in early 2001.

Patrick Scarano

Back in 1943, the war in Europe was getting worse and I was a pilot through the CPT, the Civilian Pilot Training program. I had won a scholarship after high school. From that, I started flying primary and then if I passed that, I'd do secondary and if I passed that, then cross country and then from there the instructor rating. I stayed there for a while and then the Navy man came through and was looking for recruits for the Navy. He said, 'Go to New York and take a physical at 50 Broadway.' I took the physical and they said I was a quarter of an inch short. I said, 'Oh my God, they want a 5'7"!' But then I heard that Eastern Airlines was hiring pilots, so I took a day off, went to LaGuardia Field to Eastern Airlines Headquarters, and they said they were hiring pilots for the military cargo division of the airline. Now, just about that time the government said they needed a lot of cargo pilots, so they hired me as a pilot with Eastern Airlines and sent me to school in Atlanta, Georgia. I went through their school, both the engine and aircraft instrument rating and all that.

Now, they were going to get C-46 Commando Airplanes from Curtis, from the government, and the airlines were waiting for the production. When they got that, they would put me on the Cargo Division of Eastern Airlines, flying C-46 cargo airplanes with cargo from the U.S. to Europe. In the meantime, while we were waiting for the airplanes to come in there, Eastern Airlines put me on a domestic run until the planes came.

I was on a domestic run for about four months, flying the regular routes from New York to Miami, Houston, and so forth. One day, Eddie Rickenbacker, the owner and president of Eastern Airlines, called us pilots into the operation room. There were about twenty of us pilots. He said, 'Fellas, I have good news, and I have bad news. First, I'll give you the bad news. The bad news is that we're not

THE THINGS OUR FATHERS SAW (VOL. X) | 79

going to get C-46 airplanes anymore because all the production that comes through, the U.S. Army has taken. We have a surplus of pilots, and I am going to have to let you go. That's the bad news.' In fact, he said, 'That's the end of our cargo division of the airline. Now, the good news is that as long as we trained you on multi-engine aircraft, instrument rating, meteorology, and all that stuff there, the U.S. Army will guarantee that if you go to a ninety-day officer candidate school in Memphis, you will come out of there with a commission as a 2nd lieutenant and you will be in the service.'

So, I went to Memphis, Tennessee, and was one of what they called 'the ninety-day wonders.' After ninety days, I graduated, got commissioned as a 2nd lieutenant, and there I'm in the service. From there, they sent me on my first mission, which was the Air Transport Command, ATC. So, that's how I got into it. They said, 'Well now, Lieutenant, we're going to send you to Little Rock, Arkansas, to go through the instrument flight school.'

I said, 'Why do that?' I've just come out of Eastern Airlines, I've got a rating, instrument rating, FAA, and multi-engine rating.

This officer said, 'Well that's okay, but you've got to do things the Army way!' So, they sent me to Adams Field in Little Rock. I went through instrument school and, of course, it was a breeze. They said, 'Hey, we've got something really good here. We want to keep you here as an instructor on instrument flight.'

I said, 'What the hell, anything like that.' After I instructed a few classes, they made me the chief check pilot. Now, any of the students that went through the school would take a ride with me. It was up to me to either pass them or, if they were a little bit weak, to send them back for additional training. So, I was a check pilot and had been asking to be sent overseas because of the war effort. Finally, my orders came through. They sent me to Miami, Florida, for overseas duty. The first thing they did was to give me an overseas physical. They got about twenty officers in this one room in the medical division. They said, 'Strip.' So, we stripped. The doctor came in and said, 'Okay, fellas, anything wrong with you fellas, step forward. If not, put your clothes back on and go down to the airport for 1500 takeoff.' So, can you imagine that? That's an overseas physical. I thought they were going to give me an extensive electrocardiogram, blood tests and all that but if the body is warm, you're in! [*Laughs*] I was in Miami, but the orders said, 'We want you to pack winter underwear. Get your winter clothing, winter underwear, and that's part of your winter gear to go overseas.' So they sent me overseas. I am thinking, 'Oh my God, with heavy underwear, that means I'm going to go to either Greenland or a cold country.' Two days later, I ended up in the Assam Valley of India. Hot! It was hot, during the monsoon season. Ha, winter underwear! I think the reason they said to pack your winter underwear is if there were any spies telling the direction of our movement, they would say, 'The troop movement is going this way, sending them north or to a cold country.' They really created a diversion and sent them off the beaten path.

So now, I'm in Chabua, India. When I was with Eastern Airlines, they did have a couple of Curtis C-46 transports. We had a little time in it, but not too much, just a few hours to get acquainted with the airplane and check out as a pilot. So when they got their C-46 airplanes, all they had to do was assign us to the aircraft, load up, and go to the air with the load.

The Lifeline of China

I was in Mohanbari, India. At that time in 1943-1944, there was a blockade on the east coast with submarines and the shipping was bad there. Also, China had a blockade of submarines. So the vital supplies for China came by ship up to about Calcutta, India, and then from there to the Assam Valley. They had vital supplies, and they also had 100 octane gasoline. This is for the B-29 bases that flew out of bases in China.

Air Transport Command C-46 crosses the Himalayas.
U.S. Army, public domain.

My mission was to fly the C-46 transports from the Assam Valley; we would start at the Assam Valley at the beginning of the Ledo Road. Now, they would have vital supplies going down the Ledo Road, but they were also fighting the Japs and didn't have much time or material that went through. So they had to institute something better and that's when they called 'The Lifeline of China.'

We would start at the Assam Valley with a C-46 and about fifty or sixty 55-gallon drums of 100 octane gasoline. We would take off, usually a night flight, the operation beginning with us circling up to 15,000 feet so you could clear the Himalayas; the top of the mountains there were about 15,000 feet. Then we would spread out and then head east for Kunming, China. It would take approximately two hours; this was about a 400-mile trip, at 15,000 feet, mostly in the clouds. We'd get pretty close to Kunming, China, and turn on the beacon. We would home in on the beacon, spiral down, and land in Kunming, China. The trucks would be waiting there. They would pull up and unload the airplane. In the meantime, we'd go and have something to eat. They would refuel the airplane and get it ready for our trip back home.

Hazardous Duty

Going over to China, it was hazardous due to bad weather, but going back it was even worse. We had the jet stream that flew from west to east and sometimes it would be pretty strong, 50 to 60 mph, and in some cases, up to 100 mph. Going back home, you are traveling westbound, into the face of the jet stream. So, it would take you longer. We'd head back to the Assam Valley, pick up a beacon, circle down to sea level as we broke out of the overcast, and land at the airport where we took off from. But, here's the hazard—you'd get there early morning and there would be fog. So, you'd have to circle until the fog would lift or go to an alternate airport. If the fog did not lift and the alternate airport is too far away, you would run out of gas, then you would have to jump out of the airplane and lose the airplane. A lot of ships were lost that way.

A lot of airplanes were also lost in another respect. On the C-46 airplane, which was a very good plane, we would carry 55-gallon drums of gasoline. At sea level, the procedure was for one of the crew members to go in and see if there were any leaks. If we had a bad spot or a leaker, we would take it out. If not, a crew member would come out and say, 'Captain, everything is okay.' So then we'd take off, get up to 15,000 feet, where there is lower atmospheric pressure. So, with any flaw in that drum, it would leak gasoline.

Now, gasoline fumes flow downward in the cold air, so on the C-46, as you know, the gasoline fumes would flow downward into the belly [of the aircraft]. At sea level, it's warm, but when you get up to about 15,000 feet, it's cold. On the instrument panel of the C-46, there is a red button that you press for heat. However, if you have a lot of fumes that have flowed down into the belly and you got cold and pressed the red button, it could cause a spark. The spark would ignite the fumes in the belly and that was the end of that airplane.

I just got through mentioning the hazard of flying the C-46 over the Hump, the dangerous weather, the updrafts and the jet stream over the Himalaya Mountains. The War Department considered the Himalaya Mountains and the Lifeline to China a combat zone. As a combat zone, they had a criteria of 750 hours of total time in that area and you have rotation to go home.

Medals

They also mentioned that being in a combat zone, you were also awarded certain medals for the amount of time that you had flown over the mountains. So, the first medal I received and earned was this Air Medal, this medal right here. [*Shows medal*] This medal was given for 150 hours of pilot time over the Himalaya Mountains.

The next one was given when you accumulated over 300 hours and you would be awarded the Distinguished Flying Cross, which was a very good medal. When you kept accumulating hours, you'd have another medal. In other words, after 300 hours, I would earn a cluster to the Air Medal. After another 300 hours accumulated over the Hump, there would be another Distinguished Flying Cross. Instead of giving you the medal itself, they would give you a cluster for the medal they had already given you. So, what I have is the Air Medal with the cluster and the Distinguished Flying Cross with the cluster.

The war in China back in early 1945 was getting much worse. The government had to get troops from the northern part of China and bring them to the southern part of China to fight. They thought I would do much better being transferred to China on a C-47 airplane, which is basically the DC-3 Douglas. When I flew with Eastern Airlines, I accumulated a lot of hours and experience on the DC-3. So they thought it would be a good idea to send me to China to do some service with the C-46 airplane. So, my first mission was to go to North China to pick up troops and bring them back to Shantou in the southern part of China to fight the Japanese.

As I said before, the war was getting much worse. I took many trips up there, and at one time, we had to transfer a Chinese cavalry outfit from the northern part of China to the southern part of China. That was pretty tricky. They didn't have much time so they thought they would use the airplane. They took my favorite C-47 and made some stalls. In those stalls, they would put four horses. They would have a veterinarian go along on the trip. They would put the horses on the airplane, tranquilize them enough to be calm for a couple hours until we reached our destination, and then unload them, and everything would be okay. Everything was going along fine, and we did several trips with the horses. But then one night, we went for a cavalry outfit in North China, took the usual four horses, put them in the airplane, tranquilized them for the two hours, and when I got south to my destination after two hours the weather was very bad, and I could not land there. I had to either go to an alternate airport or wait out the storm. We went to an alternate airport, which took another hour and a half. In the meantime, the tranquilizer wore off for the horses and they didn't give them any more drugs, so the horses got up and became unruly. There was really nothing we could do; we couldn't land because the weather was too bad. One of the horses knocked its hoof through the side of my airplane, a hole about as big as a watermelon. It was a lucky thing that we had a C-47. The C-47, at the time, was not pressurized, so putting a hole through the cabin was just like opening a window and didn't have anything to do with the pressurization.

The Communist Chinese

We delivered troops and several cavalry outfits from north to south. There came another time when we had to deliver medical supplies to the Communist Chinese. The medical supplies that we had to deliver were to Yunnan, which was the capital of the Communist Chinese, about 70 miles north of The Great Wall. Occasionally, we delivered medical supplies to the Communist Chinese, but it was not on a regular basis. You had to get permission/authorization from the allies to fly the medical supplies to the Communist Chinese, which was another entity by itself. We did, after a while, deliver two or three loads there. The government in Yunnan did not have adequate airports. They had a small strip in a valley. It's a good thing we had the DC-3 because it could land and stop in a small space.

About this time, we had a surprise visit at our base in Chen Yi. Our base in Chen Yi had an airport that was about 90 miles north of Kunming and the elevation of the field was about 7,000 feet. We lived at 7,000 feet, and when we flew the airplane we would go from 7,000 feet to 15,000 feet. One day, we got a surprise visit from Generalissimo Chiang Kai-shek, the head of the Chinese government at that time. We were about forty pilots in the barracks, so we stayed at attention and then passed in review in front of the generalissimo. The generalissimo said, 'Men, I want to thank you for doing such a great job in maintaining the Lifeline of China. For that, I am going to award you pilots the Order of the Purple Cloud.' [Speaking of medals], that was a beautiful medal. I saw it but I never got it because, shortly thereafter, the [civil] war was getting worse in China and the Japanese forces were coming down from the north into the central part of China and into the capital. Chiang Kai-shek had to abandon his seat of government and go to Taiwan. You probably heard that he was in Taiwan. At that time, the raid came so quickly and not knowing about it, they had to leave in a hurry. The generalissimo left behind most of his important papers right there in his office. As it turned out, the order for my medal, the Order of the Purple Cloud, was in his office, with other orders. I never got the medal. Maybe someday, some Chinese ambassador might [bestow] me the medal. I hope I do get it.

The Grand Piano

One night, my roommate said, 'Patrick, I've got cargo going to China and what do you think is on the manifest? A grand piano assigned to Madame Chiang Kai-shek!' The generalissimo's wife was a concert pianist and very good. For some reason, our government wanted to cement relations with China, so they thought, what better way than to send this grand piano to Madame Chiang Kai-shek. So they put it in this cargo plane, instead of some gasoline and other supplies. My friend flew the regular course, and the more he flew toward China with his load, the madder he got and said, 'What in the hell am I doing for the war effort when I should be flying the gasoline for the B-29s, and I've got this darn piano assigned for Madame Chiang Kai-shek?' After a while, he bent down and shut off the gasoline on one engine and the engine quit. The standard procedure when you lose an engine is to jettison the cargo because you want to save the airplane and to hell with the cargo. So they went out back, opened the door, and kicked out the grand piano over the Burma jungles. [*Laughs*]

So when they got to Kunming, China, the truck pulls up to get the piano and the guy said, 'Where's the piano?'

The captain said, 'You know, I lost an engine over Burma and there was something wrong with the cross feed and I had to jettison the cargo. Then later on, I fooled around with the cross feed and checked the tanks and found there was a short on one of the valves. I opened another valve, the gasoline came in, and I started the engine and continued the trip here with both engines.' So, that was humorous. But maybe Madame Chiang Kai-shek got mad and told the generalissimo, 'Those pilots from Chen Yi who you told were going to get the Purple Cloud—forget them!' Maybe that's why I didn't get my Order of the Purple Cloud. [*Laughs*]

The Japanese were pretty smart people. They were smart pilots. [But] we had some basic radar, and we were flying mostly in bad weather anyway. [Remember, our usual pattern] when coming back to Chen Yi, where I was based, [was to] circle until we got the beacon, which was about five miles north of the airport. After we hit the beacon and knew we were at a certain altitude, we'd fly due south for about three minutes, descending until we broke out of the overcast and landing on the runway at Chen Yi. The Japanese, as I said, were pretty smart. They would see us someplace up the line and would follow right in back of our airplane so that when the beacon would pick up our aircraft, it would only see on the radar one blip. The Japanese fighter or bomber would be so close to our tail that the radar would only pick up the one blip. They would follow us down, and when we broke out of the overcast over the airport to land, the Japanese bomber would come right over us and bomb the field, without us ever even knowing they were coming in. That's what they did. That is the only encounter I ever had with the Japanese aircraft, them following me in and bombing the field over my head after I had landed. The only [enemy] ground fire that I encountered wasn't actually ground fire; they would come over and bomb the field. If we happened to be in the barracks, the standard order was to grab our gear and canteens and head for the trenches that were around the base. We would spend the night in the trenches until the bombing was over with and the next morning, we would get out of the trenches and go back to our barracks. That's the only encounter I had with ground fire or face to face with Japanese.

*

Very rarely we would see someone that came from the reserves before the war. There were a few but I didn't know exactly who they were, and they flew with the Flying Tigers. The Flying Tigers were very active in that area, and they started in the States with P-40s, and they gradually rotated to duty in China. We had quite a few of the Flying Tigers flying out of bases in China.

Most of the pilots I flew with were regular cadets that went to flying school that came there. Very few of the pilots were from another airline. There were a few but basically most of the young fellas were trained as cadets and got to fly there. The reason I got to be a first pilot as soon as I got there was because of my experience with the airline. I didn't have to ride as a copilot for three or four months to get used to the airplane and then go on to be the pilot of that airplane. I already had that experience so when I went there, I was immediately put into left seat as the captain of that airplane.

With the C-46 or C-47, we had a crew of three: the pilot (myself), copilot, and radio man. The radio man was also the navigator. He would navigate but have the communications with headquarters and transmit all these messages via radio and they could tell him, sometimes, about where we were. So, the standard crew was the three men. As I said before, I only flew the C-47 and C-46 and those were the crew members. There was no armament at all, not a bit. All we had was our trusty .45 caliber pistols that we carried all the time. Nothing for any guns or bombs, we had just plain airplanes. Later on, I got home and flew a hospital ship, which was a different story. That had the pilot (myself, the captain), copilot, flight nurse, and medical attendant. That was a four-man crew. We always had onboard, on every flight, our parachute. The equipment in the back of the parachute was some sort of survival gear. It had the machete, a couple of flares, three or four packages of soya biscuits to eat, and possibly, if we were over water, there would be some kind of lures to catch fish. That's about it other than mosquito repellent and the parachute itself.

[We never had to bail out], but there were a couple cases where we had run into ice. I was in a C-47 in the China area and had accumulated approximately 2 to 3 inches of ice on the wings. I told the crew, 'You better get your parachutes on. I'm going down as low as I can, and if we don't break out and we run out of gas, the red lights are on now, we're going to have to bail out.' At that particular time, my radio man called in and said, 'Hey, I've got great news! We're pretty close to Shantou, and this is the first time that the government has put in an instrument landing system. Here is the number, and if you will fly a course of 270 degrees for about ten minutes, you will run into the beacon at the end of the runway, and they will turn on the instrument landing system for you!' We did that, got to the beacon, called in, they gave us the signals, turned on the instrument landing system, and we landed. This was probably the first time an Army plane landed in China with the instrument landing system. This was in Shantou, which was one of the main B-29 bases to bomb Japan.

The Chinese People

The Chinese were good people. The reason I say they were good people is because I did duty in India. When I was in India and we had time off, we would go into a small town. We would watch the people just mope around; that was their way of life. Then, when I did duty in China, I'd land and go into a town like Kunming, I'd see the Chinese people and they were walking fast and seemed like they were busy. They were hard-working, studious people. They would respect us and when they saw us they would say, 'Yīqiè dōu hěn hǎo,' which means 'everything is okay.' [*Laughs*] Every time you go to a foreign country, there are always bad words that you pick up. There are also bad words in China. If they didn't like you and really wanted to give you hell, they would take their two fingers, point them to your eyes, and say, 'Nǐ chī sǐ lǎoshǔ.' That meant 'you eat dead mice.' [*Laughs*] On the whole, I respect the Chinese people. They were good workers.

Several times, we had to land in Myitkyina, Burma, and take on gas. That's the airport in Burma. I hate to say this, there was a colonel who was trying to make general. He did make it, of course. His name was Colonel Tunner. Instead of having our tanks full of gasoline, which would be about eight hours of flight, he would tell them to give us three hours of gasoline in the airplane. The other gasoline that was left over did not go into the tank; he would put it into the oil drums. At the end of the month, he would write down 'tonnage over the Hump.' If he put five or six extra drums of gasoline in my airplane from Assam to China, he could write that off as 'tonnage over the Hump.' We would have three hours of gas in the tank, fly from India to Myitkyina, take the drums off, and put more in for tonnage. Then he would put another two hours of flight worth of gasoline in my tanks. So, in other words, there would be about 800 gallons of gasoline in the airplane, and they would only fill me with 200 gallons.

One time, I said to the gasoline man, 'Fill up the tank.'

He said, 'We can't fill up the tanks, we can only give you about one quarter of your usual capacity.'

I got mad. The weather was bad, and I said, 'I will not fly this airplane unless you fill up the tanks.'

He said, 'I can't do that.'

I said, 'Go talk to your operations manager and tell them that I'm going to leave my airplane here, stick with my airplane, and I'm not going to take off until you fill my tanks.'

He came back after half an hour and said, 'We'll fill up your tanks.' So, they filled up my tanks, I took off, finished my routine flight to China, and there it was. Two months later, I saw in the service newspaper that Colonel Tunner was promoted to brigadier general for the excellent job that he had done flying supplies over the Hump. So there you are.

Going Home

I accumulated over 750 hours over the Hump and China flying and the routine was that you would be rotated home at 750 hours. This was in China. I came home from a flight one day and Colonel Keagan, who was our commanding officer, called me into his office. He said, 'Lieutenant Scarano, I want to thank you for the good job that you've been doing here but it's time to send you home. On my desk, I have two orders. I have one order promoting you to captain. The other order is rotating you home. They are both on my desk. Now, if I send them both in, they are not going to act on both of them. What they'll probably do is send you home as your present rank, first lieutenant. I would suggest, if I put in for your promotion first and then you wait two or three weeks, then I'll send in your orders for rotating you home. That way, you'll go home as a captain.'

I said, 'Oh, that's very good.'

He said, 'It's up to you.'

I said, 'Well, I'm anxious to go home. If I go home as a first lieutenant, there won't be much for me to do. But if I go home as a captain, I'll be able to swing a good position as a pilot on a bigger airplane. So, I'll take my chance. Send in the orders for my promotion first and then wait to send in my orders to go home.'

That's exactly what happened. He sent in for my promotion, that came in, and then, two weeks later, he sent in for my rotation home, and that came in. So, I went home as a captain. The bad thing about that, at that particular time, my orders said to leave Chan Yi, China, and fly by military aircraft to Karachi, India. From there, I would get a shuttle and go to Casablanca. [However,] when I got to Karachi, the minute I got into the airport and showed my orders, we heard about VE Day! The people in Europe capitulated. The problem was that they froze all orders to go home right then and there. They said for me to wait until further orders, and I didn't know what to do. There was a rumor that we were going to concentrate more on ending the war with Japan and that, instead of going home, they were going to divert us to another part of China.

I was downfallen. I was anxious to go home. While I was sitting there, a friend of mine that I knew back in the States at OCS came by and said, 'Pat! What are you doing here?' I told him that I was being rotated home, but my orders were frozen. What could I do?

He said, 'I'm flying a supply ship from Casablanca to Karachi. I'm going to unload that, get something to eat, refuel, and I'll be taking off again in about two hours back for Casablanca. But I cannot take any passengers. I have a C-46 airplane that's parked in the north ramp, number 766, but I cannot take passengers.'

I said, 'Oh, thank you, Jim. Good luck to you.'

So, after he left, I took my bag and snuck over to the north ramp, got into the airplane, got in the tail where the toilet was, and closed the door. An hour later, I heard the engines start up and then take off. About ten minutes later, I got out of the can in the back, went to the cockpit, and said, 'Hey, Jim!'

He said, 'Pat, I knew you'd take my hints.'

We landed the next day in Casablanca, the end of his trip and the end of my trip. I went up to the operations manager and asked, 'When is your next flight home?'

He said, 'How did you get here?'

I said, 'I came by military aircraft.'

He said, 'Let me see your orders.' The orders said to go home but that I was frozen in Karachi. He said, 'You know what you're going to do? You're going to take the next airplane going back to Karachi. You stay right here. You did something wrong, and you can't go home.' I sat there, downhearted, of course.

An hour later, the same officer came over to me and said, 'I hate to tell you this, but I've got some important papers to go to the States and they are to go by courier service. I can't send them with just anyone; I have to send them with an officer. You, as a captain, are eligible to take it. Would you like to take the courier to the States?'

I said, 'Do I ever!' Was I happy! They took this pouch and hand-cuffed the strap to my wrist with the important papers. I got on the airplane, and we had landed in Bangor, Maine. That was the end of overseas. Oh, I was so happy. I was the happiest man in the world. I came back to the States and went home on leave. I saw some of my family. I saw my daughter, who was born while I was in India; my three-month-old little girl, Charlene. She was a beautiful thing. I was so happy to be home. I was home for thirty days and then had to go on my next mission.

The Hospital Ship

They sent me to Romulus Air Force Base in Michigan to be a captain on a hospital ship. In Romulus, they gave me a copilot, nurse, and medical attendant. There were four people in our crew, and we had a C-47 airplane. We would take off from Romulus with a pocket full of money because we were going to be gone for a month. We would fly to either Metro Field on Long Island or Fort Dix in New Jersey. We'd take patients that came from the European Theater, usually about six litter cases and four or five ambulatory cases. We would fly them from the east coast, Metro Field or Fort Dix, westward and drop off these patients to a hospital nearest to their home. It could be St. Louis or Cleveland, and we'd pull up, land at the airport, drop off the patients, and work our way west from St. Louis to Kansas City to Denver. After dropping off our last patient, we would proceed to Hamilton Field in California. After a few days of maintenance on the airplane, refueling and something else, we would get ready for our mission going east. When we were in Hamilton Field, CA, we would take patients that were injured in the Pacific Theater and fly them east. We could drop off a couple patients in Ogden, Utah, and continue on to Wichita, Kansas, then Cleveland, and so on. When we finished dropping off all our patients, we returned to Romulus; after several days, we would do the same routine again.

While I was flying the hospital ship, one night in South Dakota, I was homing in on a beacon. Back in those days, they didn't control the airwaves. We had a radio beacon on this aircraft, and it would home in on a broadcast station. They would have music, etc. This one night I was tuned in on a station in South Dakota and heard that the Japanese capitulated and it was VJ Day. So, there was the end of World War II, flying at 12,000 feet over South Dakota, heading west. Shortly after that, I came back to Romulus, went home on leave, and was sent to Rome, New York, for separation from the service.

The Reserves

That was not the end. I stayed in the reserves. I retired in about 1972. I stayed in the reserves and was made a liaison officer for the Air Force Academy. I would go to a high school in uniform, talk to the seniors, men and women, tell them that we would like to have them in the service and after they finished high school and graduated, they could pick going to the Air Force Academy, Annapolis or West Point. They had to get to their Congressional representative and tell them they would like to be picked to go to one of the academies. The congressman would then have two or three students that he or she would send to these academies. I was a liaison officer and spent two weeks of active duty during the summer at the Air Force Academy. I would get to see the students I helped to get through there.

I stayed in the reserves for twenty years. We would meet once a month at an armory near our hometown, Cortland or Binghamton. We put in our fifty hours of studying or duty and that would be a satisfactory year toward my pension for retirement. It must have been about 1947 when the orders came through for making the Army Air Corps into the U.S. Air Force. They gave each one of the officers $200 to go out and buy a blue uniform. I took my uniform and went to Rome Air Force Base, went to the commissary or PX, and picked out a nice blue uniform and hat. From then on, I was U.S. Air Force. That was a memorable occasion.

[When the Korean War broke out], I was waiting to be called up. They never did call me but I had everything ready so if they said, 'Let's go,' I would have all of my household things in order and go just like that [*snaps fingers*]. So, I never went to Korea.

Another duty that I enjoyed very much was being a liaison officer for the Civil Air Patrol. One time, they sent me to Harris Hill as the commander for the encampment for the Civil Air Patrol

Cadets. They would send the cadets to Harris Hill, give them ground training, put them in a glider, and teach them to fly the glider alone so they could get their license as a glider pilot. I was in charge of fifty or sixty Civil Air Patrol cadets, both male and female. That would be my two-week tour duty at the encampment. Later on, I would go to the encampments and do whatever I could do to help the Civil Air Patrol. I got this Air Force Commendation Medal for the work that I did with the Civil Air Patrol.

Keeping In Touch

[I didn't really keep in touch with any flying buddies after the war]. Some nearby, I would, but they were from all over the country, including California. I did have a couple of buddies from Michigan that I kept in touch with. There was one officer from California that called me in the middle of the night. He said, 'Patrick Scarano?'

I said, 'Yes.'

He said, 'You flew over the Hump, right?'

I said, 'Yes.'

He said, 'I have your name here and about once a month I go down the list, pick out a name, call that person, and see how they are doing just for the hell of it!' I never went that far.

[My time in the war] was a good experience and the Lord was with me. The main thing back then, and I don't know if you could do it now, is if you are the commander of that aircraft, it is up to you as a commander to make sure you have a safe return of the airplane and your crew. In fact, to go back to that C-47 flight at 15,000 feet, when I flew the Hump I would tell my crew, 'Wear your sheepskin underwear and sheepskin flying suit, because when you fly with me, I do not turn the heater on. I fly blue and cold, but I return and so will you.' It is up to the captain of that aircraft to look after the crew and the aircraft, and return come hell or high water. There was a good many times when I was in China sleeping in an operation room at the airport and an officer would come up to me and say, 'You're Lieutenant Scarano?'

I'd reply, 'Yeah.'

He'd say, 'I'm going to take your airplane, we need it.'

I'd say, 'You're taking my airplane? How are we going to get home? Where are your orders? Look, you see what I've got over here? [*Points to his hip*] This is a 45-caliber pistol. You touch that airplane and you're going to get it! Get someone else's airplane!' He never touched my airplane. Like I said, take care of your airplane and bring it back home. When you're in Burma and they want to get you short on gas, you say, 'No way, put the gasoline in there or I don't fly the airplane.' As a captain of that aircraft, remember to do your duty.

Civilian Life

After the war, I went back to the airline and said, 'I'd like to come back because you promised me that when we got back from the service that we could come back here. How long will it take until you can check me out as a captain, because I've been in China and probably have 2,000 more hours in a C-47 and that's what they're flying; I'm a much better pilot now than when I left here.'

So they asked what my service number was, and I told them, '527.' I was a copilot with the airline then.

They said, 'Oh my God, you've got a very low number here. It might be two years before we can check you out as a captain.'

I said, 'Hey, I'm not going to fly as a copilot for two years waiting to be captain.'

As it turned out, about six months later, aviation expanded, and I could have been a captain. But I went home and got into the furnace and appliance business because there was a big demand for appliances and opened my store. I did that for a couple years and then I figured since I was still a young man and had a lot of flying left in me that I'd go back to flying. I made out a resume and sent it to some of the big manufacturers, stores, and firms in the Syracuse area. One man, J. Stanley Coyne, who ran the Coyne laundry system, called me and said, 'Patrick, I love your resume. Here is my airplane, you can come and fly with me to Maryland to see if you like it. You can fly three or four days a week and the two days that you don't fly, you can go out in the field and do some selling for me. You can sell garments to General Electric.' I went back to flying. I flew for this man out of Hancock Field for about twelve years. After that, I came back home and did charter work. That was about it.

I'm a member of the Hump Pilots Association and also joined the VFW when I got home. In fact, about two months ago, I was given a pin and emblem of fifty years for being a member of the VFW for fifty years. What else can I say, except that I was born in New York State, I'm going to die in New York State, I think [the governor] is a good man, it's an Empire State and I think I like it here. I want to thank the governor for giving me the opportunity to get my experiences documented for the people now and the people of the future.

Patrick Scarano retired in 1967 from the Air Force Reserves with the rank of lieutenant colonel. He passed away at the age of 97 in January 2013.

CHAPTER FOUR

The B-24 Radioman

Dr. Norman Handelman grew up in Brooklyn, New York, and became a radio operator and gunner on a B-24 Liberator bomber flying the Hump on several missions in the 10th U.S. Army Air Force, one of which included bombing the infamous bridge over the River Kwai. He sat for this interview at the age of 82 in 2005 in Manhattan, New York City.

Norman Handelman

I was born July 14, 1923, in Brooklyn, New York. I was in college at the time of the war. The college was very affected by the war, of course; a lot of people were being drafted from the classes. They started making edicts of all sorts. If you took enough courses of your major, then you could be forgiven the courses that were not major courses like arts, music, philosophy. Then as it came to 1943, I was drafted. It came down to that if you passed the midterm, you got credit for the term. I was drafted shortly after the midterm, which meant I got credit for the term, which also meant I got credit for the courses that I was forgiven. So, I had an abbreviated college degree; it was like a two-and-a-half-year college, I missed a lot of courses a lot of people take. So, I went into the service right from there.

[When I heard about Pearl Harbor], I was in my apartment and I was listening to a football game, the Giants or the Chicago Bears. That's where I was, and all of a sudden, there was a break in of some sort. Somebody announced that 'Pearl Harbor's been bombed.' Pearl Harbor, I had no idea where Pearl Harbor was. Anyhow, slowly the news started to trickle out. I think the game went on to the finish because nobody knew the enormity of it.

I ended up in the Air Corps. When I was drafted, I went down to Lexington Avenue Grand Central Station,the post office. There were several people there representing the Marines, the Navy, the Army, and the Army Air Corps. They all looked you over, looked your records over, and I was selected for the Air Force, the Air Corps.

[I went for basic training to] Miami, Florida. We were dressed— it was late spring—we were given winter clothing. We were put on a train, a coal burning train, I remember a lot of soot and all of that. I don't know how long it took us to get down to Florida, but we got down there. Nobody was going to tell us where we were going. It was top secret and all of that. There we were in winter clothing, going down to Miami Beach. Of course, we changed. So, Miami Beach was where I trained, staying at a small hotel off the beach. I have visited a couple of times just for reminiscence' sake. It was a beautiful beach; training was not hard. My image of what infantry training was like was that it was very arduous exposure to all kinds of things, but down there I just remember marching, learning right face, left face, about face, present arms, the right way to salute. There's a right way to salute!

After six weeks to eight weeks, we were on a train again out to St. Louis. At that point, they had done all kinds of orientation tests and the like. I wound up in radio school. We learned Morse code basically and we learned also how the Air Corps radio system worked. The planes were equipped with long antennas and there were what they called 'command units'; you have to change the frequency. It was a big, bulky tube kind of arrangement. So, we learned Morse code in varying steps. They gave us mock-ups occasionally. We wound up in a little compartment by ourselves. We were fed Morse code at varying speeds. I did well enough to get some kind of special days off when my parents came out to visit. I must say, for a sheltered boy living in Brooklyn where everything was gray and concrete and that sort of thing, it was a treat for me. St Louis was a treat because of all of the greenery. There I was in St. Louis with beautiful parks and wide streets. In Arlington, it was also lovely with very wide avenues, very big skies, palm trees, and a lot of exciting things to do.

From there I went down to gunnery school in Arlington, Texas. They gave us all kinds of instruction; we were taught to lead enemy planes. For planes coming in, you don't fire at him up there. You know he's coming in, so you lead him; depending on how far away, you lead him by what they call 'rads,' the circular vision of what the aiming thing is. So, we were learning to lead. We wound up with shotguns. We wound up with clay pigeons. We wound up riding on open trucks around a course where suddenly a clay pigeon would come out and you were supposed to get at them, you know, by leading it. I had a great time. It was like target practice for me. For me, it was kind of like an unreal experience. First of all, the [Army] Air Force was kind of sheltered. From basic training you're in the mud all the time, basically;n the Air Force, we weren't. Not quite coddled, but it was nice. So, we enjoyed ourselves. We were young kids playing at shooting and all those things. As I said, for me a sheltered boy from Brooklyn, the idea of shooting bullets and shooting [was fantastic!]

One of the things we had to learn at gunnery school was [stripping a 50-caliber machine gun]. Again, I told you I was a sheltered boy, as I said, I had never really done anything with my hands, I'd been studying all of the time basically. I learned, as everybody else did, to take a 50-caliber machine gun apart and put it together again blindfolded. You got to know the names of every last piece. I remember it got down to the smallest piece that had the longest name. I couldn't do it again, of course.

At gunnery school, we would go up in AT6s at the time. They're two-seaters. The pilot would take us up and there would be some [washouts].Later I found out Women's Air Corps—WACs—would fly target planes pulling some targets for us to shoot at with this machine gun that you were given. I did poorly. So did most of us. That was the only exposure I had, the only experience I had firing a machine gun.

By that time, as far as we were concerned, the war was never going to end. It was something that you didn't think was ever, you lived in a war time, and that was it. For all you knew, you'd be an old man discharged from the service and the war would be continuing.

Shipping Out

So, I got orders to ship out. We went down to a collection point in Newport News. I went with a bunch of my friends from gunnery school and others that I had met in this collection point. One of them became a real good buddy of mine. We went on this big ship, the USS *Randall*. I remember that it was its maiden voyage; it was a troop ship, it carried thousands of troops. It was fast, it didn't need an escort. We went around to the Panama Canal, I remember watching us go through the canal, down to the South Pacific, all the way up through the New Zealand islands around to the west coast of Australia, where we docked in Perth thirty days later. Thirty days aboard ship!

To India

We stayed two nights in Perth. Some friends and I took suburban trains into Freemantle, things like that. Then we got on board ship again and fifteen more days. Again, we were not told where we were going. When you're going down [from the United States], and you're not going to Europe, and you're going someplace south, where could you go? Who knew we were going on into the CBI? It wasn't like until a couple of days out of Bombay that we knew because we went all the way around Madagascar to avoid submarines. At Bombay we were told we could let our people [at home] know. How could we let them know? We couldn't do anything, really. From there, again, we were waiting to find out what we were going to do because we were replacements. We got on board a train again and went across India by Indian third-class trains, where we'd sleep on slatted benches. You'd see exotic scenery. You'd see stuff that newsreels were made of.

We wound up in Calcutta. It was monsoon season at that point. So, we waited; I remember waiting with my group outside. Nice weather. All of a sudden, it just seemed like that, it poured. Beautiful blue sky, it just turned black in no time. It poured and then it stopped. The sun came out. We were soaked and then we were dry.

We stayed in tents for a few nights. Then we were transported up somewhere north of Calcutta. I've been trying to locate it on the maps. Kermatola, [on the east coast of India], stuff like that, not on the maps. This being the monsoon season, we hung around for a couple of weeks trying to get used to what was going on. I remember how I said it was like a game and all of that. When we got there, the bombing mission time was ending because you don't bomb during the monsoon season. You can't see your target. So, I remember a mission when we were in an orderly room or something like that there were guys coming back from a mission, coming in. The operations officer, a big, strapping Swedish guy, was crying and furious about the fact that his buddy had been shot down. I still remember—it registered with me, but nowhere did I feel like, 'Oh my God, this is terrible, I could die, it could happen to me!' That didn't register; I don't think for any of us it really registered. It was like it was your job. You're here. Something could happen down here on your way [to work], so you just do your job.

Missions

After a few weeks, we were assigned different planes because we were replacement radio operators. There's attrition of some sort. Sometimes people got sick, they got wounded or they died or opted out or whatever. So, we were assigned and then we went on gas hauling missions. We flew the Hump. We took gas. Every time I flew it was a different B-24. We flew on a lot of these hauling missions, which were dangerous, but being a kid and it being a job, it didn't feel dangerous.

[We were not under attack] on these missions. By the time we were there, the Japanese had finally been stopped; they had encroached into Burma, they were there close to the border of India. At the time, there were some Indian troops that really didn't like the British at all and were likely to throw in their hands with the Japanese. So, the Japanese were pretty close to getting into India, but there were all kinds of reasons why they were stopped. Supply lines got short; the jungles were terrible. By that time, they were starting to retreat a little bit.

I remember flying the Hump. The mountains there were very sizeable, I don't know, 15,000 feet or something like that. When you got over them, there'd be a sudden down drop midair. I remember I was never scared. I keep on saying that. I wasn't scared until, as a radio operator, I sat on the parachute. It was on the seat under me. I don't know exactly where I would have jumped out from. I sat on the chute until one day over this Hump, the engineer, a great friend, suddenly started to put his parachute on. I had never seen this before. I said, 'What's wrong?'

He said, 'Nothing.' I thought, he's putting the chute on. I thought if he's putting the chute on and he's the engineer, he must know something. From then on, I had my chute immediately available.

Later on, we went on bombing missions when the monsoon season ended. Then we came back, and yes, then we'd wear flak jackets. Sometimes flying high, we wore heat suits.

We took Atabrine, I believe, which was maybe a little bit later. Atabrine, we found out, turns you yellow. I started noticing my eyeballs were looking a little strange. It was the Atabrine. We were told to watch out for the waters, that sanitation levels were different. Someplace early in India, we were told to watch out for Indian alcohol, liquor. I was not a drinker. It didn't matter to me, but we were told to watch out because it can blind you. I remember seeing a guy coming back having drunk a lot and he was blind. It didn't last, but he was blind. He was terrified, of course. So, [we were warned of] that kind of disease or the idea of maybe consorting with prostitutes. A 'Pro Kit' included a condom to use and some kind of prophylactic ointment to put inside it and then something else to use after you finished the intercourse to inject into your penis to protect the penis from any intrusion of germs, and to wash, maybe some special soap. I think it was given to you on your leave.

For the Air Corps, the Air Force, between missions, there's nothing to do. We had it easy, I have to stress. I did not have a bad war. We didn't see any women except the Indian women, and we saw them at a distance. We had USO shows. One of them I remember was like the last USO show we got, because several of the guys got very disorderly and started making all kinds of obscene remarks about the girls—what he wanted to do with them, that sort of thing. The orders came down from the bigwigs, that's it, no more. We can't trust you guys.

I had this friend, as I said, who I see every couple of years or so. He's surviving nicely. He was my buddy in the war, in the India war; I know I have pictures showing me with a .45 automatic in a holster around my shoulder. We carried them around. There was a place for two automatic clips. Maybe we were given the clips when we left, when you go on a mission, even on a flight to haul gas, because there was always a danger of something happening to the plane. The jungles down below us were infested with Japanese. So, we were given kits to carry with us. One of the things we had, I regret not having taken it with me when I came home, we were given two small buttons. We had a flight suit, which had buttons on it, like copper metal buttons or something. We were given two of them to replace two of the buttons on the suit. When you do that, they're indistinguishable from the other buttons. One of them had a little bump on it, the other had two bumps. If you need it, you put them together and they were a compass. You put them down and they would magnetize, and they pointed north. So, that was one of the escape things we were given.

We also had carbines, small 30mm rifles. I don't remember where they were. They may have been in the planes.

The planes themselves, when we flew on bombing missions, we might have had some fighters had we flown into the Hump. We had these 50 caliber machine guns. By and large, until we flew the Hump, we flew at relatively low altitude. It was warm there, so we didn't have to wear too much. We could fly with the open waist window.

This war was never going to end.

Weightless

I was just remembering something, my lifetime experience with weightlessness. I hadn't flown for about a month overseas. My best buddy from all of the war from the beginning was shot down. We went on this mission. It was great fun watching the bombs dropping and all of that. He went on a mission a few days later and he didn't come back. I'm a little more upset now, thinking of it, than I was then. I was upset, though. I just felt like I couldn't fly. I just can't fly. I knew the policy there was you wouldn't be charged with any kind of major offense. They'd just ground you and get another replacement. So, it took me a long time.

Finally, I was going on a mission. We were awakened at 3:30 or 4:00 depending on how long the mission was, and we got very long missions from up in India all the way down into Burma. Sometimes they would go for twelve hours, fourteen hours. We bombed the bridge over the River Kwai. That's a long distance from India! That mission would be like sixteen hours.

Anyhow, I got grounded that month. I finally decided that I can't live this way. I want to fly. I want to fly, and I have a better chance of coming home at least for a furlough than if I just stay on the ground. This war was never going to end. So, I volunteered to fly on a training mission. The pilot was being trained for night flying, instrument flying. The training involved all kinds of maneuvers and the like, up and down.

With the B-24, way up front was the bombardier and, I think, the nose gunner. I'm not sure about that. Yes, the bombardier and the nose gunner way up front, downstairs. Then there was the cabin cockpit where the pilot and co-pilot were, then there's a narrow partition. On the right-hand side was where the radio operator sat with the radios. The major job of the radio operator on a flight was to listen to see if the flight has been cancelled or diverted. You have to know the code and the code name for the day. If a message comes, you put it down and you decode it. So, we sat with the headset on, on the right-hand side. On the left-hand side was the engineer. He's got his own desk as we did. Also, the plane that we flew there's various models. The plane we flew in you went up through a little trap door underneath the plane. You went up the trap door and then you were in a compartment. There was a gallon of fuel for a little engine. We called it the 'put-put' engine. It kind of warmed the major engines. It got them primed for starting. You got one more trap door, you open the trap door and come up and you've got a floor. That's where the radio operator sits, and the engineer sits. Then you walk straight through the walkway, the catwalk, through the bombs. There was a narrow catwalk about this wide. Then you got to the waist.

In this flight that we're talking about, the pilot was doing various maneuvers. At one point what he was doing was apparently checking out a stall instrument. He went up, then stalled it. This big B-24 started falling. I had no idea. We had no idea what he was doing. He was just being told by the instructor what to do.

All of a sudden, I felt like I was being pressed up against the ceiling of this plane. I thought we must be upside down. I started to try to right myself and I couldn't do that. Then I saw the trap door open and up comes floating this one gallon can of gasoline. I think something's wrong; I don't know it was weightlessness. Guys who were sitting in the waist—as I said, it was warm there—had the waist windows open and they were just hanging around. Before they knew it, they were starting to float toward the windows and float out and they were grabbing things. Of course, nobody got hurt. That was exciting. That was my experience with weightlessness.

To go on a mission, you're awakened. You go in, you have breakfast. You go into the room, and you'll be told what the mission of the day is. You'd be told, at one point, 'Watch out, here's a prisoner of war camp. See to it you don't bomb the prisoner of war camp, but you want to get the railroad station and tracks here.' Then, we would go out into another room to pick up our parachute. We also picked up a belt, it's like a life preserver belt like what we had onboard ship. Only the belt had, I forget what else it had in it, but it has a whole bunch of things to be used in case you're downed.

We had the blood chit[8] to help in one way but there was also a tin, and the tin had opium in it, it turns out. There was also American dollar bills, old bills. The old bills were so that if you were downed, you gave them to the people who were helping you, so that they couldn't be accused by the Japanese of having had these recently because they were so old. The opium was a special bribe to people to help us get out. I have a friend who was downed and was indeed taken out by the Chinese and it did help him all the way through. There were quite a few like that.

Anoxia

Let me brag about something else that happened. We were shown the dangers of anoxia in our training. We were taken into a decompression chamber where we were told that you want to wear a mask when you are above 12,000 feet because oxygen deprives your brain of the capacity to work well. It was hard to know so we're going to show you guys. Groups of us were taken into this chamber

---

[8] blood chit- military notice for civilians who may come across a 'friendly' armed-services member in distress, requesting assistance.

and they would slowly reduce the oxygen content. They reached 25,000 or sooner than that. Whatever it was, they showed at twelve, thirteen thousand your judgment is off.

I remember watching one guy. We are now pretty high. He was asked to write your name, rank, and serial number. In my case, it was Norman S. Handelman, 327...or whatever. I forgot what it was. Just keep on writing it. Just keep on writing it. I remember watching this guy writing and writing, then his hand started to tremble. He was uncoordinated. He dropped the pencil. He just stared blankly into space. He was out. Somebody gave him the pencil back, gave him some oxygen. We had this oxygen mask on. They're plugged into the oxygen circuit. He was told, because we were all wearing it by this time, he was told to unplug his. It was a male to female plug. Unplug it and do this exercise. So, he did. He was passing out. 'Plug your oxygen mask in. Plug the mask in. Plug the mask in!' He lost it. He just passed out. They plugged it back in for him. They gave him the pencil. He immediately started writing his name, rank, serial number as if nothing had happened.

I thought I was going to experiment with myself. I volunteered. What a jerk. Permanent brain damage. [*Laughs*] But I volunteered. I remember they told me this to unplug it, okay. I remember name, rank, and serial number. I felt so wonderful. I had never seen my handwriting this good. It felt so good, that's how it felt to me. They gave me this pencil. I started writing and all of a sudden I realized that I had passed out because there was a scrawl there and I hadn't known it. I figured that this is routine. I'm going to try something else. So, I volunteered again. I figured that I'll do the Gettysburg Address. So, 'four score and seven years ago our fathers brought on this continent. Four score....and dedicated to liberty'... and started repeating myself. They gave me the pencil again. At this point, I didn't know what I was doing. I just stopped and realized that I had passed out. But a routine matter, and you'd think you had been doing it all along.

For some reason, they needed more people in China so a bunch of us were sent into China to Luliang, which is near Kunming. We were established there, and we were to fly back and forth. We had flown over the Hump from Luliang before during the monsoon season. We were to be established there for how long we didn't know, of course. Where we would go back to India or pick up something in Luliang and fly to Sichuan or Guilin or other places where the Chinese were holding back or trying to hold back the Japanese and also supplying the 14th Air Force—Chennault's Flying Tigers. We supplied them with gasoline and stuff like that. We were in China for two or three months. I think two or three months. While there, I shared a tent with Bob.

Detached Service

When you come back from a mission, you'd be given a slug of whiskey and you'd work your way back to a room where they'd debrief you, tell what you saw, what happened, how much the flak was, where was it, the fighters, what the results of the bombing were, and so on. I came back from this mission. You're kind of tired. You got up early and it's intense. I got back and I'm starting to relax. Somebody comes from the orderly room saying the major wants to see you.

I said, 'What for?' I didn't know. I went to the office. They said, 'Pack up your clothing, you're going on a secret mission.' A secret mission! The hope of everybody there was that the mission would be to go back on a bond selling tour in the States! All I was told was that it's a secret mission.

I got back to the barracks. The barracks, by the way, we had it easy. We had bearers. We had men who cleaned the barracks. We slept on string beds with interwoven material on top of which were blankets and four posters so that there were mosquito nets to cover you. The cleanliness was taken care of. We had somebody we hired, all of us, probably eight to twelve of us in this room. So, I came back and everybody else was taking off their clothing. Here I am packing my bags. 'Where are you going, Handelman?'

I said, 'I'm going on a secret mission.' I figured that I've got something over them.

'What do you mean a secret mission?'

'That's all I've been told, it's a secret mission.'

'What do you think it is?'

'I don't know. Maybe it's a bond selling tour.' What could it be?

So I pack up. The next day, the truck takes me to the airport, to the airstrip. I get on the plane. God knows where I am going. Who knows? Maybe to Delhi. Maybe home. I get in. I get on the truck about twenty minutes later. Then we get on the plane. Twenty minutes later, the plane lands. That's a pretty short trip. I figured, that's not home. Maybe you've got to change planes there because it's a secret mission. For God's sake, its only twenty minutes.

We wait for the other plane. A truck comes and takes us to another airstrip where we were then—there were a whole bunch of us, several crews of us, we were replacements for combat cargo. We did then become part of combat cargo on detached service.

What we did then, we carried all kinds of cargo to the front-line troops in Burma. It was all kinds of stuff. We may have carried some ammo. I don't remember that.

That was out on detached service. Then, I came back. I logged many, many hours. We went by hour in terms of citations and the like. Well, it was a number of flights, but they were all varied. Some carried gas across the Hump. Some were bombing Burma or Thailand. Some were giving food and ammunition to front-line troops. In total, I had 60 flights flying in planes with high octane fuel, carrying fuel and carrying dangerous cargo into dangerous areas. So, I had 60 flights. That's the way it worked there. I came back and most of my friends had gone home by then because they had served their bombing missions, and I had been doing some lesser than bombing missions. I came back but I was scheduled for return home too. At the time, as I said, you got medals based on the number of hours you had put in. You got an air medal if you put in, I don't know, a hundred hours. You got an oak leaf cluster if you put in two hundred. You got a Distinguished Flying Cross if you put in three hundred combat hours. You got a third oak leaf cluster for another hundred, and another hundred would be another DFC.

I had just a few hours short of an oak leaf cluster. I did something that you're always told time and again, don't volunteer for anything. I figured I'd like to get that oak leaf cluster. So, I volunteered for a mission even though I knew I was going home I was told. Thank God, I'm here.

I was all set for the mission. It was supposed to be an easy mission, what they called a 'baksheesh,' a milk run. I get awakened. I get to the front line. Our plane is scrubbed. Something is malfunctioning. So, okay, I'll go. That's a mission from hell. The guys…some didn't come back. Some came limping back. It was not a good mission. It was Rangoon where all the Japanese had concentrated their flak and planes and that sort of thing. I got it, but I volunteered for a foolish thing. So that was my detached service.

Coming Home

Just to add insult to injury, when I came back, I didn't fly back. I came back by boat again. I got on a troop ship in Calcutta, went through the Suez Canal, the Mediterranean, the Strait of Gibraltar back at the same place I debarked from. Thirty days this time. I put in two and a half months at sea. Then, of course, I was one of the earliest people back. I came back because I got points for overseas time, combat time, medals, and all different points. I came back, and I was a changed boy by that point. I had experiences that I never dreamed of having.

I was onboard ship when Germany surrendered. There was a celebration, but at the same time the war was still on with the Japanese. I had been fighting the Japanese. It felt like it was okay, it was very nice that the war is over, that the Germans surrendered, but we're going back again. That was the prospect that we'd go back, and it would be worse because the Japanese would be concentrated. I was at home on leave when the atomic bomb dropped. I was delighted. So were all of my colleagues because that ended the war.

We were overseas when President Roosevelt died. He did. Oh my God, that's awful. That's terrible. Who's the vice president? Nobody knew who the vice president was. Nobody knew the name Truman. That was shocking, of course. What's going to happen next? I was discharged in New York City in October '45.

I made use of the GI Bill, very much so. We got the 52-20 club. Fifty-two weeks and twenty dollars a week unemployment. After a few weeks, I couldn't just hang around to collect the money. I had been trained basically as an accountant. I knew I didn't want to be an accountant. I just didn't. I had too many opening experiences in life at that point. An accountant sitting in an office scribbling numbers didn't appeal to me anymore. I was advised by a cousin, a knowledgeable cousin, who was a counselor to try it out. I tried for six months. Terrible. I just sat and wrote numbers, and I hated every minute of it. Finally, after six months of it, I quit. I started looking for what to do.

I went looking for schooling, looking for something to do, maybe journalism, maybe use my radio skills in an airline piloted plane but there was nothing there that I knew of. The journalism schools were closed by the time I looked to get in. So, I didn't know what to do. Somehow the idea of psychology, the idea of understanding people, had come to my mind some conversation I had through lunches. I went to visit the dean of the psychology department at NYU. He was very discouraging. There was no way to make a living. You can't make money or whatever. At the time, there really wasn't a way for a psychologist to make money basically. Not for many, but just around that time, a lot of veterans were coming home with a lot of mental disturbances. The Veterans Administration was swamped. They didn't have the facilities or the people to work with them. The number of psychiatrists was limited. I don't know how they got the idea, but they established training programs under the National Institute for Mental Health, the VA. They had a training program just at the time I was looking at getting into psychology. I took a test, and I apparently passed the test. I was accepted for a four-year training program in clinical psychology. At the same time, you were going to school, you'd work twenty hours a week. I had a lot of good training that way.

I joined AMVETS briefly. I didn't like the American Legion. I felt it was much too bound with tradition and didn't have the right political slant for me. Veterans of Foreign Wars. Jewish Veterans. They all seemed like organizations. So AMVETS came around at that point too. It had a very short life, but again, that attracted me, but I really wasn't focused on that. I was focused on getting my life together and becoming something.

I met my best buddy who had been with me in radio school and gunnery school; he was shot down in India, in Burma. Coming across on the ship, I met other people. I met this other fellow Bob La Canto, and we became quick friends. We had a lot of great conversations and shared a lot. We shared a tent in India. We became very close friends. However close you are, you're still at war. He went back to Ohio. I stayed in New York City. I contacted him briefly after the war, then I got involved in my own life, getting married, that sort of thing. Then about six or seven years ago—his name always stayed with me—I thought I'm going to look him up on the internet. I found several Bob La Cantos, five of them. I sent a postcard to each one saying I'm looking to get in touch with Bob La Canto. I got a call from this guy enthusiastic about hearing from me and so on. So, we became friends again. It turns out he became a professor of journalism in Illinois and other things too. I visited. We still share so many of the same interests, really, it's remarkable. We had very different backgrounds; we share much the same with one exception. He's crazy about flying. He has his own plane, which delights me, because when I go to visit him, I fly with him and it's fun. Here's this other old geezer flying a plane!

For me, I remember somebody once said you had a good war, and I did. I was fortunate. People there, I saw things I never would see. I escaped unscathed. I met friends with whom I still correspond and visit with.

CHAPTER FIVE

The B-29 Radarman

Robert D. O'Brien was born at home and raised and educated in the Bronx. He entered the Army Air Corps in 1943, and within two years he had survived thirty-six combat missions as a B-29 radar operator, gunner, bombardier/navigator in the China-Burma-India Theater and from Tinian Island in the Western Pacific. He was awarded the Distinguished Flying Cross, four Air Medals, the Asiatic Pacific Medal with silver star, and other awards. Unfortunately, right when he entered the service, his only brother, James O'Brien, was a victim of the war.

'Our plane was named before we got it. We got a war-weary one because we were new over there. It was called 'The Untouchable.' It was a good plane, and after several missions, they decided to change all four engines on it. Then we were assigned to take that plane and test run it, I guess good fortune for us. The officers were given a three-day pass. The rest of us took off to parts unknown. We didn't know that we had been assigned to that plane to test fly it. A young fellow that I had met just the day before who had graduated from grammar school with me, a fellow by the name of Morrisey, he took my place, and the plane went up, caught fire, the wing burned off, and the crew plus, I think, fifteen joy riders were all killed. Strangely enough, though it scared me afterward, it was almost

the anniversary of my brother's death. All I could think of, if I was on that plane and my folks got that message just one year after my brother, it would have been devastating.'

Robert D. O'Brien

I was born August 11, 1925, in New York City. I attended DeWitt Clinton High School in the Bronx. I really don't recall my reaction [to the news about Pearl Harbor], but what I do recall was going back to school after hearing of it. All of the windows were taped up. It was a scary proposition for me. It looked like the beginning of a war-torn area. There were all crosses, so the glass wouldn't shatter when the bombs hit us. During that time, I worked forty hours a week as an usher in Radio City Music Hall. I enlisted in the Army Air Corps after completing a testing program for pilot training in 1943. I wanted to be a pilot and after being called up, actually when I was called up I got my orders to report for February 2, 1944, and I left my orders on my parents' dresser, so they'd know when I'd be called up. I imagine they were very delighted to see my name wasn't on the list. They never turned it over to find my name beginning with the next list on the back page. I just couldn't understand why they weren't concerned about me going into the service. So, I got up early in the morning of February 2, prepared my breakfast. My father heard me stirring about, came in, and said, 'What's going on here?'

I said, 'I'm going into the army!' That roused the household. I guess, like all teenagers, I had that failure to communicate. First off, I went to Fort Dix for indoctrination. Then I went to Greensboro, North Carolina, and just about twenty days after reaching basic training, I got the word that my brother had been killed overseas. That was rather upsetting. He was in the Coast Guard. I thought it fitting that I should go home to be with my parents at that time, but I was told emphatically that no one left basic training for any reason. I went to the Red Cross to appeal to them, which was a waste of time. I went to the chaplain, which was a waste of time. I went to the base commander, and I don't know where I got the nerves, but I just let them know that I either go with a pass or I go without a pass. Lo and behold, I never saw the base commander, but a WAC assistant came out with a five-day pass for me and I went home. I had no money and appealed to the Red Cross and they weren't very helpful. My barracks mates, who I really didn't know at all, chipped in and collected money for me to go home. Years later, I realized that I never repaid them, and they never asked to be repaid.

The B-29s

I left basic training, and we went to flight training school in Florida. We never reached there. We found out that the flight training school had closed. The train reversed route and went off to Arlington, Texas, for gunnery school. After gunnery school, I went to Clovis, New Mexico, for flight training and to meet a crew. I was very fortunate the crew I joined had an experienced pilot. He was a pre-World War II pilot. He was a little older than the rest of us. It was a very intelligent group of people, so I was very fortunate they were so good. In Clovis, we had a lot of bad experiences. Many B-29 planes went down due to poor maintenance. A B-29, at that time, was still loaded with bugs. There were many crashes due to the [malfunctioning] engines of the plane, plus very, very poor maintenance. It got so bad that the commander of the post issued an order that there would be no permanent personnel on the base allowed to leave until the crashes stopped. Lo and behold, they stopped almost immediately—very poor maintenance.

When our training was finished, we were then assigned to go to a place called Kearney, Nebraska, to pick up a new plane to go overseas. We had no idea where overseas would be. Anyway, we got to Kearney, Nebraska. We saw the crews that were waiting there for their planes. They'd been there weeks after weeks, which didn't upset us too much. We figured we'd be safe for a while. Two days later, we were sent to Florida and put on a converted B-24, then took off for parts unknown.

Radar

When I was in Clovis—going back a step—I was trained as a gunner. They had already filled the slot for a tail gunner, right gunner, left gunner, top gunner, and I figured where's my position? They called me a 'roving gunner,' so I had to learn all positions as well as the bombardier's position.

In a quick order, they said to me you're a radar operator. I had never heard of radar. They sent me off to school, radar training. The radar sets were on a platform, and they showed us the switch one way to turn it on and one way to turn it off. Then they showed us how to read a map. So, that was my training. On the way overseas, I went to my navigator who I knew had been trained in radar.

I said, 'What is the radar all about? What does it do?' We were never told that.

He said, 'That's a military secret. I can't tell you.' [*Laughs*]

Missions

Anyway, we went overseas and wound up in India in a place called Piardoba. I was with the 58th Bomb Wing. We started our missions from there flying over the Himalayas into China to bring bombs and other supplies. So, it would be back and forth on several occasions. That was in November of '44. Then we started our serious bombing missions. A lot of missions, it took fourteen hours. You flew round trips. We were based in India. We were also based in China. We'd either bomb Singapore or Bangkok, those areas, from India. If we went to China, we had one bombing run into Japan and others to Nanking, Manchuria, and so on in that part of the world.

One disastrous one for many of us was to Omura in Japan where we were lost. One of the reasons we were lost, we didn't know about the jet stream at the time. We're blown so far off course. The navigator just couldn't understand how the winds could be that strong. He kept on compensating. He did find us. Actually, they were giving the order to bail out over the Himalayas some place, but he found our way home. One mission after another. Altogether, I had thirty-six.

Our plane was named before we got it. We got a war-weary one because we were new over there. It was called 'The Untouchable.' It was a good plane, and after several missions, they decided to change all four engines on it. Then we were assigned to take that plane and test run it, I guess good fortune for us. The officers were given a three-day pass. The rest of us took off to parts unknown. We didn't know that we had been assigned to that plane to test fly it. A young fellow that I had met just the day before who had graduated from grammar school with me, a fellow by the name of Morrisey, he took my place, and the plane went up, caught fire, the wing burned off, and the crew plus, I think, fifteen joy riders were all killed. Strangely enough, though it scared me afterward, it was almost the anniversary of my brother's death. All I could think of, if I was on that plane and my folks got that message just one year after my brother, it would have been devastating.

Singapore

We went and bombed Singapore and Bangkok on several occasions. By the end of February, we learned that we were going to be off to parts unknown. Our plane was no longer with us, so we had to go by ship. We went off and wound up in Tinian Island forty-seven days later. It was on Tinian Island that we completed most of our missions. We were finally assigned a new plane, which was unnamed and unpictured because some leading admiral or general's wife decided it was obscene to have the pictures on the planes and they didn't want any other names on them. So our final plane had no name. It just had a number.

We had one mission to Singapore I remember. We were very, very tired. The whole crew was very tired because we had been kept very busy with one mission after another when we were in India. But we went off on this one mission to Singapore. The pilot said to the copilot or vice versa, 'I've got to take a snooze. Put it on automatic pilot.' He reached over to put it on automatic pilot and, as he did it, he fell asleep.

We went in a very slow circle for I don't know how long. It was a question of should we abort this mission and go home and face ridicule. Everybody was sleeping on the plane except the navigator, and he was watching for a break in the overcast so he could take a fix on the stars.

Finally, there was a break, and he looked up and the stars were not where they were supposed to be. Immediately, he corrected our flight. We went on to Singapore and joined up with another crew bombing. We returned; we landed just about on fumes in the plane. That was seventeen hours and forty-five minutes of flying. The next mission, which was just a few days later, was three hours shorter. They didn't usually give us enough fuel to waste three hours of flying time. Due to our very bright engineer, he was able to save fuel.

I don't know if you knew about one of the raids into Singapore. One of our crews, I don't know which one it was, but they dropped a bomb right down the funnel of a ship, which was in the dry dock in Singapore. Rumor has it that the English government sued us for repair of that dry dock because we blew it to pieces. Then I went on another mission to Singapore a few days later with a crew that was without a radar operator. I was assigned to it. I was told it's going to be a 'milk run.' A 'milk run' is, don't worry about it, there's no danger whatsoever. So, we went on this recon mission that had no danger whatsoever. My duty was to take radar pictures over Singapore to see what was going on there. They issued me a 35mm camera to take pictures with. I had never in my life seen a 35mm camera. I had no idea how to operate it and they said press a button. That was my training on a 35mm. So, I went on the mission and took pictures galore. I have no idea if they ever came out or not. [But on this mission], we were attacked by a horde of Japanese fighters. They shot us up pretty badly, knocked out all communications on the plane, gave us a few scrapes, though nothing serious. We had to land at a place at the border of India and Burma. It was an English base. Our plane was repaired and fueled up. The next day, we flew back to our base in India, but no one had ever communicated the fact that we were alive. My crew were rather shocked to see me walk in.

Bombing Japan

I received the Distinguished Flying Cross. Actually, there should have been a couple, not to me especially, but to other members of the crew. We went to Japan. About the time we hit Iwo Jima on the way to Japan, we had a lot of engine trouble. Again, should we just land at Iwo Jima and abort the mission? Should we try to get back to our base on Tinian? It was decided to go on. We bombed Japan with one engine that was completely out. By the time we got back to our base, we were flying on two engines. By the time we landed, one was just about ready to quit. We landed actually with one engine. They thought that was a gutsy thing to do. I believe that's what it was for. But, as you know, they give out medals quite often based on the number of missions you complete.

On one mission, the doors just opened up and stayed open, which caused a lot of drag on the plane. The right gunner, the bombardier, and the engineer had to go into our bomb bay doors. There's two bomb bays—two doors in each bomb bay. These three people went into the bomb bay doors after we descended. We were just off the island of Japan and open to attack by planes. We were all alone because we were falling behind our squadron. We went down to a lower altitude. The three of them went into the bomb bay doors without parachutes, without oxygen. The tallest was the right gunner—Jim Sewell. They took turns sitting on his ankles as he lowered himself down into this open bomb bay door and hooked a cable to the bottom of the door, then he went around to the other side and hoisted it up and locked it in place. He had to do that four times, I believe, at a height of 17,000 feet. You get yourself killed at fifty feet! I read that other people doing the same thing got the Silver Star, other medals. He was never put in for anything at all, and he deserved it.

'We Lost Our Pilot'

We lost our pilot just about July of 1944. We were all assigned, again fortunately or unfortunately, we were assigned training missions. That July, we knew the war was winding down. New crews were coming over and needed a little bit of training. I was out goofing off swimming when my crewmate told me to get myself up to get on a plane for a training mission. I rushed up after a long delay. I was assigned to two different planes, one with my pilot and one with another crew, Captain Gay I believe it was. I had to train the newly arrived radar operators. They knew more than I did. They'd had a year's training in the States. They were all officers. When we landed, we found that my pilot's plane, which I was assigned to as well, had crashed and all aboard there had been killed. I think there were twenty-eight people on that plane, joy riders and so on. He was killed in July.

A Secret Weapon

In August, we had the atom bombs dropped. We didn't know what it was all about. When the bomb was delivered to our island, a rumor started. You may know the story about that ship the bomb was delivered on, the *Indianapolis*. When that ship came—we'd seen ships coming in before—that one delivered the atom bomb. We had no idea about it. The rumors started that a secret weapon was on the island. I don't know how the rumors started but most of us didn't pay any attention to it.

In August, the two bombs were dropped. I guess it was almost forty-five years later I was reading a book saying that our missions just prior to the dropping of the bombs were decoys. We had a mission to Japan. On our way back, the Enola Gay was going to Japan. The same with the Bock's Car. On our way back from Japan, the Bock's Car was delivering their bomb on Nagasaki. In September, they sent us home.

After The War

[You're asking me] how I think the war changed or affected my life? I actually only thought about that very, very recently. I think maybe I get cold. There had been many, many deaths around me, and for some reason, they don't affect me emotionally. The last one, my most emotional since the war, was my father. That got me; my mother's death didn't. I don't know why, except she had suffered, and I was glad to see her die. She was suffering. This wasn't lack of love or feeling. I just don't know. It just doesn't hit me emotionally.

After the war, I went to Manhattan College on the GI Bill, completed that. Went into industry, but my big desire always had been to study chiropractic. I was an accountant and financial analyst and even back then, I saw hanky-panky games with accounting. I didn't like it and unfortunately made my feelings known on a couple of occasions, saying things like, 'If it was that complicated, it has to be wrong.' Playing games is going to catch up with you. I got out of it. I got married, in 1957, I believe it was. She kills me because I can never remember. It was after college, anyway. I got married and was fed up with industry and decided to study chiropractic and talked about it at least. My wife said more or less do something or get off the pot. So, she signed me up for chiropractic college. I was still in industry. We had one child. She's going to kill me. I think it was 1954 when we got married. Let's put it this way, next year it's going to be fifty years. You can figure it out. We had one child. By the time I was finished with school, we had four and one on the way. That kind of killed my chiropractic career for quite a while because with that number of children you can't be that independent to just take off. It took many years later before I finally opened up my office, so I went into practice. Still practicing.

I joined the China-Burma-India veterans organization. Actually, the first one I joined was the VFW. I stayed in that a year. I joined that right after I came out of the service. I joined the China-Burma-India veterans because I kept on getting letters asking me to join a local 'basha.' I had no idea in the world what a 'basha' was. So, for ten dollars to join, I joined to find out exactly what a 'basha' was. A 'basha' was the [native type] barracks we lived in in India. My group called them 'barracks.' The old-timers called them 'bashas.' I joined that. I joined the American Legion. I joined the VFW again. I joined the 58th Bomb Wing Association, I joined the 20th Air Force Association. You name it, I belonged to it. I went to one reunion, the 50th anniversary of the B-29, which was in Seattle, which was unbelievable. They treated us like royalty there, an excellent reunion. I formed my own reunion. I found my crew after many, many years. I just made a concerted effort to try to find them. I found them all. I found that one was dead, and one was dying. We had a reunion. All but two of the remaining ones showed up at the reunion. That was in Chicago back twelve years ago, I guess it was. We made a pact that at least every two years we were going to have another reunion, [but we never had another one].

Robert D. O'Brien passed away August 2, 2010, at the age of 84.

PART THREE

FLYING COVER

"We were over Merrill's Marauders' heads from, God help us, their origin to their demise."

—Thunderbolt pilot, on covering missions for Merrill's Marauders in Burma

CHAPTER SIX

The Ace

Randolph Reeves was born in Texas on November 4, 1922. He joined the Army Aviation cadet program in April 1942 at the age of 19. Following flight training in California, Reeves graduated from the single-engine fighter school and then attended operational training in P-40s in Florida. In Karachi, India, Reeves received combat training and was then assigned to the 530th Fighter Squadron at Mohanbari in Assam, India. His combat missions were flown in P-51B Mustangs from five bases in India and Burma and eventually in Chengdu and Xi'an, China; he was credited with shooting down six Japanese aircraft. Following the war, Reeves served for three years on occupation duty in Japan; he built a career of service in the Strategic Air Command, retiring with the rank of lieutenant colonel with 25 years of active duty in 1966.

Leonard Randolph 'Randy' Reeves

I was born in Lisbon, Texas, on November 4, 1922. [I was raised on my grandfather's farm in DeSoto; my parents bought a house and moved the family to Lancaster in 1935. I graduated from

Lancaster High in 1940.] On December 7, 1941, I was seventeen and in Sunday school at the Baptist Church in Lancaster, and just as we were walking out of the church, somebody comes running up Henry Street. We lived on North Henry Street. They're saying that the Japanese had attacked Pearl Harbor. And, of course, I had no idea where Pearl Harbor was. I knew about the Japanese, but I had no idea where Pearl Harbor was. And so everybody's gathered around him. He said, there's probably going to be war. And that's when I heard about the attack on Pearl Harbor.

Pilot Training

I enlisted in the Army Air Corps Aviation Cadets in April of 1942, and I went to pre-flight at Santa Ana, California, to be a pilot. And then I went to primary flying school at Visalia, California, and basic flying school at Minner Field at Bakersfield, California, and advanced flying school at Luke Field at Phoenix, Arizona, where I graduated and was a second lieutenant and a pilot. And from there, we went down to Dale Mabry Field at Tallahassee, Florida, to get operational training in P-40s. But Dale Mabry Field was converting over training pilots from P-40s to P-47s. So we stayed there about a month, and all we did was dance with the co-eds at Florida State College for Women. [*Laughs*] They finally transferred us to Sarasota Army Air Base in Sarasota, Florida, and we got 85 hours of training in the P-40. We finished that up in December of 1943, went down to Florida to leave for overseas. We left the airport there at Southern Florida and flew down to Pelican Field, which is now Ramey Airport Space in Puerto Rico, and from there to Trinidad, and from there down to Natal and Belém in South America, and then across to the Ascension Islands and into the Gold Coast of Africa and from there down to Khartoum, from there up into Aden,

Arabia, they called it at the time, and from Aden we left and flew into Karachi, India.

India

We trained there at Karachi, India, with pilots that were coming back from combat. They flew with us, and we got 35 more hours training in the P-40, and after I finished that training in Karachi, India, I was assigned to the 311th Fighter Group, the 530th Fighter Squadron at Assam up in northern India; Assam is the northern state of India. And from there I joined the 530th Fighter Squadron and we flew combat in India until General Stilwell and General Wingate started moving down through Burma, and then they cut strips out of the jungle, and we would move down to these strips and fly against the Japanese and do strafing and bombing for the troops on the ground.

First Kill

First, we went down to Akyab, which is [in Burma] close to Chittagong on the coast of India, attached to the British. General Wingate had parachuted into Burma; they parachuted behind enemy lines and fought their way out, so the only way they could get supplies was by airdrop, but the fighters of the British Air Force didn't have the range to escort the C-47s they called the Dakotas, the Spitfires and Hurricanes didn't have the range so they sent us down there to escort the Dakotas so they could resupply them. After, we would get the Dakotas back across what we call the bomb line, which is back into friendly territory. We went on a fighter sweep, and I was flying what they call tail end Charlie, and we had 24 planes up that day, and a Japanese got on my tail, and I was trying to holler that there was a Japanese on my tail, and the squadron operations officer who was leading it, Captain James England, was hollering, 'Randy, there's a Japanese on your tail,' and our transmissions were cutting each other out. So I finally just broke away and dove down and then I climbed back up and I saw a Japanese Zero and I was making a head on passing this Japanese Zero, and I could see his guns are blinking and I'm scooching down behind my instrument panel in my P-51, but just kept firing. And as he passed overhead and as I passed underneath, I pulled up in the chandelle and came around on his tail, and there was his plane going down. There was a parachute, the Japanese pilot had bailed out, but that was my first aerial victory on my way to becoming an ace. I had six aerial victories, four more probable, and had five that I destroyed on the ground.

*

In September of 1944, they decided to transfer our fighter group to China and remove a P-47 fighter group that was using too much gas, because everything had to be flown over the Hump to supply the troops. They moved them to Burma where gas came in by rail. They sent our squadron up to Xi'an China, the 530th Fighter Squadron, and we flew most of our missions out of Xi'an, China. I flew in all sectors of the China-Burma-India Theater. I spent a year in China flying against the Japanese.

'I Believe I'm Going To Get Killed Tomorrow'

I don't ever remember being scared at all. I guess we were so young and innocent that nothing scared us, and a lot of us had the idea that we went over to die for our country, so we didn't really think about dying—I know I didn't, but some of my friends did. After we moved up to China flying out of Xi'an, we went in on Christmas Eve of 1944 and destroyed 45 planes on the ground. And they ordered us back in, go back in on Christmas Day. Now I wasn't flying on Christmas Day, but a good friend of mine was flying in that day. And at night we were sitting around talking and Courtney Richard, said, 'Randy, I believe I'm going to get killed tomorrow.'

I said, 'Nobody knows when they're going to get killed.'

He said, 'Yes, I feel like I'm going to be killed.'

And I said, 'Well, let's go see JJ, and I'll fly for you.'

So we went to James J. England, who had become a squadron commander after we moved up to China. So we went to find Major England, and he and the operations officer were in Xi'an at a dinner that one of the warlords had given for the CO and the operations officer's squadron. So we couldn't find him to where we could change, and I could fly for Lieutenant Richard. And finally he said, 'Oh, heck, Randy, [you're right], you don't really know when you're going to be killed.'

I said, 'Well, I'll fly for you.'

He said, 'No, just forget it. So the next day they went out and attacked the same airfield, and destroyed 35 more planes on the ground, but there were some Japanese flying top cover, and they attacked them, and Courtney Richards was shot down in flames and killed. I guess a lot of people have a premonition of things. I never did have, but I guess if it's going to happen, you can have a premonition it's going to happen.

Purple Heart

I got the Purple Heart while we were flying out of Akyab to support the British. A Japanese got on my tail, and I couldn't shake him. And they shot 20-millimeter cannons where we shot 50 caliber machine guns. And one of the 20-millimeter shells hit the top of my armor plating and exploded and shattered all my instrument panel and what have you, and I got some shrapnel in my back and neck.

'Pete, Don't Shoot!'

[Despite that], I never was [nervous about flying]. In March we were sent to a forward base at Ankang in China, and it was just an airstrip with pierce planking, we called it, which was steel planking that they hooked together and made a runway. There were three squadrons on this base. Everything had to be refueled by a hand pump out of a 55-gallon drum. Major Fritz Coleman was the squadron commander at the time. Major England had rotated to the station, and he was taking eight or twelve planes down to the airfields around Nanking, China, and I was supposed to take eight planes and provide the air cover. The Japanese had twenty planes supposedly flying air cover over Nanking to protect the bases, and I was to take eight planes in to attack the twenty planes that were flying top cover. Well, four of our planes didn't get refueled, so four of us took off and two had to go back because they had [problems]. So Pete Beck and I were the only two left to go in and attack these twenty planes over Nanking. Pete and I went in at around 20,000 feet, and we saw the air cover up there, and the Japanese would send a slower plane out, and it acted like the pilot didn't know how to fly, and it sort of flubbed around in the air. And this plane got too far ahead of its cover, and I shot the plane down. Then we had really a dogfight with the other planes that were up there, and I shot down another plane that day, but I ran out of ammunition. So I called Pete Beck, who was my wingman. I said, 'Pete, I'm out of ammo. Let's go home.' I was watching Pete joining up, and it looked like he was pulling a pursuit curve on me, and I could see his guns firing, and I'm hollering, 'Pete, don't shoot! This is old Randy!'

About that time, something hit my plane, and it sort of blew it out of the sky, and I flipped over and went into a dive, but I managed to pull the dive out at about 5,000 feet and was flying back to Nanking by myself. And I looked around, and part of my wingtip was shot off, and the back part of my horizontal stabilizer was shot away. So as I got back to the base, I checked it at altitude to see if I could control it, because of all the parts that were shot away. I put my gear down and I could still have enough control of the elevator to pull my nose up; I put 20 degrees of flap down, but I didn't think about pulling full flaps to see if I could control it, so as I came in on the final approach and put down full flaps for landing, I didn't have any more back pressure, and I couldn't bring the nose up high enough to make a real smooth landing, and so I dumped my flaps really quick, and when I did, I just hit the ground real hard. I thought the struts were coming up through the wings the way I hit. And I taxied in and told Sergeant George Dobner, who was my crew chief, I says, 'Sergeant Dobner, do you want me to write up a hard landing?'

He said, 'No sir, I saw the landing. We'll take care of it.' I told everybody that Pete Beck was the one that shot me up, but unluckily, Pete didn't come home.

We went back to Chengdu, and about ten days later, here comes Pete. The Chinese had picked him up and brought him back to the base. 'Of course, I jumped them, but you shot me down.'

Pete says, 'No, Randy, there were three Tojos on your tail, I was shooting at the Tojos. That's what shot you down!'

He had run out of gas and had to bail out, and his idea of bailing out was getting his feet up in the seat and jumping toward the wing and the plane would move forward while he would miss the wing and bail out. But his foot slipped down the side of the seat, and when he leaped out, his ankle, his foot, was caught there, and while he was kicking trying to get loose, he fractured his ankle, but he finally got out, of course, and opened his parachute and landed. I said, 'Pete, it's a good thing you came back, because I'm going around telling people that you're the one that shot me up!'

87 Missions

I flew 87 missions over there in about twenty months of flying. In Burma, we flew quite frequently every month, but in China, we just didn't have the gasoline to fly. We were used a lot to protect the B-29s that were coming in out of India and flying up into Manchuria and to Japan Islands there. And so we had to reserve fuel so one of them had to land in the forward base, which one did, and I went over on patrol to fly until they could get the B-29 repaired and get it off, and get it back to Shantung and back to India. So we didn't fly as frequent as we did in India and Burma.

[When we were not flying], we played poker until four or five guys would corral all the money. And then we'd play bridge on a credit until the end of the month, and then when we got paid we'd pay our bridge debts off and then go back to playing poker. And we didn't have much to read and, of course, no officers club or anything like that. We lived in tents mainly and we just lay around our tents and talked or played some sort of cards there.

The Chinese

We had this one second lieutenant that was our interpreter from the Chinese Army, and the warlords would throw parties every now and then out of Xi'an there, and we'd go to parties like that. They had a lot of coolies working on the runway. Our group commander, Colonel Tex Chandler, was an ace. These Chinese thought there was an evil dragon following them. And if they could get by in front of one of those planes that were just landing, that prop from that plane would kill this evil dragon. A lot of them didn't make it, and Colonel Chandler had killed five of those people; coolies were working on the runway trying to get across in front of his plane to get rid of that evil dragon that was following him.

War's End

[When the war ended], I was onboard ship coming home. We got this ship out of Calcutta and there were eight of us, eight officers living in a state room, and from Calcutta we stopped in Ceylon, which is now Sri Lanka. And from there we went down to Fremantle, Australia, and we got to stay overnight. So some of us went into Perth, Australia, and visited. And the next day we went up to the Philippines. And while we were going up to the Philippines, the war was over. After we got out of the Philippines, they sent us up to Okinawa to pick up around 5,000 Marines that had been fighting when they took over Okinawa, and they were supposed to rotate to the States, so we picked them up and we went into Pearl Harbor and spent a night there. And from there, we were supposed to go into San Francisco to disembark. And the war being over, the long-shoremen were on strike up at San Francisco, so they diverted us down to Los Angeles, and we pulled in to Los Angeles. And from there, I went to San Antonio, Texas, at Fort Sam Houston and got 45 days R&R to my home. And after that I reported back into Fort Sam, and signed up for an indefinite period in the service. I ended up spending 25 years in Army Air Corps and United States Air Force.

[My next assignment] was going to a fighter gun refresher course at Chandler, Arizona, but they were letting all the crew chiefs out. At Williams Field, they didn't have enough crew chiefs to man all the planes that would be found at gunnery mission, so they just closed the fighter gunnery school, and they sent me up to Wright Field, and that's where I met my wife and my downfall. I ended up getting married there after I met her. She worked at Officer Simon's section in Headquarters AMC and right after we got married, we went to Japan. We got married on the 7th of December 1946, and on the 22nd of December, I got orders to Japan. I went to

Japan in December of 1946, and my wife got over there in June of '47 and our first daughter was born in Japan. After Japan I went back to Wright Field. I was in the flight test division, and I was there for a year, then they sent me to a school at Lowry Field in Denver, Colorado, and I became a transportation officer, staff transportation officer. And so from there I went to Hill field, Utah, and then Los Angeles, California, and then from there to Biggs Air Force Base in El Paso, Texas. From there I went to Newfoundland for three years. My wife came to Newfoundland and my youngest son was born in Newfoundland and my oldest son was born when we were in my second tour at Wright Field. We spent three years in St. John's, Newfoundland, and then from there we went to Westover Air Force Base in Massachusetts for three years. And from there, we went to Seymour Johnson Air Force Base at Goldsboro, North Carolina. I was flying KC-135 jet tankers. And that's where my last daughter was born. I spent eight years at Seymour Johnson Air Force Base at Goldsboro, North Carolina, before I retired.

Japan Occupation Duty

When my wife got over there, we were assigned to a base outside of Japan, Showa Air Base, which was right close to Tatsukawa. We'd go into the city quite frequently to shop on the Ginza there. You could see all the embassies, just about all had been destroyed there with those firebombs. And most of Tokyo was destroyed, except for the Emperor's Palace. He was right in the middle of Tokyo there and had a big moat around the grounds and everything. I don't guess a bomb ever touched anything there, because I guess they were ordered not to bomb the Emperor's Palace. We had a house girl for free, and it cost us $6.50 every month for a house boy. So my wife sort of got spoiled with them, all these servants, and since we were just married, she thought that's the way the Air Force lived.

Randolph Reeves passed away on September 4, 2014, at the age of 91.

CHAPTER SEVEN

The Thunderbolt Pilot

In the China-Burma-India Theater, Kenneth Wilbur Thomas of Oklahoma flew strategic bombing and strafing runs in the 10th Air Force, 80th Fighter Group, 88th Fighter Squadron in support of the Office of Strategic Services. His missions included covering Merrill's Marauders on their long-range penetration missions in the Burmese jungle. He sat for this interview in 2006.

Kenneth Wilbur Thomas

[When Pearl Harbor was attacked], I was at my home in southern Iowa, still on the farm. At that time, I had a brother four years older than I who had enlisted in the Army. At the time, he thought he was enlisting for one year's training and then was going to come back in reserves, but it didn't work out that way. He was put in the MPs, and he was enjoying a truly great life. This would have been in late '30s or early '40s, because he was being assigned all over the country to watch the depots where they were transporting the soldiers to go and make sure the soldiers were conducting themselves in military manner, as long as they're in uniform. These were groups of seven or eight guys. They'd be stationed in an apartment, usually with a commanding car at their disposal, and getting more money than you could make anywhere else, because they were getting a per diem for their food.

He tried to persuade me to enlist and join him; of course, it was a great life. I thought, 'Hey, that's worth a try.' I went to Des Moines and sat down in front of a recruiting sergeant and told him I want to do enlisting in MPs. He looked at me like he thought that I was probably a little bit unpossessed, and said, 'You know, son, I've heard of military people being sentenced to serve the MPs, but I've never accepted that enlistment could be MPs. Why don't you think about it for a while?' [Laughs]

The Test

I knew at the time I very much wanted to be in the Air Corps. However, the Air Corps at that time required two years minimum of some college credit, which I didn't have, nor did I figure I could get it and in the end still get in the service. One September I was in Des Moines, Iowa, big sign on those sidewalks that said, 'College requirement no longer required.' I noticed it was right in front of the Air Corps, U.S. Army Air Corps enlisting station.

I went in and talked to him about it. He says, 'Yeah, you don't have to have college, just pass an equivalence test.' 'When are you giving it?' 'I'll be giving one at eight o'clock in the morning.'

'I'll be here!' I went out and took the test, of course, I reviewed it. There were several pages up. There were supposed to be 150 questions, and as I reviewed it I noticed there's about three blank pages. I thought, 'Well, that's funny.' I saw the room was crowded, and I thought, 'Well, I've got these three blanks, this guy probably got three other blanks. That way we don't copy each other.' I hustled through it, seemed like an awful easy test. Finished it up, looked around, and everybody else was still busy at their desks. I checked them one at a time all the way through. Everybody's still busy at their desk. Checked it again, took it up to the sergeant.

He said, 'Don't you want to check it?'

I said, 'I've checked it twice.'

'Fine, have a chair. I'll read them in a little bit. We'll know who passed.' At that time, the test was graded by an overlay sheet with a bunch of slots in it. Our answers were all marked with black and a slot. He just put an overlay sheet over it, and any slot that wasn't blackened got a red mark.

Then he'd count the red marks and total it up and find out what we made. He read the names of those who passed, and mine wasn't read. We had to get 85 out of 150 to pass the test. I said, 'Sergeant, would you please look...' I can remember the test number, we recorded not by names, but by test number. I said, 'Sergeant, will you look and see what number so and so had?' He looked. '78, not quite enough.'

I headed for my sister's house. She lived in an apartment in Des Moines, and I kept booting myself in the rear as I walked along.

'78 out of 150, what an idiot could I possibly be?'

Finally, the 150 number started eating at me, and I realized that I didn't have 150 questions, because the last sheet could begin with question 29 and after I got the blank sheet it might be question 41. I don't know, but I didn't have 150 questions. I hustled to the phone booth. They were a nickel at that time. I hustled to the phone booth, dropped the nickel in, and called the sergeant and said, 'Would you check the test number so and so?'

'Why should I do that?'

I said, 'I just got through taking it. I don't think it was all there. I had some blank pages at one moment.' He looked at it, came back. 'What the hell did you take this test for?'

I said, 'That's the one you gave me!'

'Well, it had 'INC' right on the front of it.'

'What does that mean?'

'Incomplete, would you like to take it again?'

'When?'

'Nine o'clock in the morning.'

I'll be there!' First thing I did was to look at it, and all the sheets were full, all 150 questions. I went and passed through it. When they read the scores at that time there was only one boy who beat me. He was from Iowa State College, a second-year physics major and he had 138 out of 150. I had 135 out of 150 correct, with my high school education.

Called Up

I waited for my call. It was the following January, and I was called into a regular U.S. Army enlisted recruiting base, Jefferson Barracks, Missouri, in January. Bitterest winter I believe I had there; while we were there, they positioned us in these little old square huts, built out of green shiplap lumber with a square-pointed roof, and they had a little inverted funnel-shaped stove sitting in the middle of the tent. The pipe was a four-and-a-half-inch pipe that runs straight through the roof, a bit cold. Being a farm boy, I went out gathering wood, dead limbs and remnants of the construction, built a fire. That old stove got red hot in minutes. That worked pretty good, except the siding lumber was green, and the next morning when we woke up, there was a crack between each and every one of those green boards, and the snow would blow in, and was lying on our covers, not even melted, just white streaks. [*Laughs*] Well, we managed to survive it; we got extra blankets. We burned up the scrap lumber, but they got coal in there, and we survived that pretty well. We spent exactly 30 days in Jefferson Barracks learning how to soldier. 'That's how you march. This is your right foot you always start with it,' or whatever it was. They gave us another battery of tests there; never knew what it was for at the time, but that segregated us into groups. The first group spent one month in Jefferson Barracks, and then we got shipped out to a school. The purpose of the school was to try to replace this college [learning] that we didn't have. I got assigned to Creighton University in Omaha, Nebraska, beautiful Catholic school teachers, first time I'd ever seen a school uniform. It was a marvelous experience. At the end of the month, I had stuff all packed waiting to ship out, and lo and behold, I got the mumps.

They sent me to the Fork Brook Hospital. Mumps was treated with ice at the time. Of course, I developed the rarest case yet, swelling in every possible area at the maximum. This Texas nurse was always kidding me about my swollen organs, how horrible they were. That wasn't enough, because about the first week I was there, I saw her leading through a group of teenagers in civilian clothes. They were planning on going to nursing school, so she was showing them everything that she had in her hospital. Lo and behold, they moved into the mumps area, and I thought, 'Good Lord, she's always talking about my swollen organs. I wonder if she will talk about me?' Sure enough, here they came. 'Notice the swelling here, ladies, see how it's equal and how it looks, jaws and everything else.' Next move, 'Take off the ice pack.' She showed them what she claimed is the most classic case of mumps swelling she had ever observed. Of course, I was red enough to light a match to the cheek, and she recognized it. She thanked me profusely for being such a 'patient patient' so she could show this to the girls. I don't recall finding any other thing in the entire four plus years of service that was as embarrassing to me as that was. Guess it didn't shorten my life any. [Laughs]

Pilot Training

After we got through with Omaha, then they shipped us to San Antonio, which was all cadets at that time. That consisted of many months of pre-flight training, we called it, and a month of classification. We went through that, and then at the end of that preflight training, they divided us up into training schools. We all went to the same primary trainer, a little single-engine Fairchild PT-19, and my assignment was to Chickasha, Oklahoma, which I enjoyed very much. It was operated by civilians at the time. Next assignment was Coffeyville, Kansas, back in the army, tar paper shacks, forty men on one floor, and we took care of ourselves, marched the mess hall and everything else, beyond that was [like] basic training. We spent just about two months there, and then went to Victoria, Texas, for the advanced training and classification. They divided us into fighter pilots and bomber pilots. Much to my joy I qualified for fighter pilots and went to Victoria, Texas, for training in the AT-6. I'm training to be a fighter pilot, but I had one question left in my mind. I had heard of the Thunderbolt. I'd never seen one, but I wanted to fly it. That was the thought harboring in my mind: 'Maybe, just maybe, I'll get the Thunderbolt.' When we saw the assignment posted at the end of graduation, lo and behold, Richmond, Virginia, P-47s.' I got my last wish granted and we finished our training.

The number one thing [they would look at when classifying us in training] was how we handled the single-engine plane, and number two was our response [to emergencies]. They'd give us all these emergencies, like, you're out of fuel. They'd shut off our gas, make us find the field, go ahead. They'd make us go into the final approach to the landing before they'd switch the gas back on. Now, the responses we had to all of those things that the instructors could dream of, whatever it might be. And if we had at it and solved it with a great deal of vigor and glee, well, they kept us on the fighter list. Now, this is something I can't understand. The bomber, of course, is like driving a bus compared to a sports car. But the responsibility of a bomber pilot just boggles your mind. He's got ten men there he is responsible for, and one of them is a navigator, one of them a tail gunner. That's a lot of area to cover. And I am not sure what the criteria for the separation of it all was. Some of it was choice; some of the guys made that choice early on. The bombers were big and heavy, and they enjoyed driving big equipment, sort of like the guy that loves to drive a truck, so bombers were their choice. But I had opted for fighters and the thing that worried me at the time, I was at the exact height and weight limit for cut-off. Exactly. Six feet even and 180 pounds. And that kind of worried me, and I was mighty glad when I was given the decision.

The Thunderbolt

I'd seen a picture of the Thunderbolt, and I read that it was the most powerful and the most heavily armed fighter we had ever built. And I don't know. I worked with big horses; I wanted to have a big machine. Growing up on a farm with a big, two-horse team, a really big horse has always impressed me, so 2,000 horses was something I started vying for. Actually, it was a very easy plane to fly. Now, I didn't really get to understand the flying of the Thunderbolt until I got overseas. In training, we flew old, war-weary Thunderbolts on 90-octane fuel. Well, with the 90-octane fuel, we couldn't put that through [what the plane could really do]; I had to wait until I got overseas before I could really run that thing out and understand the joy I had in my hands. The only weakness I would say would be the fact that it required a pretty sturdy field to work from. Now, the British and the Americans in Britain flew them off grass fields. Their grass, I am sure, was quite different from the grass we had in Burma. I didn't see a single field in Burma that I'd want to put that seven tons down on. But they did that in England, and in France, and in Germany after the war was settled. I wouldn't say that there was a weakness, as much as it was a requirement. Its strength, of course, was the fact that it had eight 50-caliber guns, and we carried 420 rounds of ammunition for each gun. It would handle two 1,000-pound bombs or napalm tanks or whatever, and we could still carry a 50-gallon belly tank to extend the range. Its one weakness probably was the fact that it was a pretty good gas guzzler, but we learned how to cope with that, too. We had recommended settings for various altitudes, various requirements, but we discovered that if we boosted the manifold pressure beyond the recommendations and dialed the RPMs back to where we could hear the detonation from that specific setting, we could get by with about 85 gallons an hour instead of 120, so we stretched its range quite a bit just by learning what it could do. And that was, I would say, its only weakness, the fact that it required a great deal of fuel. As a weapons platform, I can't imagine anything nicer, because seven tons, you don't feel a lot of thermals in it. You can feel the jolt, but it doesn't move the plane. When you line that thing up on the sightline, that's where your bullets went, exactly where it went.

To The CBI

We had partial training in Richmond, and then moved on to Dover, Delaware, for gunnery and aerial bombing. Then we were shipped back to Richmond to await assignment. We were issued our orders to go to England, but we had a storm at sea that canceled our ship. We waited for the next ship. We still kept our cold weather uniform, so we again assumed Europe, England, somewhere. Just before we ship out, we get word that there's a German U-boat wolf pack off the Atlantic coast, so they delayed that shipment again. We're still sort of in limbo land there, getting tired of eating field rations in Richmond, Virginia. They loaded us on a train, and we headed south, still with our winter clothing. Where in the world would I be going, south with winter clothing?

We finally got to Miami Beach. They checked us in a hotel down there, and we turned in our winter uniforms and got some summer uniforms and started a round of tropical shots. We finally got that round completed, and they loaded us on a C-46 and we were jungle-hopping over northern South America. When we finally got to the town in Brazil, they parked C-46s and C-47s and gave us a B-24. We still didn't know where we're going. We'd take tropical shots and have summer clothing, and we were joined there by another U.S.O. tour, which included James Faulkenberg, Pat O'Brien, and three starlets whose names I don't even remember. Well, their first words, were, 'Oh, you guys are going to CBI too?' We didn't know, well, that's where we are going. Now we know! [*Laughs*]

That was an interesting trip too; the most interesting part of it for me came in the middle of the night. I was awakened by strong gasoline fumes. I looked out in the darkness, I could see our far-right propeller on the B-24 was feathered; the gasoline fumes were so strong that I couldn't sleep. I thought, 'We must be in trouble!' I looked down, all I could see was the fluorescence from those white caps and they rocked in the ocean for a mile, mile and a half below us. Next thing I noticed is another engine was shutting down. I looked and it was the other right-hand engine on that side of the plane! I hadn't flown four-engine planes, but I knew that if you had two on the one side that were bad, you had a problem of some sort. He's revving up these two left engines full forward and we're still doing pretty good. After a while, I see the engines finally restarting everything else. I was the only guy who observed that everybody else was sound asleep, snoring, and enjoying the trip. When we finally landed at Ascension Island, I cornered the pilot and I said,

'You're going to have to tell me, why do you shut down two engines on one side over the Atlantic Ocean?'

'Oh, we do it all the time. I was transferring fuel out of the bomb bay into those wing tanks, and that fuel line goes right behind that exhaust of those two engines. You've got to shut them down.' [*Laughs*] Well, that was educational to me.

Burma

We finally got across West Africa, out of the B-24 and back in twin-engine planes, and they got us across the African continent, across part of Asia, to India, one of the northernmost [British] colonies. We were assigned to the 33rd Fighter Group for orientation, they called it. I flew only three missions with them; within a month I was transferred across the mountain into a little strip of Shingbwi-yang, Burma, which was in the most northern province of Burma, and joined the 80th Fighter Group. At that time, only the 88th Fighter Squadron was at that field. I got a thorough orientation and started the missions there.

When we got to Burma, the AVG had worked out of a field in Rangoon for a while, but by the time we went over there, by the time I got overseas, the AVG had been disbanded, and they were brought into the U.S. Army Air Corps, or they could leave the AVG if they wanted to. And we ended up with some of their mechanics on our flight line. They were good boys.

There were two typical missions we would fly. For a close support mission, most of the time, we just used the guns. We were over Merrill's Marauders' heads from, God help us, their origin to their demise. And what we would do, they would direct us in a direction, following the Burmese landscape. They could tell you to follow a river, but that was about all we had to follow. So they usually just gave us heading, and we'd fly, and we'd know that we could chart on the map what the distance was, so we judged it. And when the right number of minutes elapsed, we'd call in on the two-way radio, just like walkie talkies, 'Oh, yeah. We're close.'

'I can see you up there. You need about another minute.' And then we'd get down, they'd say, 'You're right overhead. Now circle. We'll describe the area.' And they would describe that area right down to the last detail of the land that they could see [where the target was]. They were looking through binoculars, and they could see the lines. And when they'd finally get it described, and we'd agree, 'Yeah, we think we got it,' they'd ask us for a short machine gun burst to make sure we were in the right spot. Well, often we were. And every now and then, we'd be asked to make a correction of a few yards one way or the other; if they asked us to make a correction, we'd give them another square at that correction. And then they would start bragging to us. 'Boy, get them. You're right exactly where they ought to be. Give them everything you got!' Then as we went through the motions, circling and passing—it was almost like a landing pattern—we'd make a pass, circle around, make another pass, circle around, make another pass. [*Rotates hands in the air*] Now, you wonder why we made so many passes? Well, those guns were bore-sighted for 1,000 feet, so if you're doing about 240 miles an hour, you've got an effective pass time of about three seconds, that's all. And in three seconds, you're probably going to square it up; out of all eight guns, you'd get probably less than 200 rounds total, so you'd make a lot of passes. Every so often they'd say, 'Well, that's pretty well wiped out there. Let's look at another one.' And then they describe another place. We'd move over there.

Marauders' Support

On the Marauders' early missions, the [Japanese-controlled] Myitkyina airstrip still had the problem of a Japanese gun emplacement off the far end of the runway. And so we'd take off, make short circles around, drop a bomb on it, come back and get another, take off. It was a totally crazy war. Some of those boys got in as many as six missions a day, but we eventually wiped them out of there and got them on the run. And then we, of course, after we occupied Myitkyina, we had to push them farther and farther. Burma was an area that was fought for very diligently. I had several missions in that area. And Merrill's Marauders, we actually patrolled over their heads as they were going down through the mountain, because the Japanese were famous for leaving back some expendables just to shoot people because they went by. They'd leave them there with nothing but a gun and a bag full of ammo. They could kill rats and eat locusts and whatever they could find to eat. But when these Marauders go by, shoot a few of them, you know. So we'd patrol over their heads, and if that happened, we'd zero them in and we'd take them out of the trees sometimes.

When we were carrying bombs, those would usually be loaded on only for specific purposes to go after a storage yard or a building that they thought was being used for storage or an actual weapons dump that they could see through the binoculars. All the bombs would be dropped one at a time for the very good reason that if one bomb does it, we got another [target] for the next one; see, all of our equipment—ammunition, gasoline, bombs and everything else—were flown over to us, and they always told us it took seven gallons of gasoline to deliver one gallon that we could burn, so seven-to-one was the ratio. A 500-pound bomb or a thousand-pound bomb took 7,000 pounds of fuel to deliver one bomb, so we used everything quite sparingly and for good reason.

The first place that we were based was located right in the middle of the rainforest. They'd whittled out a runway that was downhill. It didn't matter where the wind was; we took off downhill, we landed up here, and wind didn't matter because there were these huge trees on both sides of the runway. And at that place, it rained almost every day. The summer we were there, we had 200 inches of rainfall in that one summer, so everything was wet. Our uniforms, we'd have to try to hang them outside to air out so the mildew didn't set in. And with the rain going on, we couldn't always do that; everything around us was wet and soaked and sodden. We did, however, have latrine facilities and bath facilities. I don't remember anywhere where we didn't have that. We had dried eggs, dried potatoes, and dried powdered milk. But we were also blessed with a mess sergeant that understood all of those things, and he could make mashed potatoes. I couldn't have distinguished his from fresh out of the patch. He could take that powdered milk and the powdered eggs and make scrambled eggs, I couldn't wait to have them every morning. I was only one of the few idiots that they considered dumb enough to get up for breakfast. Growing up on a farm, breakfast was always the main meal, you know, 6:00 AM. If you didn't get that under your belt, you weren't fit for the day's work. So that was a habit I formed, and to this day, I still enjoy breakfast.

The Native People

[The local population, the indigenous peoples], they didn't really like the British at all then. The British had been there too long. And they were a little bit, I don't know what the word is, but they were treated like colonists. And it was their land, but the British occupied it, so they weren't colonists. And they seemed, when they worked in our tents and everything, they couldn't do enough for us, the Americans. They managed everything for us. They took care of shoe shines, making beds, sewing, making sure that the laundry was done and done right. We couldn't speak the language, but our house men would take care of it.

The other place where we were based was Myitkyina, [after the field was taken], in a prairie-like area. We had a lot of green pastures around there. Now, the farmers didn't use the pastures, but the wild water buffalo did; you could always see herds of those grazing around. Now, the air was nice and fresh, you could hang clothing out to dry, then you didn't have to hang them out just to air out. And that area was really quite nice, I enjoyed it. We had good facilities there. The area was so nice, the Red Cross girls even had a station around. We could get donuts and coffee down there, like that.

War's End

Within a few months, we moved forward to get closer to the battle lines to the strip the Japanese had built at Myitkyina. I flew the remaining combat missions from that strip. About May of '45, the British patted us on the back and said, 'Hey, you've been great, but we don't have to have you anymore.' I thought, 'Fine, we'll go home.' [Shakes head] Didn't. We went to an old B-29 base at Candi, India, which was about 90 miles west of Calcutta.

We got over there. There were a couple of bomb groups, the old 33rd Fighter Group is over there with their fighters. They've gone to P-38s, and we're being formed into something called the Far East Air Force. 'But the war is over. What's this for?'

'We still haven't beat Japan.'

We're bombing the heck out of them with B-29s, incendiaries killing them by the hundreds of thousands each and every night, but they weren't convinced that we were going to win. We were organizing that group for the sole purpose of supporting a land invasion of all five islands, one at a time. I had already heard what had happened in Okinawa. They had occupied that, and I knew that the Japanese mothers had thrown their kids over the cliff [at Saipan], and then followed them with the last leap. I thought, 'Good Lord,

five Japanese islands. I wonder if the Japanese race will really survive, or will they all commit suicide?'

[The war ended]; we got all of our people who wanted to go
home, and I had the points. I had 100 missions behind me, but I
hadn't seen a single enemy plane in the air. In my mind, I hadn't
really been [tested] yet. We were flying all these missions over the
heads of the OSS, and they were cheering us like a winning football
team. I landed our group at Djakarta and they told us, once we got
on the ground, that the war was over, that we're going to pack up
and go home. I get a screwdriver out. I want to recover that eight-
day clock out of my personal airplane for a souvenir. I just parked it
two hours before, but by the time I get out there, there's a tall soldier with a turban and a shroud. He must have stood six and a half
feet tall. He was carrying an old British Enfield that was nearly as
tall as he was, and as I get close to that airplane, 'Halt.' He pointed
his bayonet about this close to my chest.

'You halt!' It turned out to be the only word he knew in English
was halt. I tried to reason with him that I wanted to recover that
eight-day clock, but the bayonet didn't move. I finally moved, and
two days later, I watched the Corps of Engineers crush that plane
with bulldozers at each end of the wings and to the tail until it was
as small as they could get it and then sold for scrap.

Home

It took us about a month and a half to get on a boat and finally
head for home. That was a tremendous experience because we
boarded in Calcutta. They told us it'd take us 30 days to get across
the Atlantic and home. For some reason, instead of coming across
the Pacific, we went back around the Indian Ocean and refueled in
Ceylon, then up through the Suez Canal and Mediterranean and
back to New York, and then I reported back for my extra year that

158 | THE THUNDERBOLT PILOT

I signed up for. Mind you, we docked in New York City. I went home to Iowa, spent 30 days there, then got on a train and went all the way to Santa Ana, California, for reassignment. The reassignment turned out to be St Louis, Missouri. I got to see a lot of the U.S., but I didn't get all the way around the world.

That last year in the military was probably my most memorable year. I ended up inheriting the last totally segregated black raw Air Corps recruits. They had been trained previously in Texas and Louisiana, but things were getting a little touchy at the time, and I'd read about some near riots. We had a bad colonel in St. Louis that was hoping to get one star before retiring. The colonel was trying to operate the segregated troops with all white non-coms. Those other white non-coms weren't accustomed to black troops. By that time, I understood the convenience and necessity of my black acting sergeants. I said to the colonel, 'Remove every white non-com from that area and let me appoint my own.' He didn't get his star, but he didn't lose his ego either. It worked out very well.

Interviewer: How do you think your experiences in World War II affected you later in life?

[Well, learning how to] just get along with people was one thing. Ninety-nine percent of us were shelled out of the same pod, and I think that the most remarkable achievement that any military group could attain was to establish a procedure that would pick up this very narrow strip of people, from here to there. That was the first thing. And then the second thing, of course, was getting accustomed to the fact that all of them were nice guys. Some of them hadn't been [raised] the same way we were, though, and things would come up missing. We had to learn to hide our stuff or lock it up or put it away. And then of course, [we learned to] the best of our ability to get results from people who you couldn't communicate with by language, the house boys and the various people we worked with. And probably the greatest thing was what coordination and cooperation can do. Soldiers on the ground, tired, not sufficiently armed, our planes in the air over-armed, doing the work together that had to be done. It was a marvelous training, [to see the coordination to achieve a common goal].

'They Were Soldiers'

I also learned I had absolutely no aversion to colored people in any way. I hadn't known any, and to this day, I don't have any, because some of those guys are the finest people you'll ever meet anywhere, and what I marveled at about that was that they could sense anything—just like a dog knows when you're afraid, he'll attack you and tear you to pieces, but if you're not afraid, he's your friend. Sensing that I had no enmity, they became the finest group of soldiers you'll ever see. I've got a picture, I guess it's at home, but I grew from that group of boys. I discovered we had enough musicians to make a band, so we formed a band. I had a second lieutenant there that was a musician. I had a band music major. And we put together a band and we held our own little Saturday afternoon marches. They loved that, anything, to march. And the colonel learned that we had a band, and we were marching, so he declared that every Saturday afternoon, we'd have a competition for every unit on the entire base ground field. And each winner of each Saturday would get a prize. So we went into that. And by golly, we took the prize off the first time. And when next Saturday came along, we took the prize off. Finally, we didn't always win, but we did win more than we lost. Finally, one Saturday there was a deal with Lord Louis Mountbatten, who was visiting the base for some reason. And we had this big old deal, my guys loved marching so much. When they'd hear the music play and we'd do the big eight-man turn, they practiced that. Eight men at the time, with an eight-man pivot, and to practice, they'd bump their head on each beat and take the short steps and bob their head, and it's kind of beautiful. Eight heads going up and down all at the same time! And so when we got in that last competition, I told the guys, I said, 'Hey, we're going to have to cut out on this because everybody else is here and everybody doesn't bob their heads.' But this day, I just got them in, lined up, and was ready waiting for the call to march off.

'Whose name is Thomas?' Well, I turned around and the colonel's pointing his finger at me! So I went double timing enough to see what he's doing. He said, 'Lieutenant, if you take the trophy home today, you'll be excused from any further competition.'

'Oh, yes, sir!' [*Gestures with a salute*]

'And just a minute, Lieutenant, do you suppose you could coax your men into doing their special pivot?' [*Laughs*] He wanted to see it! So I went back and told the troops, I said, 'If we win the trophy this time, we won't do this anymore. And not only that, but he wants to see our special turn.'

Oh, boy, did we mow them down! You get a lot of pride or something like that, and the fact that here are guys, some of them hadn't done anything, hadn't been responsible for anything until they got that uniform on. They conducted themselves with dignity in that uniform, and I recognized it by addressing them as soldiers. They were soldiers.

PART FOUR

THE MARAUDERS

"We are the forgotten people. Nobody ever recognizes the China-Burma-India Theater, but as far as I'm concerned, I think it was one of the most integral parts of the war effort because we were the back door running to Europe, and also it was important that we open up the road to get supplies from India on into China."

—*Officer, reminiscing on Merrill's Marauders*

In August 1943, the top-secret First Quebec Conference opened at the Hotel Frontenac in Quebec City, Canada, ostensibly to begin planning the invasion of Europe. The Southeast Asia Command, headed by Vice Admiral Mountbatten, had fielded an experimental long-range penetration force in Burma that spring to strike back at the Japanese and their astonishing inroads seemingly everywhere. This force would be comprised of British and Indian Gurkha elite soldiers skilled in jungle warfare and led by the veteran guerrilla campaigner in Africa and Palestine, Brig. General Orde Wingate. This force, nicknamed the Chindits (after the mythical stone lions protecting Burmese temples), was organized into columns that could act independently and move unseen and strike with deadly force seemingly out of nowhere, living off the land and traveling in the most inhospitable environments, but in a revolutionary twist, being primarily resupplied by radio and airdrops. They suffered huge casualties in Burma and had mixed results but were lauded for their ability to hit the Japanese repeatedly, which was played up in the press as a morale builder. Wingate was called to London to be presented to Churchill, brought to Quebec, and made a favorable impression on FDR, so much so that on September 1, George Marshall put out a call for three thousand volunteers for a top-secret dangerous mission. Codenamed GALAHAD, this force was to be modeled after the British long-range penetration force. But there had been an important American precedent—Major Robert Rogers and his hit-and-run Ranger companies of the French and Indian War days struck terror in the heart of the garrisons of the French empire in North America in the Champlain Valley region of the Adirondack Mountains, living outdoors in extreme conditions, in all seasons, moving under cover, striking quickly, taking prisoners for information, and blending back into the mountains like their native counterparts, the eyes and ears of the British Army in North America. Like their successors, the Rangers who landed in North Africa, Sicily, Italy, and Normandy, the newly formed 5307th Composite Unit (Provisional) would go on to become legends in their own right. Merrill's Marauders were born.

CHAPTER EIGHT

The Virginia Farmboy

Lieutenant General Samuel Vaughan Wilson was born on Sept. 23, 1923, in central Virginia, where his father ran a generations-old tobacco farm, and his mother was a schoolteacher.

He joined the Army in 1940 at the age of sixteen, and taught guerrilla and counter-guerrilla tactics at Fort Benning in Georgia. At the age of nineteen, he was on his way to Burma as 'Lt. Sammy,' becoming a chief reconnaissance officer for Merrill's Marauders. The lessons he learned and taught in the field behind enemy lines shaped his military career. This interview took place at Hamden-Sydney College in Farmville, Virginia, founded by his fourth great-grandfather in 1775 and where he served as president after a long and distinguished military career, which included awards and decorations such as the Distinguished Service Cross, Defense Distinguished Service Medal, Army Distinguished Service Medal with two Oak Leaf Clusters, National Intelligence Distinguished Service Medal, U.S. Special Operations Distinguished Service Medal, the CIA's Distinguished Intelligence Medal, Silver Star with Oak Leaf Cluster, Legion of Merit with Oak Leaf Cluster, Bronze Star for Valor with Oak Leaf Cluster, Army Commendation Medal with two Oak Leaf Clusters, Purple Heart, Vietnamese Gallantry Cross with Palm, and the Vietnamese National Administration Medal for Exemplary Service.[18]

Samuel V. Wilson

I was born twelve miles from here on a 150-acre corn-tobacco-wheat farm. I went to a small country high school and graduated in late May 1940. On the 9th of June 1940, I believe it was a Sunday, I was in the parlor in the farmhouse, which was our home, twiddling the dials in mid-afternoon, we would call it surfing the channels today. When I heard a man speaking, I noted that it was not an American accent. It sounded like an English accent that I had heard before. I was listening to WPTF from Raleigh, North Carolina, We Protect the Family, that particular station, which still exists. The speaker was Winston Churchill, and it was a rebroadcast of his speech on the floor of the House of Commons on the 4th of June, the day that the British Expeditionary Force and the French First Army were evacuated from Dunkirk. If you recall the speech, the words that have been lifted from it are, 'We will fight them on the beaches, in the fields, on the landing grounds, in the hills, in the streets. We will never surrender.' I looked around and said, 'Where's my hat?' That is what provided the impulse for my getting into military service.

'I Lied Like A Rug'

The next day was a Monday. It rained all day. I climbed up in the loft of the old stable to read, but I could not get away from those words that were echoing in my head leading up to, 'We will never surrender.' I knew enough about what was going on in the world to know that the Western world was in trouble, at least the free part of the Western world, including ourselves. Along about night, I could not stand it any longer without saying a word to anybody. I set off down to Fawn Lane on the right on Country Road, and ran through some thickly forested woods, several miles into the town of Farmville. Company G, 116th Infantry, was gathered there for its drill night that evening, the monthly drill night. I went in, raised my right hand, all 139 pounds soaking wet, lied like a rug, and told them I was eighteen; I was sixteen. That is how I got into uniform.

When they were asking me about the things that I studied, what skills I had and so on, I mentioned that I had studied music and that I played a couple of stringed instruments and bagged away on the piano, and that I also played the clarinet. They said, 'We've got ourselves a bugler.'

I said, 'No. You kiss a bugle or a trumpet, but you put the clarinet in your mouth, and you use your tongue to make the proper kind of noises.'

They said, 'Son, a horn is a horn. You are a bugler.' Took me three months to get rid of that bugle. I had to find my replacement in training.

Forced Marches At High Speed

My Christmas present, given to me along about Thanksgiving, was to exchange my M1A1 bugle for a 1903 Springfield, be promoted to PFC, and become lead scout in the rifle squad.

We were federalized and brought into federal service on the 3rd of February 1941. We trained for three weeks out of the Army and followed, and then we were trained up to Fort Meade, Maryland, by this time as an active Army unit. Our basic training and so on was accomplished there. I remember it well. Scouting, patrolling, long marches. Our battalion commander was from over in the Valley of Virginia. He was very much an aficionado of Stonewall Jackson. He wanted us to be able to move like grease lightning, so we went everywhere in a sort of jog or trot. We did move fast, and we moved great distances. He marched the dickens out of us. Every chance he got took us off. Forced marches at high speeds, which stood me in good stead later. We spent a lot of time on the range, firing all of the various infantry weapons. We learned, of course, everything about the school of the soldier. Extended all the drill formations, signals that would allow you to get quickly into the right kind of combat formation if you were in the field with fire upon, that kind of thing. These were things I took very much to heart. I was promoted to corporal, then to sergeant, then to staff sergeant. Wound up doing a lot of teaching myself as a non-com, which I loved.

At the age of eighteen, Sam Wilson was the youngest 2nd lieutenant in the U.S. Army.

I had graduated from OCS, and I had been kept back from my class for one year to teach light infantry tactics, raiding by infiltration, scouting and patrolling, and these kinds of subjects, there on the red hills of the Fort Benning Reservation, which meant that I had a year to contemplate, conceive, and teach the very things that I was going to be required to do in Burma. A very fortuitous combination, which meant that I was better prepared than I otherwise would be. I wound up in Merrill's Marauders as a first lieutenant, initially as a rifle company executive officer, and subsequently, after a few weeks, I became one of the intelligence and reconnaissance platoon leaders of the Marauders. I and another I&R platoon leader were used frequently, directly, by General Merrill on missions for the whole unit. We were behind the Japanese lines.

Stilwell's Goals

The Japanese were almost on the border of India; India was in a state of seething political unrest. The Japanese were toying with the idea of extending their reach into India, although they were already vastly overextended themselves. Stilwell, on the other hand, felt that the American objective in Southeast Asia and in China, Burma, and India was to keep the nationalist Chinese fully involved in the war and to ensure that the one million Japanese who were then occupying huge swaths of Chinese territory would be held there and would not be able to be transferred back to the home islands to assist in the defense of the home islands when the inevitable invasion by Allied forces, mainly American forces, occurred. So his immediate goal was to reopen the Burma Road.

We were trying to get supplies to Chiang Kai-shek and his Nationalist armies, but we were flying them over the Hump in C-47s and C-46s and providing only a trickle of what was needed there. We could only provide the tonnage over land that Chiang Kai-shek needed. Stilwell felt that the key to that part of the war was to get the Burma Road open and to be able to move supplies from India across Burma into Southeast China, to Kunming and that general area so that Chiang Kai-shek could continue to fight the Japanese sufficiently successfully that he tied them down where they were.

Winning Support of the Indigenous Peoples

We were behind Japanese lines. In most instances, when we moved to the Japanese, we were outnumbered. We had to rely on the combat multiplying factor of surprise, good intelligence, again, speed marches and mobility I referred to earlier, to be able successfully to stand up to the Japanese. We were fighting mainly the Japanese 18th Imperial Guards Division; the victors at Singapore who had come across to Rangoon and marched north had acquitted themselves extraordinarily well, driving Stilwell and two Chinese divisions out of Burma. This was in 1942. We had a tough enemy. We were in his backyard, and he didn't like it. What I'm leading up to is the assistance and support of the indigenous population was the sine qua non to our survival, let alone successful operations. That particular factor emerged as one of the most salient factors later in the war in Vietnam. Except in Vietnam, the situation had been reversed and the Marauders and the VC had been playing the same role. The fact that we had been teaching the same kinds of things that we would be facing in Burma was a great advantage. Then what we learned in Burma was a great advantage for me from then on.

Inspired to Learn

The story [of my becoming a foreign area officer and my subsequent military career] is a little complex, maybe a little long, but I'll try to tell it. As you know, there are lulls in combat. There are times when there's no firing when you're resting, recuperating, repairing equipment, cleaning your weapons, and so on. We had such periods in the areas of Japanese and North Burma. On those occasions, we would sometimes set up our wireless radios, SCR-284, for example, and experiment with the antenna around trees and bushes and so on, orienting them in different directions, to see what we could pick up from the outside world. It was amazing what we could pick up, especially when we were at altitude, when we were up in the mountains of Burma, the spurs that extend down from the mountain range. On one occasion, it was just before our third mission, we were kind of on our last legs, and by the time I was down, we'd lost a lot of people. We'd been watching the mountain pass, the kind of glade, the flat area. Set up our radio that night, and built fires because the monsoons were rolling in, and there were clouds between us and the valley, the Japanese were in the valley, but they couldn't see our fires through the clouds, but we knew it. We were wet and tired and hungry. It gave us a chance to warm up and dry out. We began to play that game with the radios, put our aerials up, and we began to pick up Radio Free Rangoon, which was a joke because it was under Japanese control. Radio Free Manila is another joke. BBC, some Chinese language stations. I knew only a few words in Chinese, but I could pick it up enough to know that they were speaking Chinese.

One station coming in rather indistinctly through the static was in a language I'd never heard before. One of my muleskinners was of Russian ancestry, and he said, 'Wait. That's Russian. Let's see what they're saying.' We fiddled a little bit, brought it in a little more clearly, and he began haltingly to interpret what was being said. They were talking about the Battle of Kursk, which took place in August 1943 and was a turning point in their war on the Soviet-German front. It was a propaganda broadcast. It was designed for home-front consumption, home-front morale, and so on. But as he talked, I realized more fully something I'd already felt, that that was where the war was really being fought. On a front that extended between 2,000 and 3,000 miles, involving from 100 to 150 divisions on either side, a war being fought on a scale and scope that we could hardly imagine, where we were, of human suffering and so on, involving a huge swath of the population. I sat there, and it dawned on me, we're pipsqueaks, we're sideshows, all the war we can handle right here because one man firing and being fired at is all the war anybody wants. But I listened to that, and it dawned on me, here we have a whole nation really fighting and sacrificing, dying by the thousands. Actually, they eventually lost 26 million, as you are aware. I stood up by the fire and I said to my guys, 'Fellas, when this is all over, I'll be a captain, I'm going to study Russia, and I'm going to get myself assigned to Moscow as an assistant military attaché. I'm going to find out what motivates people to fight, sacrifice, and persist in these horrible conditions for so long. One has to try to understand what are the dynamics at work, and I'm going to go find out.' And I did. It was my interest in the Russian performance during World War II, which was only possible because of the Russian people's willingness to sacrifice for the motherland. I wanted to comprehend that. I wanted to get my mental rope around that.

At the end of the war, Sam Wilson, as a Russia specialist, was assigned to the Office of Strategic Services in Southeast Asia and later worked as a CIA officer in West Berlin and a defense attaché at the U.S. Embassy in Moscow during the Cold War. In 1959, he became the director of the Army Special Forces School at Fort Bragg, pioneering a program of instruction for counterinsurgency operations that evolved into the 'hearts and minds' approach used with varying degrees of success in subsequent wars. As probably the most militarily distinguished surviving Marauder, he introduced the 1962 Hollywood film based on their exploits. He headed the Defense Intelligence Agency in the mid-1970s and is considered a father of the U.S. Army Special Forces; in 1977, he helped create Delta Force, the Army unit devoted to counterterrorism and hostage-rescue operations.[19] He passed away on June 10, 2017, at the age of 93.

Philip Piazza, WWII. Library of Congress.

CHAPTER NINE

The Heavy Weapons
Commander

Philip Piazza was born in Connecticut in 1917. He passed up a basketball scholarship to enlist in the Army, a year before the attack on Pearl Harbor. He was posted to the Caribbean and then with Merrill's Marauders in the China-Burma-India Theater. Philip was wounded in the field; being evacuated under jungle combat conditions was no small feat. Like some other of the storytellers in this book, his family was mistakenly notified that he had been killed in action weeks before they learned he was alive.

'*I was just telling someone recently about an instance that I saw on TV that this young ranger had just been wounded half an hour before and he's on a litter and he's talking on the telephone to his wife. I'm glad that they do what they do today. I think it's wonderful for the families because obviously when you're in combat and away from home, it's very stressful. I think it's as stressful for families at home as it is for the man up at the front line. In my particular case, my family didn't hear from me for over two and a half years, and initially, my mother received a telegram from the War Department stating that I was killed in action! Two weeks later, they sent a second telegram saying I wasn't killed, but I was missing in*

*action. Two weeks after that, she got a third telegram stating that I wasn't
missing in action, but I was seriously wounded, but they couldn't tell her
what the nature of my [injury] was, so you can imagine it was rather
stressful on my family, so I'm glad about what they are able to do with the
communication that they have today.'*

Philip was awarded two Purple Hearts, a Bronze Star, and a presidential Unit Citation. Wounded and evacuated, he spent a year and
a half in the hospital and then returned to active duty as an instructor at Camp Blanding, where he was tasked with finding the highest
mountain in Florida to build a simulated Japanese village to teach
the soldiers infiltration techniques. In 1995 he was inducted into
the U.S. Army Ranger Hall of Fame; he was also the president of
the Merrill's Marauders Association, which held its annual meet-
ings since 1947.

He sat for this interview at their 59th annual reunion in Virginia
in 2005 when he was 88 years old.

Philip Piazza

I was born in Stratford, Connecticut, in 1917. I'm the permanent
president of Merrill's Marauders Association. Formerly with the
Marauders, I was the commanding officer of the heavy weapons
unit in the 2nd Battalion of the Blue Combat Team, Merrill's Marauders.

'I'm Not Asking You'

I went into the Army the year before Pearl Harbor because it was
obvious that we were going to go to war, and in those days, the
young people were pretty gung-ho about going into the Army because of the feeling after Pearl Harbor. As a matter of fact, I passed

up a four-year basketball scholarship to Ohio State. I went in as a private. Within six months, I was promoted to first sergeant and then was sent to officer school at Fort Benning, Georgia. Immediately after that, once again, I volunteered to go fight in Africa. I was on a Dutch ship with three Dutch officers who were PT boat commanders. We were heading for Africa. We made a stop in Curaçao in the Dutch West Indies. While we were there, they got a radio message that they needed a junior officer in Trinidad. We had an air base in Trinidad, and we had an Army regiment in Trinidad at that time. They sent a Navy PBY plane to Curaçao to pick me up and flew me on into Trinidad. When I arrived in Trinidad, you had a certain rigmarole that you go through, what an officer does to report to the commanding officer and so forth. When I reported to the commanding officer, the colonel said to me, 'I'm going to assign you and three other officers, and you are going to build a camp.' It was the original Special Forces Mountain and Ranger Training Camp.

I said to him, 'Colonel, I'm a city boy from Bridgeport, Connecticut. I was never in a jungle in my life.' I remember the colonel laughed, and he looked me in the eye and said, 'Lieutenant, I'm not asking you.'

Well, the funny part of it is, nobody knew anything about jungle fighting or mountain fighting because we had just been involved in the war. What we did, we actually even built the buildings. We wrote the manual for the training and everything. The unit that I had been assigned to there was the 33rd Infantry Regiment, which eventually became the 2nd Battalion of Merrill's Marauders. They had been for many years guarding the Panama Canal. That was their duty. They were sent from Panama to Trinidad to occupy the island there and secure that area in the Caribbean because we had an airfield there, and at that time the route to the combat area in

Africa was from Florida to Puerto Rico to Trinidad and then to Africa, so it was very important to have American troops there.

A lot of people are not aware of the fact that at that time of the war, believe it or not, we had a French unit on the island of Martinique, right in the middle of all the Americans. That was before, remember when the French were siding with the Axis powers? My battalion's job at that time was to attack Martinique. My duty at that time was to take a squad, cross the Nariva Swamp, hit the island of Martinique, scale the cliffs there, and take out the harbor guns. Well, our intelligence informed us that the French soldiers that were guarding Martinique used to go into town to visit their girlfriends. We figured that what we would do then was hit the place at the time that they were not there. It's a good thing because those cliffs with the harbor guns controlling the harbor were rather steep. Fortunately, the morning that we were going to attack, they capitulated so we didn't have to attack Martinique. We had trained for three months on amphibious maneuvers, but fortunately didn't have to go.

'A Minimum of 90% Casualties'

A lot of people were not aware of the Marauders, nor were they interested in how we were organized. [The backstory is that] the British had just been kicked out of Burma; they had taken an awful beating. They had the British commandos, known as the Chindits, retreat out of Burma. At that time, General Stilwell had been training Chinese troops, and General Merrill, who at that time was a major, was one of his aides. They walked out over the Himalayas, back into India. When we went back in, we actually retraced their routes. Well, at the [August 1943] Quebec Conference in Canada, President Roosevelt met with Prime Minister Churchill, Lord Louis Mountbatten, General Stilwell, and General Merrill, and Churchill had requested from President Roosevelt to have a large contingent of American 'commandos,' they called them at that time, to go back in with the British commandos and try to recapture Burma; President Roosevelt was going to give Prime Minister Churchill a regimental-size unit, which was 3,000 men.

After the president had told Prime Minister Churchill that he would allow them a regimental-size unit, telegrams were then sent out to all theaters of operation at that time. It stipulated that, first of all, you had to be in perfect physical condition. We were all volunteers, and suddenly, it was the first time they had ever had an all-volunteer unit of that size. Generally, you have volunteer units for small missions, but as I said, the proviso was that you had to be in perfect physical condition. You couldn't even have a hangnail because we were told specifically that, first of all, they were anticipating a minimum of 90% casualties, which actually eventually transpired. We were also told that because we would be operating behind the enemy lines, there was no way for evacuation because we were just beginning to use helicopters at that time, but they weren't using them for evacuation as they did eventually in Korea, Vietnam, and in the current conflict. We were told that if you became ill or you were wounded, it was impossible to get you out.

We were originally assigned to the British Army as part of the British commando unit. We trained with them for four months in India prior to going into combat. We had no objection to fighting alongside of our allies, the British, but we always wanted to go in carrying our own colors. We finally prevailed upon them to be able to do that. That's how the Marauders were formed.

We trained pretty extensively in mountain warfare and jungle warfare because they had both of those in the climates of India. We took a long train trip across India to the border of India and Burma. We were regimental-size. We were broken up into six combat teams, two combat teams per battalion. The idea was that when we were fighting, we would, hopefully, when we ran into any action, we would join up and be able to fight the enemy that way. But unfortunately, as happened so frequently, each one of us had our own individual [team] firefights and quite often we couldn't join each other, except for the main battle at a place called Myitkyina.

What we did was, we carried silver money and trinkets for the natives, and we were told that in the event you became ill, or you became wounded, they would try to get friendly natives to take care of us. We were very fortunate in that we eventually didn't have to rely on natives. A group of young flying sergeants from the Air Force formed what they called a liaison squadron flying small Piper Cubs and were able to evacuate one man at a time in these little Piper Cubs. In that area, the vegetation is exceptionally thick when you're down in the lowlands. When you're up in the mountains, obviously it's thick too. It was awfully hard to find a place to land, but they would pick a spot on the bank of a river, or we would cut a small path in a rice paddy when we could find one so they could land. Incidentally, I have the greatest respect in the world for the Air Force. We would never have been able to complete our mission had we not had the backing of the Air Force for two reasons: our evacuation, which was very important, but also, they had to airdrop all of our supplies by parachute because there was no way that they could get supplies to us. Even today, in Burma, there was only one main artery, and at that time, we couldn't use any vehicles, so everything had to be dropped by parachute. Now, of the original 3,000 troops that comprised our regiment, we kept four to five hundred back in India, and they were the ones that did the paperwork and kept the records. They were the ones who arranged for our supplies to be dropped to us, which was very important because, once again, we wouldn't have been able to operate had we not had these people doing this superhuman job that they really did.

We had K-rations most of the time. Once in a while, we had C-rations, which I would have loved to have. But only a couple of times we got what they called a 10-in-one ration, a mountain ration that was fantastic. It had pineapple rice pudding, it had bacon, and eggs, all dehydrated, of course, but let me tell you, when we operated under the conditions we were operating under, anything was good. We only got that a couple of times, they couldn't get that to us. [As I said], everything had to be dropped by parachute because when you're deep in behind the enemy lines like that, obviously there's no way to get supplies in, so everything had to be dropped by parachute. What we would do is we would radio and tell them in three days, hopefully, we will be at these coordinates, this position. But quite often, first of all, when you're operating continuously in enemy territory that the enemy had held for a couple of years, they knew every inch of the trail and they were all over the place. When you're getting a supply drop, a plane doesn't come in one plane and drop it. You had numbers of planes and they're circling around up there and giving your position away. Quite frequently, we were attacked when they were dropping our supplies, and we would take off and run to get out of the area so we wouldn't be captured, and we would leave our supplies for the Japanese. That's a terrible feeling when you haven't had anything to eat for a few days and you have no supplies, you need medicine, you need weapons. Quite frequently, they were able to garner our supplies that way.

Those American planes are what we call DC-3s, the best plane that was ever built, believe me. How those pilots flew, the Air Force, what I said earlier, they flew what they called the Hump from India into China under the most miserable weather conditions there were. Those planes weren't geared to fly at extreme heights. We lost an awful lot of them that would crash into the side of the mountain. As a matter of fact, in the period that I was in one of the hospitals when they moved me from the one in Ledo to a place called Dinjan, which was the airstrip that the Air Force was flying over [to], they had me in a bag, then I had them put me in a bed by the window so I could look out. I was incapacitated, but I could watch the planes take off and they had these plywood auxiliary gas tanks because they needed extra gasoline. Many a time, I'd see these fellows struggling to get airspeed and they couldn't make it, and they'd run right into the side of the mountain and explode. They were fantastic and it's a shame that those pilots never got the credit, but pilots and other parts of the world had a rough time, like the 8th Air Force and many others, but these conditions were abominable, especially during the monsoon season.

Of course, the Air Force, once again, I can't say enough about them. A lot of people don't realize that we were always called the Forgotten Theater, and we still are today. The Air Force never got credit for what they did, and their flying conditions and flying the Hump with the air equipment that they had was the toughest anywhere in the world, and they did it. We lost an awful lot of them. The same way with us. We are the forgotten people. Nobody ever recognizes the China-Burma-India Theater, but as far as I'm concerned, I think it was one of the most integral parts of the war effort because we were the back door running to Europe, and also it was important that we open up the road to get supplies from India on into China.

*Philip Piazza searches a dead Japanese soldier
for maps and other intelligence.
U.S. Army, public domain.*

Living Conditions

Living conditions were abominable. Number one, obviously, we were operating deep behind the enemy lines, as we did for sometimes as much as 250 miles behind the lines, and we did that for seven months. Also, you have to remember that operating the way we did in that period, we never had any replacements. When you lost a man either through illness or wounds, there was no way to replace them because there was no way to get them in there, and it wasn't until we captured the airfield at a place called Myitkyina, which was the main hub for anything going on into China. It was the terminus of the railroad. It was the only all-weather airstrip and the only road leading into there. That was our main objective, actually, to capture the city of Myitkyina, and the airfield at Myitkyina.

By the time we [eventually] reached Myitkyina, of the 3,000 of us originally, we were down to less than 200 men. Of course, that includes injuries as well as disease. Well, that's another thing that I don't know if I had mentioned earlier, but it's bad enough when you're fighting the enemy. You are also fighting disease, and the incidence of disease in that part of the world is the worst it is anywhere. Now, we were inoculated against anything that they could inoculate us against. We were inoculated against typhus, but we ran into a mite-borne typhus where there was no inoculation. When a man got infected that way, it was so bad that at times we had to tie him to a tree because they'd go out of the mind, and they would be dead in twenty-four hours. Another thing, if you look at the historical records, and of course, we had mountainous terrain, and we had jungle, and the vegetation is the worst it is anywhere in the world. Of course, we weren't far from where they were fighting in Vietnam. It's similar territory. As a matter of fact, when the Department of Defense sent me back [on my trip over there], when we were flying from India over to China, we had a general who was with us that was piloting the plane. He sent the colonel back.

He said, 'Get Phil to come up and sit in the co-pilot seat.'

He said, 'Look down. Do you see that down there? This time you're flying over it. You're not walking over it.'

To be honest with you, when I looked down at the terrain, I wondered how we were able to do it. It's amazing what you can do when you have to, but you've got to remember one thing, too. We were the [first] class of the Army, the best-conditioned, best-trained troops that the Army had at that time. We were young, and we were all very physically fit, but it was still pretty hectic. By the time the campaign was winding down, we had all lost 40 to 50 pounds. You can imagine what I looked like. I lost 50 pounds, and by the time they got me back to the hospital, I went in at 142 pounds, and I lost 50 pounds. My mother was shocked the first time she saw me in the hospital.

The Imperial Marines

As far as conditions are concerned, things were rough in Vietnam, and those conditions were pretty similar to what we experienced, but it's bad enough that at that time we were fighting the enemy, who were actually Imperial Marines. When you think of a Japanese as rather a small individual, a lot of people don't realize that to be an Imperial Marine, you had to be a minimum of six feet to start with, and they were at the top of the Japanese Army, the unit that we fought against. If you read any of your history, they were the ones who captured Singapore when they defeated the British. They were also infamous for the rape of Nanking, when this unit—I was at the Smithsonian Institute the other day, and they had an article there in one of the books that I was reading—in Nanking, they had taken and murdered 300,000 civilians, and they just [lined them up] and beheaded them, and then about another 150,000, they lined them up and machine-gunned them to death, because they didn't have time to go [beheading people] down the line. That's why they call it the Rape of Nanking. It was one of the most horrendous things that was ever done, next to the Holocaust, when you talk about man's inhumanity to man; you can understand why that's why I still, to this day, have such a feeling for what they did there, and also my feeling about Pearl Harbor. It's awfully hard to be a Christian and say, 'You can turn the other cheek.' I will never forgive them for that, because at that time, I also lost an awful lot of my friends in the [Bataan] death march.

Fight at Walawbum

I commanded the heavy weapons; I was commanding officer heavy weapons, Blue Combat Team, 2nd Battalion. We were set up on the British [format] because when we were first with the British, we were set up on what they call a TONE, which is a table of organization. They used streamlined units. We streamlined the size of the companies and everything. We operated with two combat teams in each battalion, which meant six combat teams. Each combat team was designated a color: blue, green, white, khaki, orange. That's why on our insignia if you notice, the colors designate that. On our insignia, we show the Star of India and the Sun of China, and the lightning stroke is us going between the two countries.

That's our Marauder insignia, which the present 75th Ranger Regiment wears today.

It was funny, when we first went in to fight, we allowed our men to handle any weapon they wanted. We didn't go by the records that said, 'Each one had to carry a certain weapon.' None of my men wanted to carry automatic weapons because that meant you had to carry extra ammunition. We were carrying very heavy packs as it was; you had to carry everything on your back. I used the animals to carry our heavy weapons and our ammunition, the heavy ammunition. The men carried very heavy packs, similar to what the Rangers use today. When they jump out of a plane, they're carrying almost a hundred pounds of weight. So they didn't want to carry any extra weight if they could help it, and we never collected souvenirs, because if you collected anything else, you wanted extra food or extra ammunition.

We fought thirty-five [engagements] out there, and it's impossible in a short period of time to relate all the incidents, but I'll tell you, the very first major battle that we had was at a place called Walawbum. Our objective was to move in and put in a roadblock to keep so that when the Japanese attacked, you were supposed to be able to stop them. Well, my combat team and my battalion moved into this area, just short of the road, in the middle of a beautiful Burmese moonlit night, and a Burmese moonlit night is like bright daylight, the brightest daylight that you get here in this country. We were actually able to move in within a few hundred yards of this Japanese unit, believe it or not, without them detecting us. When we got our air drops of supplies, we used to have some of the equipment wrapped in burlap. I had horses and mules to carry my heavy weapons, and we took the burlap and wrapped the horses' and mules' feet in burlap. We wrapped all of our metallic equipment in burlap, so there would be no sound. Another thing was, you know how a mule brays? Well, obviously, in the midst of combat, if one of them brayed, or in a case like that, we were close to the enemy, if one had brayed, it would be pretty serious. The original group of mules that were sent to us were torpedoed on a ship off of India. They had been surgically debrayed; a lot of people don't know that can be done. They didn't have time to replace them with more of them that had been surgically debrayed. We had our mule skinners, the men who were responsible for taking care of their individual mules. Believe me, they looked after them like their own children. Whenever a mule started to bray, they would reach up and grab them by the nostrils to keep them from braying. You can imagine how hectic it was at that time.

Merrill's Marauders in Burma. U.S. Army. Public domain.

We always talk to that man upstairs, and a soldier will always tell you he's always sitting on your shoulder looking after you. We were fortunate in that the Japanese in the middle of the night suddenly decided to vacate their foxholes and slit trenches and go into the city. When they did that, we immediately moved in and took over their positions; we didn't have to dig the foxholes and the slit trenches. When they returned, expecting to take over the positions, we hit them pretty hard. As a matter of fact, we killed 800 of them in that fight at Walawbum. If I remember correctly, I think we only lost a couple of men and a few wounded. But we were running out of ammunition, we were running out of food, and we were running out of medicine. We had to evacuate the position after we captured an area or an installation, and the two Chinese divisions would come in and secure it, and then we would move on to our next objective. We took off running.

We ran for five miles, carrying our wounded, feeding them blood plasma while we carried them on a litter. Once again, with that man upstairs looking after us, we ran down this trail that the Japanese had occupied, and because the whole trail was booby-trapped, one of our lieutenants took one of his horses, slapped him on the rump, and sent him running down the trail. As he ran down the trail, the horse set off the booby traps, so we had a clear path going down. The Japanese had all their guns set up and they were firing across the trail that we were running down, but they had their machine guns elevated, so they were shooting over our heads, otherwise they would have wiped us out. We ran five miles to a place called Wasaga, where we got an airdrop for supplies.

Wounded

I was wounded just before the Battle of Myitkyina. When I was wounded, we were in the midst of a terrific firefight. We knew that we were going to get hit at dawn, because all night long we heard the Japanese coming up on the only road that was there in Burma, and they were very noisy soldiers. They were good soldiers in some respects, but they were always very noisy. Well, we stress amongst our men discipline, and we stress quietness, because when you're operating behind enemy lines like that, especially, you have to be very quiet. But anyway, we could hear them getting off their trucks and banging the tailgates and jabbering away, so we knew that they were going to hit us at dawn. Then all day long from dawn until evening, they hit us with eighteen banzai attacks.

In a banzai attack, they come screaming at you. One thing about them, I have to hand it to them, their courage was exceptional. But it's like the Iraqis today, those stupid terrorists. It's an honor for them to die. As far as the Americans are concerned, we try our best not to let our men get wounded or die. We don't want to lose our men. When they attack you, it's an honor if they get killed. I had bodies piled up so high in front of my machine guns that I had to get out and kick the bodies away so we could fire our machine guns. That went on all day long.

When I was wounded first, I was outside the perimeter directing my mortar fire to my men. A machine gun got me in the head. As a matter of fact, I still have the two bullets in my head. Then later on, a 90-millimeter mortar [fragment] went through my ankle. At that time, the way we operated, we couldn't have any station hospital. All you had was medics. We were fighting all day long there; there was no way anybody could take care of me; all they could do was give me first aid.

When we pulled out of there, my men carried me on a stretcher for a while. Monsoon season was on. Conditions were abominable. It finally was getting so hard trying to carry me on a litter that I made my men put me up on a horse. I rode a horse for a while, back to Nhpum Ga (pronounced 'Niponga'), which was where my outfit was trapped on a mountain. It was seven days before I got to the hospital on the operating table. Yeah, a little different than it is today. Fortunately, today, you can evacuate the wounded so quickly with helicopters. But we didn't have those facilities. What they did at the time, one of the liaison pilots, the flying sergeants from the Air Force, put me in this little Piper Cub with my litter and flew me back a hundred miles till they had a DC-3 on an abandoned airstrip. That flew me the other 150 miles back to the hospital on the border of Burma at a place called Ledo, where the 20th General Hospital was the hospital that did such a fantastic job taking care of our sick and wounded. That was a unit from the University of Pennsylvania School of Medicine, commanded by, at that time, Colonel Ravdin, Isidor Ravdin, who eventually became a general. They were the ones that took care of us, and they did a marvelous job. I was at the hospital there six months because I was in such bad shape that they couldn't even move me. When they were finally able to move me, as a matter of fact, believe it or not, it was the day of the invasion of Europe.

I was in such a serious condition that I couldn't stand long flights or anything. On easy hops, they would put me into a hospital all the way across India to Africa. It was in Khartoum in Egypt, Africa, on the west coast of Accra. From Accra, we started across the ocean. Now, it was days and days that this took. When we left Africa, the route at that time was across to South America. As we took off from Africa, partway over the ocean, the engine on the plane kicked out, and we had to make a forced landing on Ascension Island. Now, you can imagine how barren that was. That was the island that originally they were going to banish Napoleon to, and they had decided it was too wild to put him there. What did they do? They put an American Air Force base there. Anyway, there was not a single tree on that island. Even though we had an Air Force base there, it was so rocky, there was a high cliff. When you land on the airplane, they have to run two jeeps down the strip to get the goonie birds off the strip to keep them from flying into the propellers of the plane whenever a plane came in. Also to get supplies to the men that were stationed there, they used to have to float it in barrels from the ships because there was no beach there to land on, that's how barren that place was. Anyway, they got another motor for the airplane, and then we flew from there to a hospital in Georgetown, British Guiana. Then it went up to Trinidad and Puerto Rico, and then to Miami. I was in an Air Force hospital in Miami until they could move me to what was then an amputation hospital in Atlantic City, New Jersey. In those days, when we went overseas, we spent years overseas. You didn't go away for weeks or months. You went away for years. What they tried to do when anybody was ill or seriously wounded was pick a hospital closest to your home that could take care of your particular ailment. In my case, the only thing closest was Atlantic City, about 200 miles from my home. But as a matter of fact, strangely enough, what was the hospital then was Haddon Hall Hotel. Today it's the International Casino, the big gambling casino. But once again, the feeling was so different in those days. The people in New Jersey treated us wonderfully. I spent a year there, when I was finally ambulatory, if you got on a bus, they wouldn't allow you to pay. Even a taxi driver wouldn't accept the money. If you went into a nightclub, somebody picked up the tab. People would buy your meals. It was a different feeling. It wasn't what unfortunately our servicemen experienced when they came back from Vietnam.

I was just telling someone recently about an instance that I saw on TV that this young ranger had just been wounded half an hour before and he's on a litter and he's talking on the telephone to his wife. I'm glad that they do what they do today. I think it's wonderful for the families because obviously when you're in combat and away from home, it's very stressful. I think it's as stressful for families at home as it is for the man up at the front line. In my particular case, my family didn't hear from me for over two and a half years, and initially, my mother received a telegram from the War Department stating that I was killed in action! Two weeks later, they sent a second telegram saying I wasn't killed, but I was missing in action. Two weeks after that, she got a third telegram stating that I wasn't missing in action, but I was seriously wounded, but they couldn't tell her what the nature of my [injury] was, so you can imagine it was rather stressful on my family, so I'm glad about what they are able to do with the communication that they have today.

Home

Home was Connecticut. Every stop that I made, because they could only move me for short periods, I would have to stay in the hospital until I was strong enough for them to move me because I was in a really serious condition. I was at the hospital in New Jersey for one year. I was anxious to get back to combat, but obviously, with my condition, they wouldn't allow that. I talked my way out of the hospital, went back to duty, and they assigned me to Camp Blanding, Florida. I was what they called G3, which is the operations or training officer. I was on the general staff there at Camp Blanding, Florida. I was there about six months, I'd say, before I got out.

After that, I went home. I was still in reserve, but I was in serious, still in bad condition from the head injury. Head wound, mostly. The leg was bothering me, but I managed. They managed to save my leg, even though I had been in an amputation hospital. But they managed to save that so that I eventually, even at my age, I played tennis up until just recently. But for many years after, I couldn't take advantage of the GI Bill because of the fact that I would spend maybe six months out of the year in the hospital. But I got my education in the service. I went into business in

Connecticut, but even then, for the first about ten years, as I said, I spent maybe six months out of the year in the hospital.

I was in Florida the day that the war ended. I had just built a replica of a Japanese airfield and a native village. I got orders to take my men out and blow it up. Then I was told to put myself under restriction in the bachelor officers' quarters and put my men under guard. In the barracks, they couldn't leave town because they were anticipating some really rough times with the men. It was a shame that we weren't even allowed into town. Well, I don't think I could describe to you the feeling that by then the war was over and we were going home. Of course, I stayed in a while to do some things for the general. I didn't get to participate in parades and everything that they had up north, but those of us who were in the war at that time were treated wonderfully after we came home, as you can see in the newsreels. It wasn't like what happened after Vietnam, which was a shame. We were treated terrifically. We cannot complain about that. There was a different feeling throughout the country. Well, you know what the women did when the men went away; the women went into the factories and even into the shipyards and everything. Unfortunately, if we were to go in a war, and we're not calling [the Iraq and Afghanistan operations] a war right now. But if we were to have to do the same thing today, I don't know if we could gear up as quickly as we did at that time, because we don't have the facilities right now.

'General Stilwell Just Laughed'

I hate to talk about the horrors of war, but when you look back, there are humorous things that happened at times. For instance, my battalion was trapped on a hill at a place called Nhpum Ga for two weeks until it broke out on Easter Sunday morning, strangely enough. But one of the men woke up one morning—in the Rangers, you operate in the buddy system. At night, there's always one man awake and one man asleep, hopefully. When he woke up in the morning, his buddy said, 'Boy, you look wonderful this morning. Who's your undertaker?' [*Laughs*] I always remember the one incident where I met the general, and I got the opportunity to talk to him later on a number of times. When we walked up into the Himalayan Mountains—initially, we walked 130 miles up into the Himalayas and over the Himalayas on into Burma. Well, at a place called Pangsau Pass, which was our jump-off point for combat, General Stilwell was standing there, and he happened to come through my area where my men were, and he stood there talking to me. He never wore insignia; he had a fetish [about it], he wouldn't wear his medals or all the fancy uniforms or anything. He always wore an old campaign hat. He always had a pipe in his mouth and a long coat. He was old, and some of the men didn't recognize him. But one of my men came up when I was talking to him. He took one look at him, and excuse my English, but he said, 'Jesus Christ, things must be pretty rough back in the States, when they send an old son of a bitch like you over here to fight!' [*Laughs*]

I wanted to dig a hole and just crawl in; here I am talking to the top general! Anyway, General Stilwell just laughed; as a matter of fact, he nudged me, he said, 'Don't let it bother you.' Well, I met him a number of times after that, like the time when I was in Florida and when he was a corps commander after that. He always reminded me of that. Just nine years ago when I was on that trip back to China that the Department of Defense sent me on, I was on one of the islands there, and I met his son, who was a forensic pathologist. Spent the night with him. His son told me, 'I was only a kid in those days. But I remember my dad telling me that incident.'

Going Back

In about 1996, I think it was, [I got to go back.] That was fabulous! What the Department of Defense did was they sent us and picked fourteen officers who had seen a lot of combat in that part of the world. I was the only infantry officer. The rest of them were Flying Tigers. At that time, they were just beginning to use a new C-17 plane that we have, a fantastic airplane. They wheeled in equipment and configured it the same as a first-class airline. They also sent three chefs from the Pentagon to take care of us. Every place that we went, not only there on the plane, they wined and dined us; every place that we went, either an admiral, an ambassador, or a general would throw a party for us every night! In China, the head of the Chinese Communist Party threw a party for us! It was a fabulous trip, 38,000 miles, three weeks.

We first went to Hawaii. The best part of it was that every place we went, we got three or four days to stay so that they would take us on tours of the area. As I say, every night, they wined and dined us, at either an officers' club or an ambassador's residence. I always remember the one in India. The ambassador's residence is really posh. I remember when we were having the reception, looking up the grand staircase and coming down this staircase was this Gurkha band with bagpipes! It was quite impressive. We went to Bombay, India, Calcutta, New Delhi. Then we flew over the Himalayan Mountains to China. We were at Kunming, which was the place where the Air Force in those days was supplied for their flights into China. We went from Kunming, where we had a big ceremony for the Flying Tigers, and then went on to Beijing. In Beijing, the head of the Communist Party gave us a party. Then we went from there to Okinawa, and from Okinawa back to Hawaii.

It was a fabulous trip. I wish my wife could have gone with me. As I said, they wined and dined us all the way, gave us all kinds of presents, and treated us royally. It was a wonderful trip, something I'll treasure. A funny part of it is, just prior to that, I had bought my wife a fancy new camera. Then I went out and I bought about 15 rolls of film to film the trip. Anyway, when I got back, I didn't use it properly, and all the film was ruined; I was on the verge of crying. But a week later, the Secretary of the Air Force sent me a big carton, and it had a big box full of blown-up pictures of the whole trip. Beautiful. We had his official photographer, a lady from Washington, D.C., so I had better pictures. [*Wistfully*] Yeah.

'You Volunteered For This Mission'

My final rank was captain. I had been promoted while we were in there, but obviously, when you're behind the entry lines, because my job called for a captaincy when I finally got it, my promotion was post-dated back to that. We have, of course, the theater ribbons, which all servicemen get, when they operate in [a particular theater]. We had the Presidential Unit Citation, and I was awarded the Bronze Star, and the China War Memorial Medal. I have two Purple Hearts, but actually, I was involved with three. I never put in for the third one. One thing that you'll find out, if anybody ever researches our records, and everybody is amazed at it, Merrill's Marauders has the least awards of any combat outfit that ever saw that much combat. The reason for that is that the officers put in a man for the award, you request it, and they were always rejected, in most cases, in my battalion, because the answer was, 'Look, you volunteered for this mission, so you were supposed to do the job.' After the war, I had many occasions. I was very friendly with General Merrill and my commanding officer, Colonel McGee, and they always regretted the fact that it happened, because people often say to me, 'How come an officer like yours did so much and got so few awards?' Well, it's like the Rangers today. They don't want to be publicized. You never see much about it in the paper. You hear a lot about the Marines right now, who are doing a good job, but you don't hear anything about Special Forces. They don't want the publicity. It really is sad, because I remember a few years ago when the president at that time took and awarded innumerable Medals of Honor to different youth. I don't believe you should—I'm not saying that they didn't deserve them, but I think they demean the medal when you give it out that indiscriminately. Our people should have gotten more awards than they did, but that wasn't why we were there. We weren't there to be awarded; we had a purpose, we had a reason for being there. We don't regret it. I don't. I often had people say to me, when they saw the records about volunteering for what they call a dangerous and hazardous mission, which the president had sent out to us, said, 'How could you be so stupid to volunteer for a mission that you're told that you're going to have a minimum of 90% casualties?' But once again, as I said earlier, it wasn't Vietnam, it wasn't Korea. There was a different feeling throughout the country completely.

'I'll Take Care of It'

[I encountered General Merrill several times.] As a matter of fact, General Merrill had a heart attack the same time I was wounded. So that's when we got to be very friendly. Even though he was very ill at the hospital, he used to insist on them bringing him over to my quarters so he could see me, and we got very friendly. Later years, I had a small business in Connecticut. I had a couple of retail stores, and I had a small wholesale business covering all of New England. I always made a point on my last evening before I went home to stop in Concord, New Hampshire, and visit with the general. Then after that, he attended every reunion, provided he was in the States, and he was very close to us. I think he was one of the most admired general officers there ever was. He was also, as a major general, one of the youngest field generals that we had at that time. He was in his early forties, and he was a powerful major general. Originally, when they went out of Burma when he was with Stilwell and the British when they retreated out of Burma, he was a major at that time. Eventually wound up as a major general, which is a two-star rank. When he retired from the Army and went back to live in New Hampshire, where his widow still lives, he was the highway commissioner in New Hampshire. They had a highway commissioners' convention in Florida. On his way back, he took ill in Fernandino Beach, Florida. The Governor of New Hampshire called me that night to tell me that he had passed away. So we arranged to have a ceremony up at where he went to school at West Point. We buried him at West Point. Stilwell was also buried there.

Merrill was very close to his men. Some fellows say he wasn't, but from my personal experience, I know he was. As a matter of fact, during the Korean War, I was here in Walter Reed for a brain operation, a craniotomy. General Merrill called the Surgeon General and said to him, 'This man's not only one of my former officers, but he's also a personal friend. I'd appreciate anything you can do for him.' The Surgeon General then got in touch with the commanding general at Walter Reed and said, 'You don't give him an aspirin tablet without letting me know about it.' Then he would call General Merrill and let him know what my condition was. Then General Merrill would call my wife, Emma, up in Connecticut and let her know how I was.

I got real wonderful treatment, same surgeon that operated on President Eisenhower the week before. As a matter of fact, right after my operation, that young colonel [doctor] had a heart attack because he had spent so much time in the operating room. Understand one thing, General Merrill didn't do that because I was an officer. He had always told me in our private conversations that 'if any of the men get in any problems, let me know. I'll take care of it. I don't want any publicity over it.' He didn't.

The same way with General Ravdin who commanded the 20th General Hospital and went back to the University of Pennsylvania. He always told me that if any of the Marauders had any physical problems and couldn't afford to have it taken care of, let him know. He went to bat for me a number of times where some of the men were rather indigent at the time. So it was a great relationship.

Reunions

I have been president of the Merrill's Marauders Association for fifty-eight years, since 1947, the first reunion. They can't get anybody stupid enough to take the job. [*Laughs*] [My wife will tell you the only time we missed a reunion was about four years ago, I resigned, I said, 'That's it.' What happened [at the one we missed]? They elected me back in and then talked me into taking the job again.

I think if anyone ever attends one of our reunions, [they will see that] there has never been a unit [with such camaraderie], and I have other service people tell me the same thing. We have met every year for fifty-eight years in different parts of the country. We have a special rapport. Maybe it's because of the unusual circumstances that we fought and lived under in those days, and incidentally, that applies to the present 75th Ranger Regiment, who are our successors. As a matter of fact, the 75th Ranger Regiment wears our insignia—one of the greatest honors I ever had, after the colors of the Merrill's Marauders were retired, was in 1969 at a ceremony down at Eglin Air Force Base in Florida. I had the honor of presenting our colors to activate the present 75th Ranger Regiment, which incidentally is the only Ranger unit in existence today. Those are the ones that are in—you don't hear much publicity about them, because they don't look for publicity, but they're the ones that are fighting constantly in Afghanistan and Iraq today, and we're very proud of this 75th Ranger Regiment. When you talk about rapport, I attend an awful lot of Ranger ceremonies, I go to every graduation; even though I live 250 miles from Fort Benning, I'm invited to all Special Forces ceremonies. There is a special rapport between Rangers and Special Forces people. It's hard to explain it to somebody else, but we really do have a special rapport, and strangely enough, the rapport between the old Rangers and the new Rangers is great. We meet pretty regularly at Fort Benning, and once a year we have what they call the Ranger Rendezvous for four days when we all meet, and we have all kinds of ceremonies. Generally, we have a change of command, and that's the time that we induct the incoming members of the Ranger Hall of Fame. As a matter of fact, I'm on both the Executive Committee and the Nominating Committee of the Ranger Hall of Fame.

Interviewer: How did your military experience influence your life or your thoughts about military or war, in general?

Well, if we're talking about war today or the conditions today over there, I'm not militaristic. I give an awful lot of talks. One thing I always say, 'Don't think us veterans are militaristic, that we love wars. That's not true. We don't want our children or our friends' children to have to go to war.' The same thing with what's happening over there. I'm sorry it's going on. Unfortunately, we're in a position right now where I don't see how we can back out of it like we had to do in Vietnam. To answer your question, I think the young Rangers today and the military people today are doing a wonderful job. Your young Rangers today I think are the best educated, the best disciplined, and the finest troops that we could ever have. We take our hats off to these young [people]. I don't mean just the people that are in combat, even service. I don't care if a person served in wartime or not, the fact that they're willing to wear the uniform. I admire them for it.

In closing, I can't think of anything else, offhand, but one thing I will say that in Tom Brokaw's book, he gives all kinds of accolades to us as the 'greatest generation.' I really think that the young people, today, are our future greatest generation, really. I think they should get their accolades, too. It's wonderful that they say what they do. The young people today, they're unbelievable! The problem is today the news media plays up the bad ones. They're a minority. Nobody says anything about the good ones who are doing the good things.

Philip B. Piazza passed away in May 2011 at the age of 94.

CHAPTER TEN

The Engineer

Morris Factor grew up in the west side of Chicago during the Great Depression. After Pearl Harbor, he decided to enlist, as he figured the draft was going to catch up to him, and he wanted to have a say in where he would up. The Army had other plans, and he would find himself in India, of all places, merged into the guerrilla force know as Merrill's Marauders. He sat for this interview shortly after his 91st birthday in 2012 in Chicago.

Morris Factor

I was born on October 7, 1920, in Chicago. I had two brothers. I had an older brother that died when he was 12 years old of pneumonia in the '20s. And my baby brother died, he was not quite two, also of pneumonia. You know, back in the '20s they didn't have penicillin then, and if you caught pneumonia you could say you're gone. They went to the hospital, and they died at Michael Reese Hospital, both of them, my older brother and my younger brother. I was the middle kid in between, the guy that was always in trouble. We ate every day, he paid rent, and when they got tired of an apartment, they used to move. One time they moved; they didn't tell me they were moving. I came home and they were gone. I came home from school, and they're gone out of the apartment, but I knew everybody on the block, and I said, 'What happened to my folks?'

'Oh, they moved to that building over there.'

Depression Days

My father, before the war, used to have newspaper stands on two corners, he owned both corners—I say he owned, but he had the stands across the street, and he sold newspapers to make a living. At that particular time, way before the war broke out, my father used to make if he sold 100 *Tribunes*, he made 60 cents. The paper was two cents a paper, on a Sunday he used to get two cents a paper. Of course, it was a dime a paper for the Sunday paper. And that's how my father made his living and supported the family. We ate every day. We paid rent and I went to school, and I used to help out after school or on a Saturday or a Sunday, while he used to go to sleep because he worked selling—he had to be there at 5:30 on a Sunday morning selling the newspapers. They used to drop off a whole load and he would sell them and whatever he didn't sell, he gave back, and he'd make 60 cents, or he'd sell a hundred newspapers, two dollars. Or he used to make more because he used to sell several hundred of them and I used to help out with it, and he had to go home and sleep.

Now after war broke out, my father got rid of the newsstands and he went to work in a defense plant, and he was making metal casings that they used to make for shells. He was the first guy there in the morning and the last guy to leave during the day. And the owners of the plant told my father—he was in his middle to late sixties when I came out—and they used to tell him, 'Harry,' you know they had him on a first-name basis, he never missed a day of work unless he was sick, and he was the first guy to come and the last guy to leave. He said, 'You got a job as long as you want.' And we used to holler at him. 'You're 65, I mean why don't you go on Social Security?' He didn't want to leave, you know. He was happy working. We finally forced him to leave, which was wrong. He lived 'til he was 93, I mean, but he was never as happy as when he was working. He could have worked a few more years, but the family forced him to quit.

In those years, they didn't have air conditioning, and unless you had a little fan, you used to leave the windows open, the doors open, sleep all night long that way, or we slept in the park, all the kids used to sleep in the park, boys and girls. I mean not together, I mean but we were teenagers, we'd sleep in a park at night, and nobody bothered us, and that's where we survived and lived in the Depression years.

I was always in trouble. Not criminal trouble, just trouble. I was going to Hebrew school and before I became Bar mitzvahed and I was what, about 12 years old. And the rabbi had a beard like this, [*gestures*], and I was always fascinated. I said, 'That beard must be false,' and I kept telling myself it must be false. I said, 'But how do I find out?' Finally with nobody even knowing, he walks by, and he stands there. I grabbed his beard, and I pulled. That's when I got thrown out of Hebrew school. My father came and got me back in. And I found out that it was a real beard. [*Laughs*] He didn't want me back at first, but my father was a member of the temple, so he did that. And my father was a religious man, and I was semi-religious. Most of my friends were not religious, unfortunately, even today. I go with some that are and some that are not. You know. So what can I say?

On our street we had Italians, we had Jews, everybody. And we were friends; we played ball together, softball. [Everyone got along.] If you go a block, two blocks away, then you had problems.

We had to walk three blocks to go to school. And when we crossed Taylor Street, we were in a different neighborhood, and the guys there used to come, and all of a sudden you were in a fight. Not with knives or baseball bats, I mean, or guns. With our fists, on an average of about I'd say maybe three times a week. I remember when we were playing in Sears lot, we were playing softball for the neighborhood championship, and the team we had to play was an Italian team from another neighborhood. So they came up to us and they said, 'If you guys win,' they said, 'we're going to pounce on you and beat the hell out of you,' you know, 'because we want to win and we don't want you to win.' It went in one ear and went out the other. We won. And believe it or not, there was a whole fight on the playground until they broke us up, you know. That was part of the life of growing up.

'You'll Go Where I Tell You to Go'

I went to Herzl Junior College for a year and a half before I went in the army. I enlisted in February of '42, right after Pearl Harbor. I went down to the draft board there and enlisted because they were going to take me anyway. So I figured to myself if you enlist, they told me that you can go into the branch of the service that you want. I found out then that they lied. I wanted to go in to become a photographer and go into something like the engineers or something like that. That's what I was more or less taking up in school. I was very good in math, you know. So when I went into the branch at Fort Sheridan to get inducted into the Army, when they called my name, I walked up. It must have been ten thousand kids in the place there, and they called them in alphabetical order, they called your name. So when they called my name and I come up, a sergeant was there, a corporal and a lieutenant were sitting in back, and I saluted, which I was supposed to do, I was told, I knew that. And they asked me my name and I told them. I said, 'Sir,' I called him sir, and he smiled at that. And I said, 'I understand when you enlist that you can ask for the branch of the service that you'd like to go to.'

He sat up straight like that. He said, 'What did you say, soldier?'

I says I only asked a question. I said, 'I understand.'

He said, 'You'll go where I tell you to go.' I wanted to tell him I'd like to tell you where to go, but I didn't.

He said, 'I'll choose what you want.'

I thought, okay, there's nothing I could do about it. So he sends me to the 954th Topographic Engineer outfit in Douglas, Arizona. Now their job was to make a map of the Mexican coastline. At that time in 1942, the coastline was very poorly charted in the beginning of '42. And my job was to do the math work for the surveyor on that. And they sent us in groups of four men, four men, four men and we're surveying the coastline. And they flew over by plane, photographed it from the air, and they correlated everything. And we were gone for about five, six weeks. When we came back, I asked for a furlough. I'd never—I'm in the army a couple months, I wanted to go home. And they said, 'You're in a cavalry, and you're going to a new outfit, and you've got to go up to Seattle, Washington, to Fort Lewis.' There were six of us that went there, we had a week to get to Seattle. We stopped off in Los Angeles for a few days, and we had a ball. And we come to Fort Lewis and the MPs at the gate, and we see all these beautiful barracks like Fort Sheridan. And we come up to the gate, and they asked to see our papers and we showed them. We said, 'Which building do we go to?'

He said, 'Do you see those tents out in the field about three-quarters of a mile away? That's where you go.'

I said, 'What are we doing in tents?'

He said, 'That's where you've got to report.' So we're walking over the grass carrying our duffel bags and everything, and we come there, and we see flags flying. It says First Ranger Battalion. I said to the other guy, I said, 'What's a ranger?'

He said, 'I don't know.' And that's when we found out that this was the First Ranger Battalion, and we got combat training from them for a few weeks, going out at night traveling by the stars, coming; we went into hilly country where they were training us. And finally we came back, and they'd bring us into Fort Sheridan, and we'd get assigned to the 930th Engineer Battalion, so now I'm in the 930th Engineers.

I went up to the guys and I said, 'Can I get a furlough to go home?'

They said, 'Sure.' They give me a furlough and I get on a train, and I come home. I get off in the station and I'm greeted by MPs. 'Let's see your orders.' I showed them my orders.

They said, 'You're one of the guys we're looking for.'

I said, 'How can you be looking for me? I just got here!'

He said, 'Well, your outfit's shipping overseas, you've got to go back tomorrow.'

I said, 'Oh!'

They said, 'We'll take you home, and we'll pick you up in the morning to bring you to the train.'

They wanted to know where I lived. I came home, I didn't go to sleep, I was with my folks and with some of my friends. In the morning they picked me up, put me on a train. I come back; they're all packed, and we get on a train, and we leave from Seattle, Washington, all the way to Newport News, Virginia. It took us a week to get there. Of course they stopped, but you couldn't get off. They had MPs at every door, and you stayed in the car that you were, no beds. You slept in seats.

They issued us winter clothing because we're in December, you know, and we were there two days or a day and a half and they says we're boarding the ship that's out there in the harbor at 2:30 in the morning. We were there and another outfit was there; there must have been maybe five, six hundred men on this ship, a Victory ship with bunks twelve feet high. Fortunately I was almost near the top so nobody could throw up on me.

They gave me a job clicking a counter to count how many people were coming for breakfast and lunch, that was my job when I was on the boat, because I didn't get seasick. I should have gone in the navy, but I was in the army. Now we were surrounded by destroyers, and they used to circle around us like we were nothing, looking for submarines. We were attacked by submarines, but not our boat. There were ships that had supplies like tanks and stuff on the deck that they were bringing overseas, that's the ones they went after. We were lucky, you know. It took us thirty-five days, and we landed in North Africa.

Rommel took off from Tobruk, and the war was over in Africa, and he flew to Germany. We were there and we knew that they were going to invade Europe. We thought that we were going to be in the group that invaded Europe, you know. And we're outside of the town, and all of a sudden, they said we're going back on a ship. I said, 'Oh, are we getting ready for the invasion?'

They said, 'No, you're going to the Mediterranean into the Indian Ocean, we're going to Bombay!'

We got strafed by German planes, but the U.S. planes were there, and they drove them away; nobody got hurt. We were down—we were told by the navy 'stay down below' because they had their gunners on top, and they didn't want us to get in the way, you know. I wanted to jump off, you know.

India

We landed in Bombay, and we were there for—that's when we were able to do a few things. We were there for a couple of weeks until they put us on a train and took us to Kharagpur, a town in India. And from Kharagpur, all of a sudden, we were no longer the 930th, we became [part of] the 5307th Composite Group. Our unit was the 5307th Composite Group, before we were named Merrill's Marauders. Before Merrill became the general, he was in Japan before the war, and he learned Japanese, and he became friendly with a lot of Japanese officers and generals before the war. And he knew a lot about the Japanese, he knew how to speak Japanese, and he was an engineer and very well trained, you know. That's why Stilwell took him. And the other colonels graduated West Point the same as he did. Hunter thought he was going to be the commanding general instead of Merrill, but he wasn't, he was just a colonel, and the three colonels were all West Pointers; they are not alive today.[9] They'd be about 115 years old if they were alive. None of the officers are alive. They are all West Pointers that graduated in the late '20s. They're gone.

Now I was under General 'Vinegar Joe' Stilwell. He wanted American troops to fight in Burma and he had Chinese troops, three divisions, but he didn't have [American commandos to spearhead any attack]. They had some Chindits which were part Chinese, they were like Indian Chinese, you know. And then they had the Kachins, which were Burmese. The Kachins hated the Japanese with a passion. They fought under Wingate. I don't know if you

---

[9] Charles Newton Hunter (1906-1978) was second in command, but is generally recognized as the de facto field leader of Merrill's Marauders, given Frank Merrill's medical emergencies and evacuation. He was the author of the 1963 book *Galahad*; author and field commander Charlton Ogburn noted in his own book on Merrill's Marauders that 'Colonel Charles N. Hunter had been with Galahad from the beginning as its ranking or second ranking officer, had commanded it during its times of greatest trial, and was more responsible than any other individual for its record of achievement.' Source: Ogburn, Charlton, *The Marauders*. New York: Harper & Brothers, 1956. p. 2. There is more on Hunter's story in Chapter 12.

ever heard of General Wingate. He was a British commando officer, and he trained—or he started to train the Chinese and trained some of the American forces. Wingate started the initial invasion of Burma.

'General Orde Wingate (center) with other officers at the airfield code-named 'Broadway' in Burma awaiting a night supply drop.' Colonel Frank Merrill far left. 1944. Wingate was killed in a plane crash shortly after this photo was taken. Imperial War Museum, public domain.

He sent commandos, Chindit commandos that he trained into Burma to hit the Japanese and then they pulled out. And then he wanted to train the Chinese and later the American forces in guerilla tactics up in Deogarh, India, until he got killed by accident, and we trained without him on that. But he was a commando general, I mean who trained us very well, but we trained without him on that. Now at that time they needed troops to form the American combat team. But where were you going to get American troops who are jungle fighters? So he asked, and the [British] generals there said,

'No American forces. Let the Chinese fight.' So [Stilwell] went over their heads to the States, and he got permission to gather up 3,000 men if he could, who were jungle experienced. They asked MacArthur at first. MacArthur then asked the troops that fought in Guadalcanal and the islands that they needed—these guys were out at the islands right at the moment—that he needed experienced jungle troops that are willing to volunteer for a dangerous mission; they wanted troops that had jungle experience, and they wound up with 650 experienced, tough New Yorkers to fight and those were the first group. But that's not enough. So he went to the States, and he got a group; some of them that were there were being trained in jungle warfare. So he got another group. He still didn't have enough. So he went to Australia, and he got a small group over there, and then finally the 930th came in to assist them to round out the 3,000 men that he needed.

With 3,000 men, we went up to India to Deogarh. It's a mountainous area. To get into Burma, you've got to climb up the mountains. Remember where the guys climbed up in the mountains 10,000 feet up? The Japanese figured that nobody could go over that there, especially an army because you can't go with motorized troops. So they figured that they were safe. They didn't know the army.

Combat Teams

We were trained in Deogarh with jungles similar to Burma, you know. They'd take us out in groups of five or ten, maybe ten, fifteen miles away from the camp. We looked at the stars and we took a reading, and we had to come back. They gave you a canteen of water and a cheese sandwich and you had to come back at a certain time. And we trained so that we would get harder and get in better physical shape. We were in pretty good shape, but we became even

harder until they decided at that time—we didn't have any motorized vehicles, of course, you couldn't take motorized vehicles over
the mountains. We had mules; they assigned 700 mules to 3,000
men and troops. Now what they did with the unit is, they broke it
up into three units, a thousand, a thousand, and a thousand. Now
they took the thousand units, we were still the 5307th Composite
Group. They took and they broke each unit up into two groups,
sixteen officers and about 460 men in number one, and the same in
number two, and then another and a colonel in charge. Then another colonel. There was Colonel Olson, Colonel Beach, and Colonel McGee, the three colonels that were in charge of the three
groups. Each group was broken up into a thousand men and then
each thousand men was broken up into two groups. And they didn't
give—they gave us numbers and colors. That's how we were identified.

White and red and white—or blue and green. I was in the number one group. I was in the white unit, under Colonel Olson. They
broke it up so they could form like pincer movements. There were
two groups here, two groups here, two groups there. We were not
more than a mile and a half or two miles apart, as we were there.
Anyway, we went in, we're in groups and over the mountains we
came, high out there with the mules and everything. And some of
the stuff, the mules had big, big packages on them. They couldn't
climb. So we had to carry some of the stuff that the mules couldn't
carry to bring over the mountains. And then we're walking almost
500 miles, we're walking for combat. And how many miles do you
walk in a day? We're lucky if we walked ten to fifteen miles in a day
because you're walking through jungles with cane and mud and
everything down below. We had to combat two or three different
kinds of mosquitoes, we had to combat leeches, we had to combat
the different kinds of leeches. We'd scrape them off with our
knives. You know, there's trees that were a couple hundred feet

high. And there was the cane, and we had to chop that to get through.

Now, each group were fortunate that we had three or four Kachins as guides. Now they were born in the area, so they knew how to go on certain trails with us, and they went along with us. And I was really fortunate. One of the guys that was in our outfit was Japanese-American, so he was able to speak Japanese, and he would listen to the Japanese issuing orders, and he'd tell us. We were fighting different battles going along, and our first battle that we had to go down was down near Walawbum in Burma. Well, we were fighting battles as we went along.

Now, they broke up the 460 men, they took a unit, a platoon, and they became an intelligence reconnaissance unit. They picked up all the sharpshooters for this group, and these were hardened soldiers that they had in excellent shape. And they were reconnaissance. Then they picked certain ones that they made like medics in the group that—everybody had a job. And the rest of us were the soldiers that went along on that. I was a marksman, but I wasn't a sharpshooter, you know. I could hit the target, but a sharpshooter could hit the bull's eye all the time. I'd hit the target but not necessarily the bull's eye.

We'd travel a lot by night, because at daytime they can see you. The Japanese could be anywhere. You know, each unit of 460 men with our patrols going out and our colonel, we would be group one and color white or whatever, we would go a couple of miles and then we'd stop, we'd go a couple of miles and then we'd stop until we got to our objective. We had the Kachins that were with us, we knew where we were going, but you couldn't make it more than six or seven miles, eight miles in one day, you couldn't go any further. Maybe you could go ten miles, but that would be it. Don't forget, you had to go through cane and swamps and you just—you're not chopping it down because you couldn't chop it all down, it was impossible. I mean everybody had a job and they all traveled together. But the patrols went out without us and they—sometimes they got involved in a fight with another Japanese patrol. And they'd surround them, and they would get rid of them. There was quite a good deal of that.

But we went to all of these places, and we fought the Japanese. See, the Japanese had the 18th, the 55th, and the 56th division of Japanese. These were the three top hardened soldiers that conquered China under General Tanaka. Now he was under another general, but he was in charge of all of these troops, and we're going along, and our first big combat unit was at Walawbum. We had four major battles that we had going in.

The River Crossing

We were in the first big battle that we had, which is across the Irrawaddy River, and we're on the ground over there. And one of the fellows climbs a tree, and he takes a look across the river, and he almost had a heart attack. There must have been a thousand or more Japanese getting ready to cross the river at us. They thought that they would be easy to fight. You know, especially when we only got 400 men in that spot at that moment. The others were around but not close by. And he said, 'They're getting ready to cross the river.' And he was in a tree. He almost fell out of the tree. He said, 'Don't shoot until I tell you,' you know, so we're sitting there and we're waiting until they were across the river, and they were about 300 yards from us. They got a little closer and then he said, 'Fire.' Now all we had for weapons, no heavy equipment, because we couldn't carry it. We had .30 caliber machine guns, .45 caliber machine guns, Browning automatics. We had mortars; I had a carbine, and I had a .45 automatic and a trench knife, and we waited, and they came.

When they were all across the river, and they were coming toward us, and the last of them came, it must have been 100 feet away from us when they turned around and they took off and went back, and we're waiting there in the foxhole, and they came back again, and they took off. And now the Chinese were in back on the flanks with the Chinese army in case they tried to go a different way, the Chinese would surround them, and they would get the stragglers. We were in the middle with one.

There was a reporter from *Life Magazine* with the headquarters company under General Merrill. We also had Colonel Beach, Colonel Olson, and Colonel McGee. Each one had 1,000 men under him. What happened is after the first couple of battles, the guy from *Life* magazine sends reports back to the United States. You know, he's a reporter. So he called us Merrill's Marauders instead of the 5307th Composite, and that's how we got the name Merrill's Marauders from him. And we fought, as I say, altogether in Burma, we must have killed close to 3,000 Japanese. We destroyed the 55th and 56th and 18th Japanese divisions. It must have been 20, 30,000 men there, and we—they must have killed a third of them. We were almost finished as a fighting unit. We had dysentery, we had malaria, we had jungle fever, wounded different guys. And we didn't have semi-healthy guys, we had about 300 men left that were capable of fighting yet a little bit, and Stilwell wanted to take Myitkyina. Now the Burma Road was going through Myitkyina, and the airfield was in Myitkyina they wanted. That was considered a big city with 8,000 people. Now we didn't have healthy troops. So he tells General Merrill what he had, he says he didn't care as long as they can walk and carry a gun to go in and fight and take Myitkyina.

'We Were Through'

We fought the battle on the airfield and destroyed the Japanese in the airfield, and then from there, which they wanted, which the Allies, they needed the airfield, and you've got to remember, the engineers, the 930th that I was originally with, were building the road to Kunming, China. They had to go through that area there and join up with the original road over the mountains, you know, and nobody said you could build it. But General Pick had built, I forgot what dam it was in the United States, but he had been a civilian engineer, and he was in charge of the unit, had built a road, but they needed military protection. That's how the 930th Combat Engineers went along, and they protected them while they were building. But we were the chosen few. And anyway, after the airfield, we went in to take the town. And then after that, there was no more Merrill's Marauders, we were disbanded and they formed a new group called MARS, new recruits that came in, Mars Task Force.[10] Some of the Marauders joined up with them. A few did. They wanted to go to combat, and they went up. And I went in with a group, I was with a group of special forces that went into French Indochina and then we heard that the war was over. We didn't know that they dropped a bomb. You know, we found out afterwards, and our job was to go from there into Shanghai and help to collect weapons and make way for signing a surrender. And that's when from there, that's when I started to go home.

We had enough combat, and we had not only combat. What about the dysentery? What about the dengue fever? What about the jungle fly? What about the leeches? All of that we had. The guys, in order to unfortunately to move their bowels and stuff, they couldn't pull their pants down fast enough, so they'd cut a hole, a slit in their

---

[10] The Mars Task Force was the long-range penetration successor to the Marauders.

slacks, so all they had to do was bend down and open it up so that they could go to the bathroom. And they used to go to the bathroom, they'd dig a hole in their own foxhole and then they'd cover it up because they couldn't go out somewhere and move. I mean that's the story that we had. We ate K-rations when we got them. We didn't always get them; we had the Air Force; we had a group that took care of us. We'd call up by radio, and if we needed water or ammunition or food, within 24 hours the planes would come and drop it to us. This group was absolutely fabulous.

We were in I think about four major battles, and we couldn't— we were exhausted; I think out of all 3,000, 93 were killed, but we had about four hundred something that were with diseases and stuff and wounded and different things, and the rest were—everybody had a disease of some sort or another. I don't think there was anybody that didn't have one. But Stilwell said he didn't care, as long as you could walk and carry a gun, he wanted us to go in. We wound up with 300 of us, and we took Myitkyina, the airfield and the town, and that was our last battle, and then we were through.

The End of the War

I met Ho Chi Minh. At that time the war in Europe was over, and they were going to invade Japan, and in order to invade it, they had to invade French Indochina into China to the coast so we can invade Japan. He was with the officers in the group that were there. He seemed like a nice guy. [The unit was originally helping train him and his fighters to fight the Japanese], that's what they were doing. They were the rebels. The rebel [communist] forces that fought in French Indochina were not part of Chiang Kai-Shek's group. Chiang Kai-Shek was the regular Chinese army, and they didn't like each other. After the war, Chiang Kai-Shek's troops pulled way back, and they didn't bother the Chinese [communist] forces. In the beginning. I was out of China, you know about three or four months later, whatever, they started the invasion of China, and they wanted China, the rebels. [Later], they drove Chiang Kai-Shek and his troops into Taiwan [in 1949], and they took over China.

'He Belongs To Me'

They dropped an atomic bomb, and we got word to stop what we were doing. We said, 'What's an atomic bomb?' We didn't know. And we were going to be picked up by a C-47 and were flying into Shanghai, China, to make way for signing and surrender. When we landed in Shanghai, there must have been two or three hundred Japanese soldiers on each side, you know, standing there saluting us and with their rifles at attention, not shooting us. You know, the Japanese soldier, if you would tell him to kill himself, he'd kill himself. He did what his officers told him. And they told them when we came in that they're supposed to bring all of their weapons—you know what a Quonset hut is? They were to bring them there and bring in their swords and knives and guns to us. And that was one of our jobs, and to pick out suitable quarters for the American forces that were coming in for living quarters in Shanghai. And we're riding around, and that's when I'm looking and I see I've got 146 points, and they're sending guys home with 40 and 39 and 40 points, and I never was home. So when the Tenth Air Force came in, I was by myself when I went in and asked permission to see the adjutant general, and I came in and he asked me my name and rank and who I was with, and he says he heard of us.

He said, 'What can I do for you?'

I said, 'I want to go home.' And I told him I have 146 points, and they're sending guys home, and my outfit is going on to Japan.

I said, 'I don't want to.' I made a mistake, and I'll tell you, if I had to do it over again, I would have gone to Japan. I was a single fellow, and I had an opportunity to go to Japan and I didn't go. You know, and I could have lived high off the hog there. Anyway, I didn't go, and they typed the orders up.

When I came back, my colonel said, 'Where the hell you been?'

I told him; he grabbed me and brought me back and he said to the general, the general asked him, 'What can I do for you?'

He said, 'I want you to get rid of these orders and reassign this man to me. He belongs to me.'

The general said, 'He doesn't belong to you anymore, he's going home on the next ship.' And the colonel turned around, and he looked at me and he didn't even say good-bye. He turned around, walked out, and that's the last I saw of him. A week later I got on a ship and home I went.

[Once I got back], I was going to collect $20 a week for 52 weeks. You know, 52/20 club. I thought to myself, I'll be home, and I'll be unemployed and not do anything for a year. One week home and I was working.

My girlfriend's brother-in-law owned an auto supply business. And he traveled to Wisconsin and Illinois, and he said, 'I'll give you a job.' He said, 'I'll give you the whole state of Wisconsin.' And you're guaranteed when you start to work there, you're guaranteed to make a minimum of $7,000 a year. In 1945, that was a lot of money. 'Plus expenses and we'll give you—we have 35 accounts in Wisconsin, and we'll turn these over to you.' And he showed me. I would work out of a catalog like a dictionary. You would go into a place. The guy says I want a dozen here, a half a dozen here, and you'd write up an order. No problem, they showed you pictures. This is what you did. And I'm running here, I'm running there. I didn't know what the hell I was doing because I wasn't used to it. I was working for a few weeks, and I bumped into a guy in the middle portion of Wisconsin. I saw this guy before. And he walks up to me, and he said, 'My name is'—I forgot his name—he said, 'My name is so and so.'

He said, 'What's your name?' I tell him.

He said, 'What are you doing?'

I said, 'I'm selling automobile supplies.'

He said, 'Do you got the whole state?'

I said, 'Yeah.'

He said, 'Why are you jumping around like you do like a chicken that's out of a nest?'

I said, 'I don't know how to work it.'

He said, 'Break the state up in three sections: west, middle, and east. Pick the middle. Pick a hotel and have a standing appointment at that hotel. Then you go north, and you can go south for the week, but you work out of this hotel, and you have a standing room there regardless of it's snowing or what, it's your room.'

And I did that, I worked here, I worked here, and I worked there. And I was opening up new accounts. I made $35,000 in my first year and quit. I went into the drapery business. I didn't want to work on the road, you know, and be gone. I was gone in the army, and I wasn't home and I'm traveling five days a week, and it was a life I didn't want.

Souvenirs

When I came to the States, I had a carbine, I had a .45 automatic, and I had a trench knife. I wanted to turn it in in Shanghai. They told me that, 'You can't, we don't have any records that it was ever issued to you.'

I said, 'What do I do with it?'

He said, 'Turn it in in the States.' Okay, so I came to the States in the Port of Los Angeles, and I tried to turn it in, and they said, 'We don't have any records.'

I said, 'What do I do with it?'

He said, 'When you go to Fort Sheridan, they'll take it.'

Okay. I come to Fort Sheridan, and I want to turn it in, and they said, 'We don't even know if it was issued to you.'

I said, 'What do I do with them?'

He said, 'Do whatever you want.' So some guy from Chicago, I forgot his name, wanted to buy it. I sold him a carbine rifle, a .45 automatic and a trench knife for $35. I didn't want to come home with a weapon. About five months before I came home, I sent home a Gurkha knife that was presented to me by the Gurkhas, and a Samurai sword, and I came home. I said to my folks, 'What did you do with it?'

They said, 'We never even got it.' This was six months later.

I said, 'Well, I guess I can say good-bye to it.' Two months after I got home—you know, what they did is they piled everything up in big packages, and after the war they sent it all out—I got it. Well, I had gotten married since then, and I had it and the thing was in the basement, and I lived in a house and when I had a child, I said to my wife, 'I'm going to hang it on that wall.'

She said, 'You try to hang it on that wall,' she said, 'and I'll hang you on the wall with it!'

She said, 'No weapons are going up!'

I said, 'What do you want me to do with it?'

She said, 'Sell it.' So I sold it to a police officer in Schaumburg. And I sold the three units for $100; a Gurkha knife, a Samurai sword, and a .45 automatic and a trench knife. From what I understand, if I would have kept it a while longer, I could have sold it for several thousand dollars, but I didn't know any better. My wife told me to sell it, I sold it. I listened to my wife. She's dead now. She died; my girlfriend died. And now I'm by myself again with my friends.

Once in a while I still feel the dengue fever. I talked to my doctor and two other doctors, dengue fever is way worse than malaria. Malaria is minor compared to dengue fever and it stays with you. Once in a while I go to sleep, and I wake up in a cold sweat and I'm shaking like this. And in about an hour, it finally goes away, you know. Not that often but it comes. And I say to myself, well, I'm living with it, I'll live with it and there's nothing I can do, you know. We used to take Atabrine and everything else, and it was there. [Tough service]. And the monkeys used to throw coconuts at us. [*Laughs*]

Still Alive

How many men do you think are alive from the original group? I understand about a month and a half ago up at North Chicago, they had a reunion of some of Merrill's Marauders. I didn't know about it, I found out afterwards, but there weren't very many. There's only a few that came there. I would say to myself out of 3,000, they're lucky if there's maybe 50 of them that are alive, and they're up in my age. You've got to remember the war was over in '45. That's 67 years ago when the war was over. If they were 20 years old when the war was over, they'd be 87 or more. What does that tell you? How many guys are in their late eighties that survived? And I'm very fortunate I'm still here.

I haven't heard from anybody. At first, I thought there was nobody really in Chicago. I went on this honors [flight] trip. I went with a group from Chicago. Nobody on our plane was from the China-Burma-India Theater. Now there was another group from Texas and another group from the south. So roughly there must have been five, six hundred men there altogether. Nobody came from China; I was the only one. I asked all over. And they put up a memorial there, China-Burma-India, and we took a picture of myself in front of the China-Burma-India Theater that they had at the memorial there.

We were greeted—when we came back to Chicago, we were greeted by navy personnel on both sides, you know. And there must have been two, three thousand people in the airport waiting for us to come back home when we came home. It was nice to see. I can't tell you anymore. I remember what I remember.

Morris Factor passed away in 2017 at the age of 96.

Herbert Clofine, World War II. Library of Congress.

CHAPTER ELEVEN

The 4-F Volunteer

Herbert Clofine bucked a 4-F deferment to volunteer for World War II. He was a radioman in the Intelligence and Reconnaissance platoon, 2nd Battalion, Blue Combat Team of the 5307th Composite Unit (Provisional), better known as Merrill's Marauders. He gave this interview at the 59th annual reunion of the Merrill's Marauders Association in Arlington, Virginia, in August of 2005 when he was 85 years old.

Herbert Clofine

I was born in 1919. I was a member of the Merrill's Marauders, which was an infantry unit that served in Burma. Originally, I was a 4-F, unfit for military service, but it got to a point in September of 1942 when I felt that I could be of some value in the service, and I tried to get in but nobody would accept me. And I finally went to my draft board, and I said, 'Look, I'm a 4-F, and I've been to the Army, the Navy, the Air Force, the Marines, the Coast Guard, and none of them would accept me, so put me down as a voluntary draftee,' which they did. Six days later I was on a boat for Trinidad in the British West Indies, where I was assigned to the 33rd

Infantry, which was a regular Army unit before the war stationed in Panama and had then been transferred to Trinidad. I took my basic training there, and then eventually took radio training and became a radio operator. I had charge of an outpost on the coast at that time where we were watching for submarines, and eventually the call came out for volunteers for a dangerous and hazardous mission. And most of us at the unit volunteered, and we were flown back to the States and then eventually ended up in Pittsburg, California, where we boarded the *Lurline*, which is a transport ship, and sailed across the Pacific, taking 38 days, because we traveled unescorted during the war, and landed in Bombay. We trained in India and were formed into the 5307 Composite Unit, Provisional. Our basic mission was to take the only all-weather airstrip in Northern Burma, and the Japanese occupied that entire area. I was assigned to the I&R platoon in the blue combat team.

Our unit was divided into three battalions, the entire 5307th, which was nicknamed Merrill's Marauders by the press. The three battalions were each divided into two columns, red and white, blue and green, khaki and orange. I was a member of the blue combat team assigned to the intelligence and reconnaissance platoon as the radio man. I served with this unit until we took the airstrip at Myitkyina, and then was evacuated from the airstrip, which was the only way of getting out by plane, because we were a pack outfit. There was no motorized vehicles of any kind. I was put in, I believe it was the 110th General Hospital, where I underwent some surgery and then returned to the States. When I got back to the States, I applied for OCS and was eventually commissioned a second lieutenant. I spent six months at Fort Knox, Kentucky, as an instructor in the communications department and then eventually separated from the service.

Unit 'GALAHAD'

The unit, [code-named GALAHAD], had been put together at that time with various troops. We had one battalion composed of members that had been—come up from the Caribbean, and having been in Trinidad, we were part of that. When we got back to the States, we picked up additional troops, which formed another battalion. And then when we were crossing the Pacific, we made a couple of stops on a couple of the islands—I don't remember their names, some of the men will be able to tell you the names of the islands—and picked up seasoned troops who had fought in Guadalcanal and places of that type. When we got to India, we trained and eventually walked up the Ledo Road, and entered Burma. And each battalion naturally had their assignments, and being in the I&R platoon and the blue combat team, we were always out ahead of the rest of the unit, because it was our job naturally to see what was going on, and as the name says, intelligence and reconnaissance, find out what the situation was and report back, and I would report back naturally to headquarters. The first American soldier killed on the continent of Asia was a member of our platoon, Bob Landis. And we continued on and eventually worked our way down. Our entire unit fought five major battles and 32 minor engagements. Our battalion, 2nd Battalion, was at one point surrounded on the crest of a hill called Nhpum Ga, and for twelve days we could not get off until the breakthrough came, but we were eventually evacuated from that location to continue on. I was eventually pulled out immediately with a radio, and with my radio crew, to go back to the closest village to take an air drop the following day. All of our supplies were dropped by air, because we were a pack outfit with horses and mules. I stayed with that unit where I was assigned, which was called K-Force, and so we got to the airstrip at Myitkyina, which was our major objective. Once we had taken the airstrip, and we were in a position where planes could fly in replacements, the 5307th actually ceased to exist. And with the replacements coming in, I believe at that point it became called the 475th Infantry. We stayed on. As I said before, I was evacuated and went into the hospital for surgery and stayed in part of India there until we got our orders to come back.

*

[Some of the things that stick with me], one instance in particular, we were in a certain location and the Japs had occupied an area very close to it, and we were determined that there was some telephone lines that they had strung. So Sergeant Matsumoto and myself—he was one of our Japanese interpreters—were sent out that night, and Roy Matsumoto climbed up and tapped the telephone lines and got information as to troop movement, ammunition supply locations, and so forth, gave me the information, and I radioed it back to headquarters. That was a highlight.

Sergeant Roy Matsumoto was one of fourteen indispensable Nisei soldiers assigned to the Marauders. Born on a small farm in Los Angeles on May 1, 1913, he went to Hiroshima, Japan, at the age of eight to be raised by his grandparents, returning to the U.S. at age 17, finishing high school, and working for a Japanese grocery to support his family during the Depression. There, he learned many Japanese dialects as he delivered groceries to Japanese immigrant families in California, which would prove fortuitous when later fighting in the field.

When the United States began its mass arrest and incarceration of Americans of Japanese descent, Matsumoto and his family wound up in a concentration camp in Arkansas, yet like many young Nisei men, he enlisted in the U.S. Army from behind barbed wire. He was trained as a military linguist, and signed up for hazardous duty with the group.

SGT. Roy Matsumoto

That evening, I took everything out of my clothes. I put the helmet away and left the rifle behind, and I took the canteen, and the pistol belt off, and no weapon. The only thing is I had a bayonet, then a couple of rounds of hand grenades. If I was going to be captured, I was going to blow myself up. Anyway, when I took these gears off, then I told the boys, 'I'm going to come back here, so don't shoot just because you hear the noise. Recognize me first, then let me come in. Don't open up.' Then I crawled down the hill.

They're still talking, and the voice gets louder and louder, so I know I've come very close. I just sat there so I couldn't even sneeze or cough. I was that close, a few feet away.

Then they sat down, and they were talking to their buddies in the foxhole. Then they mentioned about next day at dawn, attacks. Then the other guy asked, he just got information from the commanding officer that they're going to attempt an all-out attack on the perimeter where they're pointing out the direction. I couldn't see it, but they're saying that way. That was the easiest access to come up because there was a gentle slope there, so I knew they would come, but they didn't want to make sure, so I stayed a little longer and found out it was daybreak.

LT. Edward McLogan

Roy came back, and we were all, of course, very quiet. Roy was talking up a storm, and I kept saying to him, 'Quiet.'

He said, 'Well, your area, your platoon is going to be hit tomorrow. The regiment that is surrounding us is going to make a last-ditch effort to breach our lines, and this is the platoon that they've picked to assault.'

With that information, we went back and talked to Colonel McGee, and McGee ordered us to withdraw farther back up the hill, maybe 100 to 200 feet. Further, he directed that we booby-trap our empty foxholes and dig new foxholes farther up the hill, consolidating our lines so we were all a little bit closer together in our perimeter.

The rest of the night passed quietly, but early in the morning, we first heard the enemy talking. Then we could hear them yelling. Finally, we could hear the Japanese screaming at the top of their lungs, 'Banzai!', even that trite 'Death to the Americans,' but in fact, that's what we were hearing, and they broke through into a clearing in front of us. There were two officers and maybe fifty men or so charging up the hill. They were only slightly halted or hesitated, I should say, at the empty foxholes, and at this time, Matsumoto yelled out to them, 'Charge!'

SGT. Roy Matsumoto

They had also reserves behind that were coming up, and then they mentioned about the retreating, so I gave them a counterman order, then I gave them a charge order, and I stood up so that they could hear me, and told them to charge. Then they heard me, so they started to charge up again. Then we come to our close, probably 15, 20, or 30 yards, and we opened up with all our, the platoon's, weapons.[11]

---

[11] In 1993, Roy Matsumoto was inducted into the U.S. Army Ranger Hall of Fame. He passed two weeks before his 101st birthday in April 2014.

Herbert Clofine

Other than that, it was just general operations all the time of—when the unit wasn't fighting, we were [on the move]. We were hiking through some very treacherous terrain. And I mean by the time we got to the airstrip at Myitkyina, those men that were still around—and we lost naturally I don't know how many men, you know, through gun battles and so forth—most of the men were pretty well beaten. When I came out of the jungles of Burma, I weighed 98 pounds.

'Everybody Was A Marauder'

Naturally, we were very close. And naturally, whatever we had done, everybody supported everybody else. And fortunately, that feeling of camaraderie has existed and that's why we are now in our 59th annual reunion, to which I have been to 56 of the 59 reunions, and we've become very close. We've had marriages within the organizations, sons and daughters from various Marauders got married and it's always been a family affair. And one of the interesting things about our reunions, whenever we have guest speakers, which we usually do, we've always made it very explicitly non-political. I mean nobody cares what party you belong to, what religion you are or anything else. Everybody was a Marauder.

Like I said before, out of the three battalions, and each battalion having two columns, there were six units actually operating, and each one of these units could operate by themselves, because they were formed in such a way that they were self-sufficient. So we actually never were active—we were never in combat combined as six units. Each one—and then when the time came and it was necessary, one column would support another. When the 2nd Battalion was surrounded on the crest of the hill at Nhpum Ga, it took the other two battalions to get us released, because we had no control. We couldn't get off that crest of the hill. The Japanese controlled the only waterhole there, and to the point where even water, everything we received as far as supplies had to be dropped by parachute. And up until the time we got to Myitkyina, the only evacuation for seriously wounded was by L4 Piper Cubs. That's the only way they could get out. There were times I can remember where we would carry men that were seriously injured on litters for miles, because we had to find a rice paddy that could, number one, be secured, and which was level enough for a Piper Cub to land on. My recollection is that there were at least a couple of Piper Cubs that crashed in the attempt to evacuate, but that's the only way men could be evacuated—there was no other way, because there were no roads.

The Natives

Northern Burma was primitive. I mean the people that lived there were very nice and everything, as far as, you know, but they were primitive. They lived in bashas that were thatched huts, and I know whenever the occasion did present itself that we were in a village, the natives were very kind to us. I can remember when we were evacuated off of Nhpum Ga and they sent me back to take the air drop with my radios. I stayed in the village that night, and the head man from the village came over to the basha that I was assigned, given, and I was able to get on my radio BBC, British Broadcasting, and it was something that these people never saw or heard. They were completely flabbergasted! So we saw another way of life that we would have never witnessed before, because everything was trails. I mean the terrain, there were places there where we'd walk through mountainous areas that had sheer drops of hundreds of feet. And horses and mules can go so far. As far as I'm concerned, a man will out-walk a horse or mule anytime. I mean they weaken.

And they had to carry any heavy equipment that we had, like our heavy machine guns, and in my case, my larger radio, the SCR-284 had to be packed.[12] If I had to go any great distance, I had the SCR-284 radio that I used to have to mount on a stand, and then have somebody with a generator to generate it, and put up an antenna 25 feet, which you couldn't do in most cases, because it would be a dead giveaway to the enemy, see?

Radio communications, SCR-284.
U.S. Signal Corps manual, WWII.

---

[12] SCR-284-Paul Elisha, Joint Assault Signal Company radioman in the Pacific, noted: "Usually, we used what they called an SCR-284. It was about the size of a suitcase, on two folding legs. The lid would plop down and that'd be your workspace. The set was facing you in the rest of the suitcase. And then you have a cable going to a generator, which you turn; that was the worst job of the lot. We lost several people because the generator let out a squeal whenever you had to transmit and that gave away your position. You'd have one SCR-284, the large one with the generator. You'd have a couple of back-pack radios. Then with you, you'd have a few people for fire support if you ran into a hard time supporting your communications setup you had when you dug in."

Figure 1. Radio Set SCR-300-A, In Use, Viewed From Right Side.

SCR-300 'walkie talkie' radio. Training manual, public domain.

I personally carried a radio on my back the whole time, which was an SCR-300. And the terrain was as much an enemy as the Japanese.

General Merrill

The reason we were called a provisional unit is because according to the TO, Table of Organization in the Infantry, a regiment was commanded by a full colonel. But they gave the command of our unit to a general, so in order to follow procedures in the service and everything, they called it a provisional unit, aside from which it was organized to accomplish one mission. And from what we were told afterward, Washington expected us to have eighty percent casualties. We lost several men, but unfortunately not only through gunfire, but disease. Malaria, typhus, dysentery, which was rampant there, and we survived practically the whole time on rations. So that was it. I mean you carried what you could eat. If you were lucky enough to be near a river, you could hand grenade the river and kill some fish and have a fish dinner maybe, but that was the extent of it.

It was very interesting that in later years we found out that in 1952, General Merrill, who incidentally had two heart attacks while we were in Burma and had to be evacuated, met with General Tanaka, who was the Japanese commanding officer of the 18th Division, which is the Imperial Division of the Japanese Army, who had taken Singapore, so it was their crack unit. And when General Merrill told General Tanaka how many men he had in the field, he was absolutely dumbstruck, because he had a full division of men. And a full division at that time was probably around 18,000 men, I imagine. And we actually had in the field just our 2,400 men; the balance of the men were in the rear echelon, because the rear echelon is where they had to pack everything that was dropped to us and maintain anything, from the statistical standpoint. But when General Merrill told General Tanaka that, he was absolutely amazed, and General Tanaka at that time told him that whenever they passed an area where an American soldier had been buried, his officers put flowers on the grave. So they had a lot of respect for us. Unfortunately we lost General Merrill in 1955. General Merrill was very, very, very well-liked by all the men.

'We Had No Dancing Girls'

I mean look, we had a mission to accomplish, and we—a lot of our boys were young. I know one fellow, he was sixteen years old—how did he get into the service? —who was with us. On the other hand, we some fellows that were older. I was about 24 at that time.

We were there. There was no alternative. There was no alternative. You didn't say, 'I'm going home,' you know, or something like that. 'I'm going to go down and catch a bus back to Calcutta,' or something like that. There was no such thing. You were there, period. [There was no time when you were off the line]; any chance you got, you just sat down or rested. Did the best you could. That's right. But there was nothing else, I mean nothing else, period. I mean whenever we stopped, naturally we had to have security out all the time, because you never knew when you were going to run into the enemy. [In the field], we received no mail that I know of. There might have been mail drops, I'm not sure, but there was no way for us to send out mail or anything like that. They used to send mail home to the families advising, you know, your son is 'killed' or something like that, unfortunately the other way. Someplace that we felt was secure enough, some of the guys would sit around and talk and shoot the bull, you know, like you would. But other than that, not much for entertainment. We had no dancing girls.

Going Home

Once we were evacuated from Burma and sent back to India, a lot of us ended up in hospitals. Like I said, I went into the hospital; I was evacuated from the airstrip on June the 6th of '44, and on June the 7th, I had some surgery done. It was actually why I was a 4-F to begin with. I had a weak wall in my abdomen. I had had a ruptured appendix as a teenager, and it left me with a weak wall in the abdomen. When you came to being evacuated from Burma from the airstrip, the medical officers were there— 'Why are you leaving?' You had to have a reason. So most of the cases it was FUO, fever of undetermined origin. In my case, I said I have an incisional hernia, so they evacuated me, and once we got out of the hospital and we were in a staging area in India, we knew that we would be going back. So evacuation was just a question of when, what your schedule was. You were tickled to death when you finally landed. I know we flew out of Karachi and made several stops in between. If I remember right, we stopped in Cairo, we stopped in Tripoli, and we stopped in Casablanca. And in Casablanca, we had to be put in a staging area to wait for assignment to fly back to the States. And it was usually a case of a day, or overnight, or whatever it was. And when we got to the staging area, a friend of mine and myself, we found out that about half a mile down the road was a roadhouse that served meals and everything else, so we crept underneath the fence and we got down to this roadhouse that night, and we had a great meal and a couple bottles of wine. My friend was a tech sergeant. I was a buck sergeant at the time. And by the time we got back to the post, we looked at the bulletin board and saw that we had missed our schedule to fly back! And they were having a lot of problems with troops that were taking off at that point and staying out, away, and they said if you miss your plane, you'd be broken in rank and lose two-thirds of a month's pay. Well, we didn't want this to happen. So this friend of mine and myself, we caught a bus down to the airstrip. And when I got there, I went up to the lieutenant in charge and I said, 'We're scheduled to fly out at such and such. Where's the plane?'

He said, Up there!'

I said, 'Uh-oh. What are we supposed to do? Look, we've been overseas for over two years. We fought in Burma and everything. What can you do for us?'

He happened to be a real nice guy. He said, 'I got a mail plane coming through 6:00 tomorrow morning. Go lie down on the bench over there, and when the plane comes in, I'll let you know, and I'll send you back on that.'

Sure enough, the mail plane came in, and Bill and I were put on that plane with nothing but mail bags, and he and I flew back to the States in that, so that made it interesting. We got back, and we were given leave at the time when we got back and told when to report back and everything, and then we were assigned to a post in

Louisiana, which they had just reopened, and they were converting troops from branches of the service other than infantry into infantry for the final push in Europe. And the first thing we did in there, we were lined up and we saw what was going on there, and I approached the captain. I said, 'What's happening here?'

He said, 'Well, we're training troops to go to Europe.'

I said, 'Sergeant Angelo and myself just came back from overseas. We fought in Burma!' I said, 'No way.'

He said, 'Well, that's what it is.'

I said, 'Well, I'll tell you what. We'll both go before an OCS board, Officer Candidate School. We both qualified.'

He said, 'Well, there's no board here. We just reopened the post.'

I said, 'Well, then, get me an appointment with the IG, the Inspector General.' Well, at the time they couldn't refuse you that privilege. So I went to the IG and told him our story. He says okay, and set up a board, and Bill and I were both assigned to go before the OCS board, which, of course, was a snap. And we both applied to go to Fort Benning, which was the Infantry OCS School. That's all we knew was infantry. And they sent him to Fort Benning. They sent me to Fort Knox, Kentucky, armored force. Well, all these motorized vehicles, I didn't even know how to drive an automobile, but I stayed on and graduated number one in the class and got my commission. And like I said, I stayed on for six months after I was commissioned and taught field operations in the communications department. That was already—that had to be '45, I believe. I was always in the retail business. I was a department store buyer before I went into the service, and I went back into the retail business. That's where it was, home, in Philadelphia.

Observations

A good part of my personal life has been my activity with the Merrill's Marauders Association. I have been active since the first reunion with the organization. This is our 59th, and I've been to 56 of them, and I've been the treasurer of the outfit now for the past 20-some years, whatever it is. I mean, your family gets to know that come this time of year, you're going to be in a reunion, period. And like I say, it's always been a family affair. There are people here now with their sons or daughters, grandchildren. We exist where a lot of other organizations, divisions that had thousands of men don't get the kind of turnout and camaraderie that we have. It's important to us.

[I guess my experience in the war influenced my thinking about war today]; of course, when I see what's happening today, it's so foreign. I look and I see the equipment these people have today. I mean they walk around with a radio that's [tiny]; I carried a radio on my back that was [huge], big, heavy thing, and it would only go so far. But today, they have [the newest] technology. They have these glasses that they wear that you can see at night. I mean, armor and vests. We had what we had on our backs. I think I went for months without a pair of socks even! And then, of course, the rains over there, we stayed wet for days at a time. You could only have what you could carry on your back. You can't carry a hell of a lot on your back, because you're carrying ammunition, and you're carrying your firearms, and in my case a radio, and it's altogether different, and I see what they have today. Unfortunately, the war today [in Iraq], I mean I don't consider—that, to me, is not even a war. Maybe it's an insurrection; I don't know what it is. I mean I see pictures in the paper that the press has, and it shows the people that are actually the enemy. Well, if the press can take pictures of these people, why can't you shoot them? That's my theory. Kill them.

That's what you're there for. You're not there to have a conversation. I don't know. I don't want to get into that, because I'm opposed to the whole thing. But equipment-wise and everything, compared to what we had... [But] I'll tell you, fortunately we had great medical personnel with us. That was very important, because they had to do everything in the field under adverse conditions. I mean they did amputations when they had to. They were great, and they've stayed active with the outfit, those that are still living. I think there's one left, he was supposed to be here, and he's out there in Johns Hopkins—his name is James Hopkins. He was the one who wrote that book we have, *Spearhead*. Our medical personnel were great. And, of course, at these reunions, everybody's on a first-name basis. Nobody knows who was a captain, who was a major, who was a private. It doesn't make any difference. Everybody's the same.

*

I observed that in recent years, I think there's been more recognition of the Second World War than there was in the years before. I mean here lately, I see a lot written up about it, you know, the units and so forth. We've been documented in a lot of places; the History Channel did two documentaries on us. There's been several books written, a couple of books written by members of the organization itself. But other than that, I find that there seems to be a little—a little resurgence of interest in World War Two that didn't exist. They don't teach it in the schools. I walked into an elevator one day, and I wear these [Merrill's Marauders] shirts often, I have many of them I wear to the gym all the time. I got on an elevator one time, and somebody looked at it and said, 'Merrill's Marauders, what was that, a rock group?' Well, that's what it is. People have no appreciation, I don't think we appreciate what some of these guys in Iraq are going through today. Not knowing what's there, and they don't know what they're going to run into, because what they're doing there with these bombings and stuff, that, to me—

that's not war. First of all, that whole Middle East thing, I mean that's ridiculous. Of course, it's become very political unfortunately. I feel sorry for a lot of them, especially the married men with families at home. I mean I look at the paper, and I'll read an account of somebody. He's got a wife and four children, but he knew that when he went in. Sure, he was going to get paid for the time he put in the reserves, but you don't do that unless you're prepared to accept the consequences. That's the way I look at it. You know, like I say, I only know certain things—being isolated like we were, especially in my platoon, which was all I&R, we were sometimes a day or two ahead of the rest of the unit, the rest of the outfit. The first man killed, Bob Landis, was in my platoon. And the first man to kill a Jap in our unit was Werner Katz, who fought on the islands before he came with us, and was a refugee out of Germany as a young man. Very interesting individual. We got a great group. That's about all I can tell you; I hope it's an experience I'm not only sharing with you, but for generations to come, because there will always be wars, honey, as far back as you can read.

Herbert Clofine passed away in 2009 at the age of 89.

CHAPTER TWELVE

The Radio Wizard

Robert Passanisi was born on July 24, 1924, in Brooklyn, where his father was a bricklayer. As the youngest of twelve children, he grew up with a fascination for radio, and as a teenager learned to repair radios from his older brother. In 1942, the 17-year-old altered his birth certificate so that he could join the Army, the only service branch recruiting high-school dropouts. Soon, like most of Merrill's Marauders, he found himself in Burma after volunteering for a hazardous mission, a radio operator and repairman with the 1st Battalion. He sat for this interview in 2005 at the Merrill's Marauders reunion in Arlington, Virginia, when he was 81 years old.

Robert E. Passanisi

I come from Brooklyn, New York. I enlisted at the Number One Jay Street, I think it was, and was inducted in Governor's Island. I had gone to see the movie *Bataan*, and I was so infuriated coming out of that movie. I was 17 years old and hadn't graduated high school yet, so the first place I went to was the Marine Corps. The Marine Corps didn't take anybody without a high school diploma at that time, although they did take 17-year-olds, see. I went to see the Navy, which also took 17-year-olds, but the Army was [the only service branch] that didn't require a high school diploma, [but was] only taking 18-year-olds and up, so I had to play a little game with my birth certificate to get into the Army. [*Laughs*] So I joined the Army and was given orders for basic training with my folder stating 'Signal Corps,' because I had been repairing neighborhood radios and was into radio from about when I was 13 years old. After the induction center at Camp Upton, Long Island, I was sent to Seagate, New Jersey, for basic training and then to Fort Monmouth, where I studied aircraft radio repair. After coming out of Fort Monmouth, we were sent to Fort Hamilton in Brooklyn, an embarkation center ready to ship overseas to Europe.

Somehow or another, the orders got mixed up, and on the day that I was to ship out, I was in the hospital, which I would have signed myself out of at the time. So now I'm kicking around at Fort Hamilton for a month or two where they were giving me leftover jobs. I wasn't the best-behaved soldier at Fort Hamilton. They gave a one-evening pass for about four hours, but since I lived in Brooklyn, that wasn't going to do, so I learned how to go over the fence by the parkway at Fort Hamilton.

After spending a few months at Fort Hamilton, I believe this was sometime in the spring of 1943, I was already in the Army for a year and was sent to A.P. Hill, Virginia. I was first sent to Fort Meade in Washington and found that the outfit was in training at A.P. Hill, Virginia. It didn't take long for me to see that this was not the organization I wanted to serve with. It seemed that everybody and his brother was an OCS washout, and the worst thing is to be with a group of men who think they're officers, but aren't.

'I Wanted To Do My Part'

I had already applied for paratroop training; I also had applied for commando training, and nothing occurred. I always had the feeling that I wanted to do my part. I had brothers in Europe, and I always felt that if I did my part, things would balance out, and they wouldn't have to do as much. So when the call came for volunteers for jungle warfare, preferably a radio mechanic, since they wanted radio men in the Signal Corps, I volunteered. Out of the 247 men in the company area, there was only one volunteer. If I needed justification for not wanting to serve overseas with that group, that was it.

Figuring that I had volunteered for various things before and the Army takes forever, I thought I would still have time. That was a Friday morning. That Friday afternoon, I was instructed that I was restricted to the company area, and on Monday morning, I was on the train to San Francisco! The following Monday, I was on the SS *Lurline*, the ship going overseas.

Now at this point, the request was for volunteers for a 'hazardous mission,' which had become a commonplace term at that time. The company was told there would be a three-month training and a three-month mission, and that would end it. It was indicated that it was going to be a dangerous mission, and that's why nobody else volunteered. Well, not only that, I heard, 'What are you, crazy? What are you doing that for?' from the background.

Anyway, I was on the *Lurline*, and we were out three days; while I was on the *Lurline*, the public address system had us practicing 'abandon ship' drills every day. On the third day, we didn't have any abandon ship drill. Lo and behold, on the fourth day, the first electrician of this merchant marine vessel approaches me and asks if I was Passanisi, and I indicated that I was. He just said, 'Come with me.' So, I went with him.

He takes me up to the bridge and introduces me to the ship's captain. I had just turned 19 now, and here I was on the bridge of a vessel like this, being introduced to the captain! If there was ever a time I was nervous, that was it. He takes me to the bridge, where they have a wall with the radio equipment and four racks of amplifying systems. In those days, they used tubes, which few people know about now. And I must have had some oversight from some heavenly instructions because I look at this entire system, and I'm awed by the size of it. I assumed that since nothing worked—none of the systems worked—the pre-amplifier unit, which was in the center, would be common to everything. So, I pulled the pre-amplifier unit out and discovered that there was a charred resistor. Resistors are those things that you find in your TV set. I knew enough about radio repair to know that the resistor didn't burn by itself. So, I checked further and found a leaky or shorted capacitor. Fortunately, the electrician showed me a cabinet that had every part number of every item that was in the unit. We took the two components, replaced them, put the thing back, and with the help of God, it worked.

Well, the rest of my trip on the *Lurline* was a very pleasant trip, because I didn't have to wait in the 12-hour chow line. The chow line was 12 hours long! You got on the chow line, you had two meals a day, and we had like 3,000 troops on the chow line, so it would take all day to serve them, and you'd be in time to get back on the chow line. So, you did your sweeping, your gambling, your washing while you were on the chow line. I didn't have to go through that anymore. I was able to eat after the officers left the mess. The steward was instructed to serve me whatever they had.

The 'Song Of India'

I met at this time another fellow by the name of Milton Gray, who was a radio announcer. The two of us, now that we had extra leniency, put on a music request show for the rest of the troops. We occupied the radio room and were able to broadcast onboard the ship. Our theme song was the 'Song of India.' We had found that out from the merchant marines about where the ship was headed, see, but nobody on board knew; nobody equated it; Milton Gray and I were the only ones who knew that the theme song meant something.

So, we got to Bombay, India, after about thirty days. Oh, we picked up most of the men from the 3rd Battalion. We had stopped in Australia at two of the ports. The total three ports that we stopped at were Perth, Brisbane, and I forget the other one, but we only stopped at two ports coming up, and I don't remember which one was which. We also picked up some men at one of the islands before going, which constituted most of our 3rd Battalion.

My first impression at the time we landed in Bombay, after looking over the side of the ship, was disbelief that the United States government, our government, would send us to this godforsaken place. The natives that came aboard ship, I was afraid to brush into them because everything looked so filthy and shocking. I never knew such a thing could exist, even though I was brought up in the streets of Brooklyn.

I carried a loaded Thompson submachine gun on the train, just in case. At that time, I was a Technician 5th Grade, which is a non-commissioned grade. I was in the communications platoon. The writer of the book *Marauders*, Colton Ogburn Jr., was my platoon leader. Another officer, Lieutenant Bright, was also assigned to the platoon, but he hadn't arrived yet. He was involved in the design and procuring of the first twelve units that we used for radio communication that were able to float. If you closed them up, they floated, and they were also more efficient than the radios that the Army had up until then. At that time, they used the radios on mobile troop carriers and whatnot, and you had to crank the radio energy by hand.

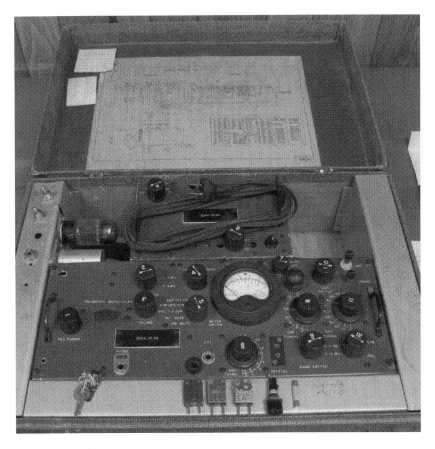

AN/PRC-1 Radio
"Originally designed for use by Army Intelligence, some of these radios were used by the Office of Strategic Services. The radio is concealed in a suitcase." U.S. Air Force photo, public domain.

The radios were the AN/PRC-1 and AN/PRC-2. One was for the lower frequencies, and one was for the higher frequencies. At that time, a megahertz was considered a pretty high frequency. So we had radios from, let's say, one to two megahertz, and the higher frequency radios were from two to four megahertz. Nowadays, your cable is transmitted at gigahertz, which is a thousand times a megahertz. Radar is now up to the area of infrared light, around the 200-gigahertz area.

So anyway, the radios weren't difficult for me. We also had these portable radios, which were 18-tube transceivers that were good for about a 10-mile range in the jungle. You managed to get two or three miles with rather reliable coverage. We also had what they called the handy talkie, which was about double the size of a cigarette carton and shaped like that, which were absolutely worthless. We eventually threw them all away as they weren't good for ten feet in the jungle.

My job was to keep that equipment for the entire 1st Battalion going. The radio mechanic of the 2nd Battalion was a great guy, but he was predominantly an automobile mechanic. So, Sergeant Bellard, who was the radio man for the 3rd Battalion, and I, from the 1st Battalion, always helped out the 2nd Battalion, depending on who they were with. The SCR-300 was a tremendous asset that weighed about 65 pounds with a 30-pound battery. It didn't have any better ability than your wrist-type cell phone, but that was state-of-the-art then. The 18 tubes required energy to illuminate and heat up, so the batteries were very sizable. The hand-cranked generators for the other radios were the only way to power them at first.

To communicate with the liaison planes, they used a frequency in the 4 MHz region. The only thing we had that could cover that was a mobile-mounted-type radio, the SCR-284, which was very inefficient compared to the others and very hard to generate power for. For the liaison planes, the Piper Cubs that we used, I eventually got a hold of one that I was able to get onto for a moment. I hooked up one of the SCR-300s and jury-rigged an antenna on the plane to replace the whip antenna that the radio came with, and we used that to communicate. Now he could communicate with the walkie, the backpack, or the portable radios, and we didn't have to set up the hand-cranked generator. But for the airdrops, we still had to use the larger radio because it wasn't as easy to hook up a portable radio on the C-47.

Mules

Everything we had we carried on our backs or carried on our mules. But what was bad was when a guy from Brooklyn has to take care of this stinkin' mule. I have to say that after a while you became dependent upon the mule, and you appreciated the mule, and you took care of him, especially when you took a ten-minute break, and the mule sits down. But now your break is gone, because now you can't get the mule back up. You have to unpack the mule, get the mule up, and repack it. There's your ten minutes. So after a while you learn how to keep the mule from sitting down. Once they're down, they're not getting up until you unload them.

Shooting

Radio repairman was like a secondary item; during the daytime or while you're on the road in the field, you are an infantryman, the same as everybody else. My baptism of fire was at Walawbum. We were on a riverbank in Walawbum, and we dug in there. The Japs were trying to cross the river to get through it, but we had the ideal position. The 3rd Battalion, which was upriver from us, took the brunt of the attacks, but we had a couple of waves down where I guess they tested our area. Probably the reason we were so successful was that the Japanese were in the habit of charging these banzai attacks, where they would come in waves. A wave would run, firing at the enemy, then hit the ground, and the second wave would come to run over them, and they would then alternate. Whether there was a third wave or not, I don't recall. That's okay if you can overwhelm the enemy, but everybody had semi-automatic weapons, such as the Garand M1 rifle, which was an absolutely startling gun from my standpoint. You could fire rather rapidly; you could put 8 rounds in less than a second, and you could fire just as quickly as you could locate a target. I had grown up, in my earlier days, with a BB gun, and that's one of the reasons why I think that restricting youngsters from playing or having guns is not necessarily a great idea. I learned to shoot, to light wooden matchsticks at 15 or 20 feet. I don't know if you're familiar with them, but a wooden matchstick is about that long, and it has a head about an eighth of an inch in height. The little tip of it, the phosphorus tip, if you just strike it, would ignite the match. Nowadays, your safety matches have to be struck on the proper surface for them to light. Well, you could hit that little tip, just about an eighth of an inch in size, with a BB and light the match. That was the game. That means that when you start to fire a regular rifle, you have a more inherent feel of how you should aim and fire.

So with the M1, I must say that in basic training with the Springfield, I barely was able to make marksman. I've got a weak right eye, and the 1903 Springfield, which was the original rifle of World War I and still used in World War II, had a very small peep sight. When I tried to view through it, it would tend to blur out on me. The M1 had a slightly larger sight, and I could clearly see my target with my right eye and keep my left eye open on the target so I could see what was going on. This allowed me to call the shot, a very important aspect of shooting. Calling the shot means that you squeeze the trigger and don't know precisely the instant it will go off, but you keep your eye on the target, so you know where the bullet actually went. If you jerk the trigger, you have no idea. With the M1, I was able to achieve an almost perfect score, except for the standing position, where I couldn't hold the rifle steady enough to hit a bullseye every time. I felt that with the M1, anything I aimed at was going to hit. Therefore, I protected the front sight on that rifle because it was extremely important to know what I could aim at and hit.

'They Would Go Wild'

Our main training, I think, was with Lieutenant Ogburn. He was a great officer in training, and he got us running double time on everything we did. We went to the mess hall, we ran; we went everywhere running, which was good conditioning. In that manner, in the field or in the jungles, I would prefer him over most any other officers. He was a college graduate, a Harvard graduate, and I got the impression that he felt he was there serving his penance and that he shouldn't mar his reputation or his record, so he was entirely by the book, but one of the things that won the war, I think, is the free-thinking aspect of the American soldier, and this group was probably the most free-thinking you could get. You could throw a switch night and day. In the training at the agoge, they were the most undisciplined people you can get. I was still very idealistic and didn't stray at all, but about half of our unit was AWOL during the Christmas holidays of 1943. A couple of guys that were drunk in the company area managed to get some stuff called bullfighter rum, and it probably had 100 octane gasoline in it or something. They would go wild, and there was one incident where they were firing through the top of the tents, through all the tents, with machine gun tracers. The officer of the day, I think at the time, I don't remember who it was, but as I recall the incident, he wasn't able to control that, and it was too dangerous to try. So when General Merrill took over a few weeks later, he made the announcement that there would be no court-martials. By the first week of January, everybody who was AWOL, though maybe like 98%, 99%, returned. They were all ready to go, and General Merrill passed the word along that there would be no court-martials, so he became a superhero.

When I read the book *Galahad,* written by Colonel Hunter, who was a true strategist and a true combat officer—not really to put Merrill down, but Merrill was really Stilwell's representative—Hunter was a combat officer, no question. A lot of us owe our lives to Hunter's strategy. Anyway, in reading the book *Galahad,* Hunter naturally got extremely mistreated by Stilwell, and Merrill for that matter, so his book wasn't very complimentary. The reason why Merrill didn't have any court-martials was that Army regulations require that a general court-martial has to operate under the rules of the regimental command. We were a unit, not a regiment, and we had no regimental command. The only regimental headquarters was formed by Hunter, and the name 5307th Regiment was what he got as a designation, but I'm not even sure whether that was official. For about three days, we were the 5307th Regiment, and then when Merrill came in, because a general leading a regiment is kind of a put-down, they changed the name to unit.

So now you have a unit and it's provisional, which I always felt meant expenditures. So he couldn't legally court-martial anybody except at the company level for company punishment and such. So he took advantage of this great moment and whitewashed all court-martials, which worked because, I mean, everybody in combat, as I started to say, it was entirely different. You never had a concern about whether the guy who was supposed to be there was there. He was there. Everybody did their job. We didn't have anybody who slacked off or anything. We had one person, when we left Ledo, who was a misfit in our group. He had a mental problem, and we tried to get Sergeant Sylvie, who at the time was a tech sergeant in command, to get the medics to move this guy out and especially take his Tommy gun away from him. So while we were on the Ledo Road on this initial 100-mile trip, on the sixth day, I think, we went by the 20th General Hospital about that time, and he had put his Tommy gun into his mouth and pulled the trigger one night. I took it that he was extremely fearful of going into combat, and I could not understand why, if you're willing to die, why didn't you at least make yourself into a hero? I mean, if you're willing to die, that's the greatest thing you need is somebody who's willing to take every chance there is. So I could never understand that; I still remember that.

Marching Past The Hospital

Talking about the 20th General Hospital, the Japanese were within 25 miles of the 20th General Hospital, and the Chinese were losing ground all the time, and they were waiting for orders to pull out, and they couldn't understand why they got so frightened that their ward boys and such, the conscientious objectors, were going behind a hospital and starting to practice shooting a rifle. And then the one morning they wake up and they see infantry, American infantry, GIs—not British, not Chinese, there's nothing better than an American infantryman—and they see this endless column. It took us three days to pass the hospital. Well, we were ten feet apart per man, and between each squad there was like twenty, you know, we were spread out—the 1st Battalion went through, then the 2nd Battalion went through, and then the 3rd Battalion went through. So for three days they had this American infantry coming through, and it's like they were getting a new lease on life. The 45th Engineers or the quartermaster that were there, they got out the band, and they marched like ten miles with us, and then hurried back to pick up another group. They carried water and blister bags, blister bags maybe 200 pounds, and they would carry water, just whatever they could do. There wasn't enough that they could do for us. Of course, this was great because if you wound up in the 20th General Hospital, you got great attention, and that's what most of our boys did.

Food And Sickness On The Move

With the food, the worst situation was to eat K-rations and not even get a full complement of K-rations. You tended to get three days' worth of K-rations, but they didn't have to be a breakfast, dinner, and supper unit. You could have gotten five breakfast units or six supper units, and you can't imagine how it works. K-rations have a K-1 cracker and a K-2 cracker, so you would eat the two crackers when you start, and you find that you like the K-1s better or K-2s, and then you would be eating only the K-1 crackers, and then you reach the point, and you're trading K-2s for K-1s with somebody else, and you reach the point you can't eat another K-1 cracker, so you now are eating K-2 crackers, and that goes on for a couple of days. Now, the cracker is a hard cracker. It's about an inch and a quarter wide or an inch and a half wide, about three inches long, and about, the one cracker was like maybe a quarter inch thick and they would fit in the K-ration meal. The breakfast unit had supposedly pork and eggs, and it was the greasiest garbage you could ever possibly imagine. It wasn't really edible, but you could manage. The supper unit had the, I think it was corn, pork, loaf, which was worse than the breakfast unit. It was so bad but you're so hungry that I found that the burnt paper liner on the corn loaf was edible. The lunch unit had cheddar cheese, crepe cheddar cheese or something like that, but you can't eat all cheese, and you didn't get it all the time. You had a D-bar sometimes. That D-bar was an enriched chocolate bar about the size of a Chiclet package or Lifesaver package, and you also had Dextro-maltose tablets, which was supposed to be good for you, but they weren't that readily edible. The lemon also came in one of the units, I think it was the lunch unit, which was like very acidy. You couldn't make lemonade and use it. The breakfast unit had instant coffee, which went like fire, and the supper unit sometimes had bouillon powder. That went great, but then cigarettes, well, they must have been packed 50 years beforehand, because if you lit one of those cigarettes up, it would burn halfway down and flame out. So anyway, food was a terrible problem. We tried eating bamboo shoots because the mules ate them, but they weren't really digestible that well. If you managed to kill a couple of Japanese that were cooking, you got some rice, but the Japanese, if they were abandoning an item, they would urinate on the rice. That sometimes didn't make any difference, you know, but other than the staying alive from day to day, that was the most difficult item, and everybody had some form of diarrhea, some amoebic dysentery, but everybody had diarrhea, and bad. Everybody ran a fever. You had to run a fever of a hundred and three plus for three days to be considered sick. So when I got evacuated for running a fever, I was shocked because I didn't know I had that high a fever; I felt all right. I get to the 20th General Hospital, and I think I got a reprieve on life. I'm great. They wouldn't let you in a hospital. You stripped, dumped the clothes in a pile, they threw gasoline on and ignited it. [Laughs] Then you showered with GI soap.

So anyway, I'm talking to this nurse, thinking that somehow or another I feel like I got away with it, [being evacuated though I thought I felt okay]. And all of a sudden, I said to her, 'I feel faint,' and she took one look at me, shoved the thermometer in my mouth, took my pulse, and then went running and left the thermometer in my mouth! I took it out, and the last thing I remember was 105.2, and I put it back in. [Laughs] About two weeks later, I woke up; I don't know whether I was unconscious [the whole time]. They loaded us with Atabrine and quinine and sulphaguanidine, and fish-filled pills, and the requirement to drink, I don't know, was 320cc's of water, so you would wind up just throwing the pills in your mouth and doing it. But anyhow, your skin was all yellow, your eyes, you looked more Oriental. It took two to three months after I got home for my eyeballs to finally clear up, and when I got home, I was 125 pounds. This is after spending three days at Fort Dix and five days on the train and a couple of weeks in quarantine in Angel Island, I think it was, in the Pacific, and I was eating well there. So now I got home, and I weighed 125 pounds; [I was 185 before that].

Home

Now the first week I was home, the family was still on meat rationing. So I ate, I didn't realize it at the time, but I consumed my wife's and son's and my meat rations in the first week. So now I was eating eggs, like twelve eggs a day. I was eating raw eggs, hard-boiled eggs, sunny-side-up, scrambled, and that went on until, like the K-rations, you reach a point and then you couldn't look at another one. And I've never been able to give my wife a good enough explanation on how I came to volunteer to go overseas and leave a pregnant wife at home. [*Laughs*] I don't think there is any such thing as a good explanation... I had a baby boy who was born while I was overseas.

Last Words

Like every Marauder, it's only now starting to fade from memory, because probably everything is fading from memory now, but it was the most prominent time of our life. It's what has been embedded into your brain, and things that happened there keep coming about, like no other happening, no other incident or three-month time, or four-month time, has been recorded so thoroughly in your brain. And probably every single Marauder, when they came out of the service, weren't great guys to live with. I certainly look back and see some of the difficulties that people must have had with me. I couldn't stand certain noises, I was on edge a lot. Let's see, in 1950, we moved out to Long Island, and my first time that I wasn't working, and I was home during a weekday, Republic Aircraft jets were flying in, which was a common thing my wife was used to, but I wasn't. This is the first time I heard them, and that sounded to me like incoming artillery. I'm standing in the kitchen doorway, my son is there, my wife is there, and I'm looking to dive on the ground there, and this is five years later! When my wife realized what was happening, she calmly said, 'Those are the jets from Republic.' I wasn't as bad off as those that I've talked to on the internet, the family members that I talked to on the internet. Some of them took to drinking and never stopped. Some of them were divorced twice. Some of them left home. It was probably the percentage of Marauders that had domestic difficulties or difficulties adjusting to civilian life were probably much more than any other group. Today, they look upon it as combat neurosis or something like that, and, well, we didn't know about it then.

I'll [close with] my favorite statement. 'When America no longer is the home of the brave, it'll no longer be the home of the free.'

Like several Marauders in this book, Mr. Passanisi was an Army Ranger Hall of Fame inductee. He passed in 2022 at the age of 97, leaving less than a handful still alive.

Warner Katz, World War II. Library of Congress.

CHAPTER THIRTEEN

The Immigrant

Warner Katz came of age in Nazi Germany, a Jewish kid who felt the winds beginning to shift as Hitler came to power. He managed to follow an older brother to Italy as the doors were closing on German Jews by smuggling through Switzerland. When that too became uncomfortable, he arrived in New York in 1938 with the help of a friend of his uncle. His mother and her sisters perished in the Holocaust; his father died in Frankfurt. His brother later followed him to New York, where Warner basked in the freedom, struggling with a new language but holding down various jobs. He was drafted into the Army before he had citizenship and wound up fighting in Guadalcanal; from there he volunteered for hazardous duty and served as a staff sergeant and one of the lead scouts with the Marauders. He was credited with being the first American soldier to kill a Japanese soldier in the Burma campaign, and he was also likely the first one wounded, an occurrence which triggered an Army 'Killed in Action' telegram back home to his brother and family. He sat for this interview in 2005 at the Merrill's Marauders reunion in Arlington, Virginia, when he was 86 years old.

Warner Katz

Fifteen years old, and I'd been through the Swiss border and into Italy; I had a brother in Italy. I can speak Italian [besides German]—but they sent me, when I'm Italian and German, they send me to the Pacific. [*Chuckles*] I was drafted. [I had been drafted] in June 1941 [when I was twenty-one], before Pearl Harbor, [and I was in until] June or July 1945. I never had any leave until I came back to the United States. We never had leave.

I was in basic training at Camp Jackson, South Carolina, and I started December 7th. I was supposed to be in Maine, but I volunteered to go with 182nd on Panama Canal to Australia. We were the first troops to land in Australia.

We went through California training and the Marine Corps invaded Guadalcanal on August 7, 1942. The Army relieved some of the Marines in September and October. I went in on October 13 to Guadalcanal. When I came from Guadalcanal, we went to the Fiji Islands and one day they lined us up and they asked for volunteers for a dangerous and hazardous mission, and I volunteered. I wanted to get the war over with and I volunteered for the Marauders. It was called 5307 Unit. It wasn't then called the Marauders; later on, it was named Marauders.

I was only at my first citizen papers and the war started after December 7, but if you were drafted, you became a citizen. I never officially became a citizen until I went into Burma. Later on, I was in the hospital in India, from where General Stilwell would send us back to the front lines. I said, 'Before I go back there, I would like to be a citizen of the United States.' So a man from the State Department and four soldiers, one Mexican, one Scottish, and I think one Italian and me, we got our citizen papers in India. Finally, I became a citizen of the United States.

'You Become A Fatalist'

I went all the way to Myitkyina, all the way through all those five battles. I had already [had special training for this jungle warfare] on Guadalcanal. You know what I mean? First, I was a machine gunner and then I used to go every second day on patrol. So what becomes a veteran, and people get killed next to you, or you kill, and you get over that fear, you become a fatalist. You become a veteran, in my opinion. You know what I mean? You're always scared like hell, but you still keep alert. You know, you do your duty. You don't do anything [special], but you know and there's such a thing as heroes, but you do your duty. The hero was the guy that gets killed.

Point Man

I was the point man in the platoon led by Logan Weston. He was called the 'Fightin' Preacher.' [13] It was an I&R platoon, intelligence and reconnaissance. You're not mature enough yet to think, but you learn. You're not mature—you become mature in action. When you're in action, they say you become fatalistic. There was [something about] these Japanese that makes them go and use banzai [charges] and all that. They were a lot different than we were.

And I was one of the first scouts, you know, when we contacted the first Japs; that day I was the first scout going into the elephant grass. [I was] dreaming about [the fact that] I was already overseas over a year and a half, you know, [and I saw a man ahead] and I thought he was Chinese, so I went forward, but I stopped—I said to

---

[13] Logan Weston-Nicknamed the 'Fighting Preacher' or the 'Fighting Parson,' Weston's service awards through World War II, Korea, and Vietnam included two Distinguished Service Crosses, five Silver Stars, seven Bronze Stars, six Purple Hearts, and the Legion of Merit.

myself, 'My God, Japanese!' He started to fire at me, but I hit him before I [dropped] down; I found an indentation in the ground. A Japanese machine gun started to open up, but I was lucky enough to find the indentation. I had a big watch on, and that watch got hit, and the ricochet hit me in my nose, so I started to bleed. If it was a tenth of an inch more, I probably wouldn't be here today.

'We Didn't Get Decorated'

I had the distinguished distinction to be the first American who got wounded by a Japanese and the first American to kill a Japanese in Asia. That was the wound I got, then my first officer came in, he pulled me back. Logan Weston, who was later on a colonel—one of the most decorated men in the United States Army, but in Marauders, we didn't get decorated. We didn't fight for decoration; nobody in the Marauders got decorated because Stilwell didn't decorate, [outside of a Purple Heart for being wounded]. It was the first Purple Heart. At the same time, somebody else almost got killed.

When I was wounded there at the time, as I told you, it was a slight wound, but it was bleeding severely. They wanted to send me back, but we were already over 120 of about 200 miles inland, and the only way I could get back was with the natives and I was more worried about that than staying, because I got all the attention. You know what I mean, all behind Japanese lines. Our platoon, the I&R platoon, was always what I would say eight, ten—maybe even twenty, thirty miles ahead of the main group and combat teams—different combat teams.

'Killed In Action'

I was officially called 'killed in action.' I was wounded, I killed the first Jap, but I was [reported to be] killed.

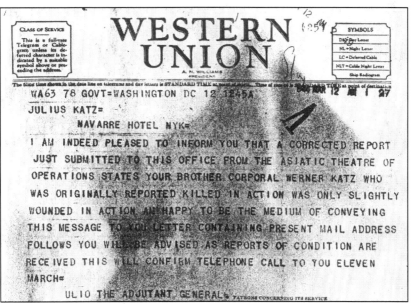

So my brother mourned me about two weeks; it took two or three weeks to straighten out. My brother didn't serve, he was nine years older, I think.

*

There were no replacements, and later on, as we went deeper into Burma, General Stilwell didn't have enough replacements, so he took the people who were wounded in the hospital and sick and sent them back to the front line. There was a little revolution [brewing] there; people didn't want to go back, you know?

The Chief

I was in more action. We went later on in a town called Walawbum, where our platoon was completely surrounded. We didn't even see the enemy. Under Logan Weston, we had with us Japanese-Americans, Mexicans-Americans. We had all types of people. We had American Indians—we had an Indian chief, [well, we called him 'Chief']. And if he wasn't there at the time, I wouldn't be alive today. I took a body of guys across a deep river, and the chief—Janis was his name—he looked in back of me from the original side, and in back of me was Japanese. It was a question of seconds, and he killed [several] Japanese and if he wasn't there, I would never be here today. [14]

---

[14] Gavin Mortimer, in his excellent book on the Marauders, elaborates on this incident:

"As we started to withdraw, Weston made a temporary litter and gave me and another fella the order to take this fellow [Lionel] Paquette across the river," recalled Werner Katz. Katz and the other man, John Clark, slid into the river with their cargo and struck out for the opposite bank. Katz glanced around and "saw a Japanese with a Nambu machine gun. I was praying, thinking 'this is it, I'm going to die.'" Katz, ever the fatalist, turned his face from the enemy and braced himself for the inevitable bullet. But on the eastern bank of the river, another soldier had seen the Japanese machine gunner. "He squatted down behind the gun, so I shot for his head," recalled Norman Janis, the Ogala Sioux known as "The Chief." The Japanese was dead before he had a chance to draw a bead on Katz. "Another one got in his place," continued Janis. "I hit him, got him out of the road. There was seven of them, dragging them away, and then another one. That last one, he kind of crawled back. I said, 'By gosh, I'm going to get you and keep you

*

I had malaria and even typhus. The doctor told me when I was in the hospital that it was probably typhus. People died next to me from typhus because we went in a certain area of Burma. I would say maybe half of us made it to Myitkyina. They were all disabled, wiped out. We were completely weak, but we made it. We had to make it. We had help from a local outfit called the Kachins, who were the natives of northern Burma. Thank God they were friends of ours because the Japanese mistreated them. [The Japanese had occupied Burma for some time, but the OSS had trained these people.] In the middle of Burma, I saw a guy in a Navy uniform in bell-bottom trousers. I didn't believe it when I went on patrol.

---

there.' So I shot him twice.'" Janis had a name for his M1 Garand: "Betsy." Betsy fired eight bullets across the river, and seven brave Japanese died as a consequence. Weston waded into the middle of the river and stood there exhorting his men to hurry, disdaining the enemy fire that threw up spurts of water on either side of him. Only when the last member of the I&R platoon was being pulled up the bank by their comrades did Weston follow "as calmly as he were out for a walk in the sun." The Japanese, furious that their prey had eluded them, charged across the river, but they were easy targets for Weingartner and his men. "They just kept coming across and we kept shooting at them," he remembered. Mortimer, Gavin, *Merrill's Marauders*. Page 71.

The Ledo Road

Marauders on the Ledo Road. U.S. ARMY SPECIAL OPERATIONS HISTORY OFFICE, Public domain.

Now, the Ledo Road was tremendous because our engineers built it; the English didn't think we could do it. The American engineers in fact were black troops, and they were wonderful. I remember when we walked and a hundred miles there was a black soldier, and they were the most wonderful people I ever saw, they were wonderful to us. I remember I stayed one night with them. I had to make an arrangement for a show; Melvyn Douglas was an actor. Later, I was down in South Carolina before the war started, and I remember I went to a football game for the first time. You know, I came from Europe in 1938, and there was a bunch of black soldiers sitting on one side and there was an overflow of people there, so they took the black soldiers off the stands, and they put white people in there. And at the time I didn't understand it; I thought it was terrible. You know what I mean?

Troops in Burma. U.S. Army, public domain.

'A Very Tough Thing'

I can tell you that Burma was physically a very tough thing. We had to walk, march, and walk. I'll tell you something. We went through terrain there over the mountains [seven hundred miles, seven thousand feet up]. I don't wish it on anybody. Even with the little breaks, I don't know how we ever made it. I'm very physically exhausted. I had poisoning of the stomach; I had to take 30 sulfa pellets a day. I was sick to my stomach a month. I had amoebic dysentery, and I had to take 30 or 40 sulfa tablets, I'd march a mile or so and lie down. I wanted to die, but they kept me moving, so we stayed in it. Yeah, if you ever would have seen our outfit going down into Myitkyina, you would have seen a bunch of dead people.

How I made it, I will never know, and I'm glad that the Japanese didn't attack us, like they attacked us later on, you know. They had gone through a lot of hell themselves.

We could really hit them, and then we run, and they didn't know exactly where we were. We had different combat teams in different places.

I know the last day when I left Myitkyina, I remember a Texan was singing 'When My Blue Moon Turns to Gold Again,' and I said—this was the nighttime, I said, they're gonna break through, and they broke through and that night two officers who had felt very secure [actually] slept in harm's way, because they got killed.

Home

All my education was minimal; really, I didn't have much education. High school, I learned in the Army. I learned a lot in life in the Army. I tell you, we had people who were in jail. We had people who went to Harvard. We had engineers. We had farmers. We had men from Oklahoma, from California, from South Carolina, from New York. We had people from all over life.

After the airfield was taken, I was brought out, they said I had a temperature of 105.5 degrees. In India I was in the hospital, I don't know if it was a month or two, and some of our people died there because they had typhus, you know. Later, I went back to the United States, somewhere in North Carolina [to an intelligence school]. It was very interesting, there were a lot of people there, a lot of language people, and I had to learn all about the German Army. I was born in Germany, you know. I got to know more about the German Army than the German officers, and I interrogated the Germans.

I was discharged at Fort Dix, New Jersey. I went into business, I got married five years later, I was married 54 years. She was a lovely girl.

This is an honor. [Thanks for listening to my story]; it was a pleasure, darling.

Staff Sergeant Warner Katz was inducted into the Army Ranger Hall of Fame in 2000. Mr. Katz passed away a little more than a year after this interview, on November 5, 2006, at the age of 87.

CHAPTER FOURTEEN

The Combat Cameraman I

David L. Quaid was born on March 27, 1920, in Glendale, New York. He was a cinematographer and director, the best-known picture that he worked on being the film *Arthur* (1981). As a young man, he had a single-minded pursuit in photography and motion pictures that would someday land him in Hollywood, after a detour to the jungles of Burma, a formative experience that stayed with him all of his life.

David Quaid

Depression Days

I was born on March 27, 1920, in Glendale, New York. I came from a typically Depression-struck family. My mother and father had five children; my father's boast of it was, 'I had five children and none of them went to jail.' But it was a typical, very difficult, Depression situation. My brother, who was absolutely brilliant, got the gold medal when he graduated from P.S. 121 in Queens. Brilliant guy, but he had to go to work. His sacrifice permitted my sister—who was also brilliant, actually, I come from a very interest-ing family—she was able to go through high school. Then I followed and I realized that this would be the limit of any education I could get, which would be high-school level. Now, strangely enough, in the years after the war, I've now taught in five major universities and no one has asked for my credentials, ever, okay? I mean, [I'm talking about] NYU, BU, School of Visual Arts, Rochester Institute of Technology, all these schools. I taught in all those schools on the basis of things I knew that they don't know. Anyway, because of obviously the sacrifices of the first three children, my two younger sisters went to college. That was sort of typical, I would say, of the [times].

Becoming a Cameraman

I was always interested in the motion picture business, and I was an Eagle Scout, so I got into the sort of senior program of Boy Scouts, and I met another young guy, Warren Rothenberger, who was also interested in motion pictures. The two of us basically edu-cated ourselves in the public libraries on the books of Pudovkin, Eisenstein, and Paul Rother, and people of that nature. Then I de-cided to become a freelance newsreel motion picture cameraman and work with basically Paramount News as a stringer, not that they ever gave me any leads. I had to develop my own. I had a couple of good breaks. Crown Princess Martha of Norway was viewing some Norwegian dive bombers who were training in Canada at LaGuardia Airport. I managed to get some very fine footage of all these, of her, of Mayor LaGuardia, of Grover Whalen, who was the greeter for New York City, and what have you.

I also picked up some other stories. There was a riot down where they were building the East River Tunnel under the river at Battery Place, and the sandhogs were fighting the hard rock miners for jurisdiction.[15] I got some terrific footage on that, and also the first camouflage clipper that went to the embattled British, but the union newsreel guys would see me, and we'd get into fights, arguments, and what have you. Anyhow, I realized two things. One, I realized that these are the guys that I'm going to want to work with someday. I was doing a stupid thing; I was embarrassing them because since I ran around with a hand camera, they didn't get the kind of footage I was getting. Two, I realized I needed a regular job. What's interesting about this, Warren and I wrote to all the big shots of Hollywood. Now this is interesting. We'd get these letters back on embossed, heraldic letterheads from the executive secretary of Samuel Goldwyn. It would say, 'Mr. Goldwyn read your letter, and he's sorry, but there are no openings in the camera department at this time.' But finally, Mr. Cone of Columbia, who was considered the toughest producer in Hollywood, wrote back and said, 'Dave, if you'd find yourself in front of the gates of our studio, just present this letter. I'd like to meet you.' But at the same time, I was trying to get work in the industry around New York City. I got a job with an outfit called General Business Films and made industrial films. That's sort of interesting in a way, because Mr. Lawton, who owned it, he said, 'I'm very interested in your qualifications. But before we discuss further, I would like to give you a test.'

I said, 'Okay.'

He said, 'You know how to run a Cine Special,' which was a very sophisticated 16mm camera of its day.

He said, 'I'd like you to go out and shoot a typical autumn scene.'

I said, 'But Mr. Lawton, this is February!'

He said, 'Well, that's part of the test.' Then he said, 'I'd like you to shoot a scene of New York City at night.'

---

[15] sandhogs- underwater or underground excavation and construction laborers.

I said, 'But you know the film has an ASA of eight? I think you're asking a lot.'

He said, 'Well, that's the test. Take it or leave it.'

We went out to a place called Alley Pond Park where we used to camp with the Boy Scouts. There was this tree up on a bluff and it was blowing like crazy. We scratched around on the ground and found a beautiful red leaf, which I tied to the end of a branch, these bare branches. Now, this camera could run at 64 frames a second, which is a degree of slow motion. I had Warren grab palm loads of leaves and throw them in the air, and it'd come through the scene, this close-up scene of one leaf. In slow motion, it was absolutely, it was ethereal, I got to tell you. It was just fantastic, you know? Then we went to the top of the Empire State Building and now this camera would also run at four frames a second, I think it was, I could run that slow and pick up exposure. We got there just before dark; I really got a fantastic night scene of New York at night. Everybody looked at the shots and they were just pleased as hell. Then I got to know Elmer McGovern, who was the film editor. I said, 'What are you working on?'

He said, 'I'm working on a picture for the Better Light, Better Sight Institute.' He said, 'Yeah. We have one problem.'

I said, 'What's the problem?'

He said, 'Well, we're missing an autumn shot, we're missing a shot of New York City at night.' I got the job. It was a good learning experience.

'We Need The Five Dollars'

The war was developing all the time. Warren and I used to do backpacking when no one did it in those days. One Saturday, Palm Sunday, I remember that we were going to hike across Bear Mountain State Park. We hitchhiked and hiked up to the western entrance to the park. We started to follow this trail. Unfortunately, Warren had high-cut boots; for five dollars you could get an excellent pair of boots. Very nice. My Aunt Nora, my godmother, had given me five dollars and I was going to buy a pair of boots for them. But my father, who is a wonderful guy, said, 'Dave, we need the five dollars.' So I had a pair of old Oxfords, which had cardboard in them for where they were worn through, and I had a pair of rubbers. We started over this trail, and the hunters had shot off the trail markers and it started to snow. Before long it was a 19-inch blizzard. It was now getting dark. Anyhow, I was at that point breaking trail. It really snowed extremely hard. There was a light skim of ice on this small stream and snow on top of it. When I went over it, of course, I ended up to my waist in the water. Then it got bitter cold, and we realized we had better stop and do something about it. But all we had were these cotton blankets. By that time, my pants had frozen solid. We spent all night rubbing my legs. But what happened was they turned black, and it took a month and a half in bed with all kinds of techniques to restore the nerves and what have you. But that's the kind of, that's the things you did in those days. You couldn't afford to go do anything. You hitchhiked; you did things like that.

'The War Was On Top Of Us'

Suddenly the war was on top of us. Since I had 2500 vision, which is legally blind, I was rejected immediately. I was a very patriotic type of guy; that offended me terribly. But one day, in the newspaper it said that they got smart. I mean, why turn all these 1-A guys into cannon fodder when there are people that have minor problems? They were called 1-B. They had this program through General Hersey, who was the head of the draft, to start a 1-B qualification in draft boards. But you had to write a letter. I wrote my typical letter. I'm an Eagle Scout and all that sort of business, I know all this stuff, which I did. Then, like overnight, the draft board called me and suddenly I was in the Army. But some of my friends, who worked as film editors at the Senior Corps Photographic Center in Astoria at the old Paramount Studios, told Colonel Gaskell, who was in charge of training combat cameramen in what they used to call the IMO school. The IMO was a Bell and Howell hand camera, it shot 35-millimeter film, same as theatrical, and it weighed about 15 pounds; it was a very good camera for hand use. Through my friends, he heard about me and arranged an interview. This was early in the war, and he said, unfortunately, the Senior Corps has no priority comparable to combat arms. It's going to be very hard to get you, especially from a 1-B outfit. But as time went on, I progressed. I was in the first 1-B unit, which was the 1st Battalion's A Battery, 701st Anti-Aircraft. Because of all these skills I had as a Boy Scout, I was teaching all kinds of classes, so I ended up Chief of Range Section, which is sort of a computerized situation where you pick up an enemy plane and zero in on it. But I told Captain Potts, who was a very fine officer, I said, 'I'm going to do my best to get out of here.'

He said, 'Well, I'm probably not going to let you.' He said, 'In fact, you're going to apply for anti-aircraft OCS.'

I said, 'I don't want to apply for anti-aircraft OCS.'

Well, suddenly I was in front of all these colonels, and I was accepted, okay? I got orders to be transferred to Camp Davis. I had my barracks bag filled, and I had a command car waiting to take me to the train station. Captain Potts came out of his office to wish me well.

I said, 'Wait a minute, Captain Potts, I have a feeling what's going on here is illegal. How can you order anybody to become an officer? How can you do that?'

He said, 'Well, it does have its difficult interpretations.'

I said, 'Wait a minute, is it legal or isn't it?'

He said, 'Well, I would say probably sort of borderline.'

I said, 'Okay. Then I'm not going.'

I took my barracks bag, went back up to my bunk, and that was it. Then what happened was two films were made. Now, the war was going on in Africa at this time. The British were pushing from the Nile against Rommel's forces, and they had a Colonel McDonald who ran a photographic unit and they made a picture called *Desert Victory*, which was fantastic, black-and-white picture, beautifully done. We had, what was that idiot's name, a big producer, Darryl Zanuck, who was in charge of an American outfit that was shooting color, and the picture was called *At the Front*. Here are shots of Darryl Zanuck with a Tommy gun shooting at Junkers 88s up at 10,000 feet and all this sort of crap. It was a terrible picture, except for some shots of artillery hitting German tanks. What happened? Secretary of War Stimson and Roosevelt would look at movies together. They ran the British picture and then they ran the American picture and Roosevelt turned to Stimson and said, 'Wait a minute, aren't we the preeminent makers of motion pictures on earth?'

He said, 'How could the British make such a magnificent document? We made this awful thing.'

This is what the Signal Corps was waiting for. Stimson said, 'Well, we know there are men in the service, but we can't get them, we don't have the priority.' Well, at that point, the collators—collators were machines that they put cards in— [went to work]. Well, when I went in, you get an army specialist number and mine was 043, that's skilled motion picture camera. At that point, my card dropped down [by the collator] and unbeknownst to me, I was transferred to a signal photo company. I had an inkling there was something going on, and when I spoke to Captain Potts, he drew this red border letter out of his office desk, and this had me being transferred.

He said, 'We're not going to let you go, Sergeant.'

Now, a red border letter is what's called an immediate action letter. There's nothing you can do about it. When you get an immediate action letter, you have to perform it. By that time, the First Army, which I was in, had rejected the whole idea of my transfer.

Then, it went back to where it started. Then the red border letter came in again, and it chewed out the First Army. Suddenly, I was thrown into a command car and taken to a railroad station, and I was on my way to Camp Crowder, Missouri, where the 164th Signal Photo Company was. What's interesting about that now, you know, I had worked making industrial films and all that, but I never equated that to Hollywood technique. I was picked up at Camp Crowder station and the driver of the jeep was telling me this was a Hollywood outfit and all Hollywood people and all this other business. By the time I got there, I was sweating, I figured they were going to find me out, you know? I checked in and they gave me a bunk and the first sergeant told me to go to this certain barracks where they had set up as a projection room for training and they were running footage. They were like, 'You have to see this shot. It was magnificent.' I came there and it took me a while to get my eyes adjusted, and I looked at the screen and I'll never forget it until I die. Here was this paratrooper coming through the screen horizontally, with a parachute, fully inflated, coming through. I took one look at this, and I said, 'Quaid, you got it made.'

I said, 'He's obviously a still photographer and he took the motion picture camera and made it vertical.' This paratrooper dropping, he made vertical out of it, you know? It turned out that really what happened was that the motion picture industry wasn't going to lose their good people. I guess they helped organize some of these companies and I don't remember anybody who was a professional. Colonel Gaskell sent some good people in, and he devised courses for these guys, and they ended up doing a hell of a fine job.

'I Won World War II'

I was in Tennessee Maneuvers after training with this outfit and then I ended up in Tennessee Maneuvers, we all did, which was a huge enterprise.[16] You have no concept. There was this constant joke on the front lines, you know? 'You think this was tough, you should have been on Louisiana Maneuvers.'

'Well, you think this is tough, you should have been on Tennessee Maneuvers!'

Anyhow, they were short of lieutenants, and a photographic unit would consist of generally four or five men. There'd be a lieutenant, there'd be a motion picture cameraman, two still men, and a driver for whatever vehicle the unit had. Anyhow, two things happened. As I said, they were short of lieutenants, so they put me in charge of this unit. Now, the three men I had were Hatfield of the original clan, Cochran, and Beelen, and they were all very deep south guys or Kentucky or borderline states. Cochran, who was a staff sergeant, had recently been demoted to private and I never knew why, but these were three of the toughest men I've ever encountered. I take them out and for a week we'd do fine, because the maneuver went from midnight Monday until midnight Friday, and at that point, you camped next to the first creek there was and took a bath right out in the open.

On Sunday, I had finished chow, and I was sitting under a tree writing a letter home, and suddenly, I feel these shadows over me and there's Hatfield, Cochran, and Beelen, and they jump on me, and they pound the hell out of me and I pounded the hell out of them. But I realized they weren't really hurting me, I was hurting

---

[16] Tennessee Maneuvers- Large-scale Second Army training exercises involving more than 850,000 soldiers between 1942 and 1944; Middle Tennessee was selected because the terrain resembled that of France, Belgium, and Germany.

them, but yeah, they are bruising and what have you, nothing serious. They all got up and Hatfield said, 'Okay, Sergeant, you can run the outfit another week.' Okay? Next week these guys are fantastic, you couldn't wish for a better team.

Sunday comes, I'm under a tree writing a letter, but this time I'm looking, and I see the three of them come over this hill and I stood up, and this time they didn't pull any punches, they really belted the hell out of me, and I belted back, and by that time I was on the deck, and they were standing over me and Hatfield said, 'It's okay, Sergeant. We just want to know whether you'd fight.' You see, these boys were not going to go with anybody into combat that wouldn't fight. I never turned them in, never, you know? Actually, I should have, but I didn't. That, I earned a great deal of respect also, so we ended up a very fine team.

Last week, a relative, a cousin who I hadn't seen since before World War II, called up and dropped by, and her husband... See, I know nothing about him. See, I've been in motion picture business all my life. I was traveling all the time on projects. Anyhow, the husband of my cousin turned out to be with 4th Armored with General Patton. I said, 'Hey, 4th Armored. You were in Tennessee Maneuvers.'

'Yeah. We were there for three months.'

I said, 'I'll tell you a story.'

I decided to go out with 4th Armored with my unit. It's like 7:00 in the morning; a new phase of Maneuver started on Monday morning. By that time, temporarily, I got a lieutenant, and he was an ex-newsreel man from Florida.

I was lying on the ground while this briefing was going on. Now, they had a map of the military area, as big as that wall, and each of the colonels of Combat Command A, Combat Command B, each one would take notice what their outfit is going to achieve, and all that. And finally, one of them, Combat Command A, said, 'We're

going to cross the Cumberland River at the bridge at such and such.'
So, at that point, the general takes over and he starts his briefing,
and I listen, and this General Wood, who was very well respected
in Patton's Third Army, extremely well respected, and so was the
4th Armored. He points out where the Combat Command A is going to go across the river. Finally, he said, 'Any questions?'

I started to raise my hand, and Cliff Paul, my lieutenant, said,
'Shut up, Quaid!'

I said, 'Oh no, it's too important.'

And I raise my hand, and he looks at me, I mean, I'm the only
one. He looks at me, and he's taken aback, like, 'What is he doing
asking me questions in a major briefing?'

I said, 'Sir, if you'll check your map, at the point that Combat
Command A is going to cross the Cumberland River—I'm a little
distant. I realize, from the map, but that looks to me like it's a ferry
symbol.'

'What?' And he goes and looks, and he goes, 'Yipe!' Now these
three colonels come, and they all go, 'Yipe!' And he gets the radio
man. He said, 'Call Combat Command A, put them in reserve.'
Combat Command B was in reserve. 'We'll go for the bridge at Car-
thage,' and they changed the whole thing and stopped this whole
thing.

Now, Combat Command A was moving out since midnight. So,
I said to the guys, 'Hey, let's go down and take a look at that ferry.'
So, we had a hard time getting there, because here's Combat Command A, all these Sherman tanks coming back the other way, [re-
versing direction]. We finally get down there, and the ferry
consisted of this cable across the river and a barge that would take
one automobile at a time. And what they did is, the guy that ran it,
by angling the bow, the current of the river would slide this ferry
across the cable, see? And all you could imagine is, what would have

been happening to Combat Command A, [with their tanks trying to get] down to this muddy embankment, a disaster.

So, people say, 'What did you do in the Army?' I say, 'Well, I won World War II.' And I explain this whole story, because this is one of the prime tank outfits that we had. So anyhow, that night, we camped back with them, and I see this group of officers circling through this whole bivouac area. And finally, somebody points my unit out, and they come over, and it's General Wood. And he says, 'Sergeant, you have no idea what you have done for us.' See, don't forget they had umpires on all these units. And if this had happened, I guarantee you, they would break up the outfit, the whole officer corps would be gone. It would have been a disaster. And he went on, spent his whole time trying to find us to say thanks, but that's the kind of man, apparently, he was. He was extremely well-respected. But that outfit would have been junked, or at least the officers would have been. So that was Tennessee Maneuvers.

Going Overseas

Then, after that, they figured it's time to send us overseas, and we went to a port of embarkation: Hampton Roads, Virginia, Camp Patrick Henry. And there was nothing interesting there, except an outfit would have to take KP for this huge mess hall. But the whole outfit, it was so big, that every man would be involved. And so I was, at that time, a buck sergeant. And so, the mess officer of that installation said, 'Okay, here's how you lay out your men. You are going to run the officer's section here.'

He said, 'We're not going to issue any Kel-Bowl Paks today,' the little boxes of cereal that you could open up and pour milk into them. Do you remember?

'No one gets a Kel-Bowl Pak. Okay.'

So certain officers would say, 'Hey, I need something to put my cereal in.'

I said, 'Sorry, orders are we're not issuing them today.'

So, finally, this black colonel came on over, and he wanted a Kel-Bowl Pak. Well, I recognized him right away, he was Colonel Davis of the Tuskegee Airmen! And I said, 'I'm sorry, sir, but they're not being issued today.'[17]

And he looked at me as though I was another redneck of his life experience, and he just didn't believe me. And since I recognized him, it was rather excruciating to me also. So I understood his problem, and he refused to understand mine, that he was not going to get that damn thing, no way. I'm not going to get him a bowl, I'm not going to do anything against orders, period.

So, at that point, I see the mess officer, I said, 'Please come over here. You talk to the colonel,' and he told him that those were my orders, period. And that was the end of it. But I always felt bad about that. The guy probably had enough of this by this time.

*

So, then we went overseas, and finally, our time came to ship out, and we were on a British ship, *The Empress of Scotland*. I suddenly was put in charge of a group of twenty men, and we were supposed to work in a galley. There were at least 10,000 men on the ship, so it must have been an officer's mess; to feed 10,000 men is something else. So the mess officer had told me to tell the men that they're going to work all night, till morning, till dawn, and they would be excused from lifeboat drill. So, the cook who I was working with, a little bandy-legged Englishman, said, 'Now look, Sergeant, we got five jobs here. We got twenty men. I need four men cutting up herring. I need four men cleaning up around here from

---

[17] Benjamin O. Davis Jr. (1912-2002) was the commander of the Tuskegee Airmen and later was the first black United States Air Force general.

the last lane. And four men are going to help me with the bacon,' and all this sort of business. So, I tell the guys, 'That's what you're going to do.' Now, we left Hampton Roads in a violent storm, and I never get seasick, but I could see the guys trying to work [here on the food prep] and they had never been on a ship before. And so, the first guys I lose right off the bat are the guys cutting up the fish. I mean, that did it, I got to tell you. I would have figured they're out to con me, so I would not have permitted that. I really had to see the results, and I saw them [getting sick].

So then, the next group, the guys getting rid of the garbage, had whole big garbage pails, huge pails, and they would go into a small room, I'd say about eight foot wide, square. In the middle of it was this huge pipe with an iron cover on it, and what they were supposed to do was to take these pails of slop and pour them down this tube, and it'd exit out into the ocean. The only trouble is the ship was rolling. So, they took this mess of slop and poured it in, and the ship rolled, and this column of water came up this pipe. All the garbage, everything, hit the ceiling, all over these men. Four more gone. Four more wiped out. So then, finally, I lost the rest of the crew before I was done, and things like that happened. So, it was only the Englishman and myself to cook the bacon. Now, the way that was done, is we had these big black broiling pans, and the ovens were in ranks, serried ranks. It went from one side of the ship to the other, many of them. So we would take this bacon and throw it into the pan and put it into oven one, and go on, and as soon as we got to the end of the line, he would take one and I'd take the other and immediately go back and start pulling these out, and they'd be cooked pretty well. And so, finally, I'm dismissed, and I go back to my compartment, and all the guys are asleep and nobody else is in the compartment. They're up on lifeboat drill. So, at that point, all these officers come stamping down the stairs and, 'Sergeant,

Sergeant, what are these men doing in the bunks when they should be up on lifeboat drill?'

I said, 'Sirs, these men have been granted an excuse. The mess officer of the ship told us that they were free to sleep through lifeboat drill. They were on all night last night and they just got into their bunks.'

'Get them out. Get them up there.'

I'm like, 'Well, okay.' So I got them up and then [I started looking for] Captain Knight, the captain of the 164th Signal Photo Company. I found out where his cabin was, and I went up and I knocked on his door and he was very surprised to see me.

'What's your problem?'

I said, 'I don't have a problem, but you can have my stripes.'

'What do you mean by that, Sergeant?'

I told him, 'We were guaranteed that if we worked right through the night that we would be exempt, and you and the other officers rousted everybody out and there's no way I'm going to be in charge of men where what I tell them is not enforced by the officer corps.'

'All right, take it easy,' and he went up to the mess officer and the transport commander both, because this is pretty serious, lifeboat drill. And we got a reprieve and, of course, he demanded a great deal of credit for it, but son of a gun. So anyhow, that was our trip across. I mean, this is the stuff that nobody will ever tell you.

Mr. Quaid's story will continue.

Kermit Bushur, center, with soldiers from his first unit.
Library of Congress.

The Volunteer

Kermit 'Tony' Bushur was born on March 22, 1924, in Neoga, Illinois. He worked for the U.S. Postal Service as a mild-mannered rural mail carrier later in life, but as a young man he had a penchant for mischief and fun, which landed him in the brig early in his military career. He kept being turned down as he tried to get drafted; he had to write a letter of voluntary induction in order to serve his country. Amazingly, he survived the sinking of a transport vessel in the Mediterranean by an advance radio-controlled German bomb, an attack which resulted in the greatest loss of U.S. life at sea due to enemy action during World War II, and the loss of his official orders and identity papers. As a man now without a 'formal identity,' he found himself in India picking up the famine dead before 'finding salvation' in volunteering for an unspecified dangerous mission assigned to the unit that would become the famed Merrill's Marauders, seemingly filling the role of 'everyman' before being evacuated with a leg wound so serious he was recommended for an amputation.

'My squad leader was a convicted felon. He had been convicted of killing a man in Tennessee; it was his wife's lover, and he killed a man with

his knife. He was sentenced to life in prison. I think there was more than Tom in our unit who were felons, but there came a time when they would let them go into combat if they wouldn't take any training, just take them right from the prison and go right into combat. Well, Tom took it. He said, 'That's better than sitting here in the jail!' And he was the best man I knew. I would follow him into the hubs of hell. He was really a wonderful fellow.'

He sat for this interview at a Merrill's Marauders reunion in 2005, when he was 81 years old.

Kermit 'Tony' Bushur

My mother was intrigued by the name Kermit from Teddy Roosevelt's son, who was Kermit. It was a heck of a name for me because I could not pronounce it. Whenever I'd go into town, the boys would ask me, what's your name? I'd say, Joe, John, Mike, anything but Kermit, because I couldn't even pronounce it. But eventually I grew to liking my own name. But in college then whenever you're playing football and you're going for a touchdown, you can't say, 'Go, Kermit, go!' So I used my middle name, which was Anthony, and Tony. I became Tony and I've stayed Tony most all of my life since then.

My brother and sister are both older than me, my brother John William was fourteen years older and my sister Helen Marie was sixteen years older. We were a poor family that did not know we were poor. My father provided us with a comfortable life, nothing fancy, just adequate, never going hungry or without clothing. He owned a 56-acre farm that started out at first being a fruit farm, then as the trees died off, it was converted to a grain farm. I do not remember the fruit farm. Sis used to tell me of Father's maverick ways of not conforming to the norm. Most fruit farms sold their products to cold storage houses that then shipped the fruit to the larger cities, such as Chicago and St. Louis. Father instead would load up the wagon and hawk his wares in neighboring communities. She remembered him coming home with a fistful of money. By the time of my birth, Father was in the grain farming mode. Again his maverick ways was seeking a greater return from the land, so he improvised to making it a pig farm. He would raise what grain he could on 56 acres, but that was inadequate for the pigs that he would prepare for the market. Therefore in the fall of the year we would scour the area to buy more grain to make pig feed. I walked many a mile driving a team of horses with a wagon of corn, walking to keep warm as this was usually a job for the fall and winter.

My education consisted of six years in a rural one-room school house, today it might be termed 'one size fits all.' The 7th and 8th grade was in a Catholic school, me being sent there for the purpose of confirmation into the Catholic religion.

Pearl Harbor happened the first year I was a freshman in college. I remember coming back to the frat house and everybody was glued to the radio, and they were being bombed at Pearl Harbor. It was a devastating blow, and I remember the look on many of the boys' faces. They couldn't believe it and some of them just wandered around in a cloud for a while and some even went down and they volunteered immediately to go into service.

'You Have To Stay Home And Farm'

I completed the year of schooling and then that summer, wanting something to do and trying to sort out what I was going to do, the government made available schooling, which was called NYA schools, and they were teaching machine shop, sheet metal work, and welding. I chose machine shop, and I took their training, and I then went to work in Chicago in a plant and that's where I was really then getting ready to go in the service.

I thought, well, I want to go in the service. I lived about 200 miles from Chicago, and on the way home one time, I went to the draft board to see why I wasn't being drafted—everybody my age was being drafted! Well, to my surprise, the factory had made my work very, very much needed, so they got me a deferment. Well, I went back up and I quit that job immediately, came back home, and I thought surely I would be called back up. Well, I was not.

Weeks went by and I was not being called up by the draft, so I went back to the draft board, and they said, 'Well, now you're the only son left on the farm. Your brother has been drafted and he's in service, so you have to stay home and farm.'

I said, 'I am not a farmer. You have drafted the farmer.' I said, 'I'm going to go in the service.'

They said, 'Well, I'm sorry. You're going to have to stay home and farm.' So I went home, and I left the farm to go to visit a sister in another area, and I thought, well, surely they'd see I'm not farming, they'll still call me. But they didn't.

I went to the draft board again and they said, 'Well, the only way you can get into service is by writing us a voluntary letter of induction,' which I did. I wrote them a voluntary letter of induction, and lo and behold, the next week I was on the train going to the draft board or to the examination area, which is in Chicago. Now in basic training, I went to Little Rock, Arkansas, and it was B-I-R-T-C, which is Branch Immaterial Replacement Training Center or Company or whatever it might be, but we were being prepared to enter almost any one of the branches of the service. It might have been quartermaster. It might have been engineers. It might have been many different things, but that's why they called it Branch Immaterial. So at the conclusion of the training we were put on the train and we ended up at Sharon, Pennsylvania, at the place, they call it Shenango.

'You're The Son of a Gun That Went AWOL'

I got word that my brother was getting married, and he asked me to be his best man. So I went to the company commander and asked to be on a leave to go home for the wedding.

He said, 'I'm sorry, we can't give you no leave because you're on orders. You're going to have to be going overseas.' So I just politely turned around and walked out, but I picked up a pad of passes, three-day passes on the way out and I went back to the barracks, and I started ironing clothes like mad.

I was charging a dollar a whack for a pair of trousers and a dollar for a shirt. And if they wanted the military crease in it, I'd charge another dollar. So when I had enough money, I went to Youngstown, and I bought me a round trip to go to Illinois and back. Now here's where those three-day passes came in. The passes would get me 300 miles. And that was the limit of the extent that you could travel on a three-day pass.

So every time I was at the extent of 300 miles, I'd write myself another pass. So, finally I got to Chicago. And from Chicago to home, you have to go through Rantoul, Illinois, which is an air base that they were teaching weather, I think, and some other Air Force-related things. But the train was just loaded with GIs and MPs. Well, I thought, oh, I don't want to get stopped this far from home. I'm really close now. So I spent about 50 miles in the bathroom while everybody was—when they got off at Rantoul, then I came out of the bathroom.

We had a very, very good wedding and I decided it was time to go back to camp because I was only home, I think about eight days. And I was in town at the bus depot. I had to take the bus to a train station. It was right across from that Western Union Station. And while we were sitting there, my brother and I, here came the

Western Union messenger. He came over to me and said, 'What are you doing, Kermit?'

I said, 'Well, I'm going back to camp.'

He said, 'Are you sure you're going back to camp?'

I said, 'Yeah, yeah.' So I showed him what I had and my round-trip ticket. I said, 'I'm just ready now to get on the train going back to Ohio and Pennsylvania.'

He said, 'Well, if you're going back, I won't show this to your parents.'

It was the telegram telling them that I was AWOL, and if they knew where I was, they were supposed to let the government know and they'd pick me up, you know. Well, he let me go and my brother took the telegram, and he tore it up. He said, 'Dad will never see this!'

So I get back to Pennsylvania into the camp where I'd come from, and it was empty; the area that I had been in was empty. There wasn't a person around. So I talked to one of the soldiers that was walking around on the street. He said, 'You got to go down to the dayroom down about a block.' So I went down there, and I saluted the lieutenant, and I said, 'Private Busher reporting from AWOL, sir!'

He looked up at me and he said, 'Oh, you're the son-of-a-gun that went AWOL before I got to see you. Well, your unit has shipped out!' So he said, 'I'll tell you what. I'll give you this quarter number and I'll set you up for a summary court martial tomorrow or the next day,' whatever it was, within three days.

So, at the summary court martial—in fact, it was early in the morning, and he hadn't even got out of bed yet when I had knocked on his BOQ, which is Bachelor Officers Quarters. And he just lay there in bed, and he turned the light on and picked up my papers and looked at them. He looked at me. He said, 'Well, you look like a pretty good kid. You weren't going to go—or desert, were you?'

I said, 'No, no, no, no! I bought a round-trip ticket, and I just came back to camp on my own!'

He said, 'Okay, that's good, in your favor. I'll tell you what I'm going to do. I'm just going to fine you fifteen dollars. You'll be on a shipment to go overseas; we'll send you on out just like you had been originally.' So that's how I got to Newport News. And at Newport News we got on the liberty ship, the *Betty Zane*, and we landed at Oran, Africa, after 21 days.

In The Brig

On the *Betty Zane* I befriended a fellow German; I'm of German descent. But his father had been in World War I as an officer for the German Army. And he came to the States after the war and brought his family to the States. His name is Ed Truckenbrote. Ed became a very close, a very good friend. He was a manipulator, and there was nothing that he wouldn't try to do. But we had a lot of fun onboard the ship. In fact, he and I made up a little skit, like he was a German submarine commander, and I was the crew. Oh, we sank a lot of convoys. And you know, it was funny that we had the crowd laughing and stuff like that, but somebody didn't like it. When we landed at Oran, they turned us in as maybe being spies. So we went to the brig.

Ed and I spent about a week and a half in the brig, and they ran security checks on our parents and everything like that, you know. And finally they decided—I remember some of the questions they asked me, which was ridiculous, but then it's just like they said, 'If you were on the battlefield and you had your sights set on a German soldier, would you pull the trigger?'

I said, 'Well, sure I would,' you know. These are the kind of questions that they would ask you and it would be irritating, but finally they let us go and he went one way, and I went another, and I did not see Ed on my stay in Oran. On Thanksgiving Day of 1943, I boarded a boat or a ship that was going to join a convoy in the Mediterranean. I had no idea where it was going, but we were just out a short time, and we were attacked by a group of German bombers and pursuit planes. They strafed us and things like that.

'My God, A Torpedo!"

We made it through that day. But the second day I was on the ship—I now know the name of the ship was the *Rohna*, but at the time I did not know the name of the ship. And I remember seeing this thing coming down from the bomber. It was very large. And my thoughts were, my God, a torpedo! It was so large. It wasn't a conventional bomb. So we were hit, and we were sunk in the Mediterranean there.[18] We lost 1,015 men, and I was picked up and found to be fit for duty. So they sent me on in the next convoy and I ended up in Calcutta—Bombay, then Calcutta. Now Calcutta or India at that time was in the midst of a famine.

---

[18] *we were sunk in the Mediterranean*-1,149 men were killed in the sinking of the HMS *Rohna* on 26 November 1943; 1,015 were U.S. personnel, with another 35 later succumbing to their injuries. The ship was sunk by a radio-guided, rocket-boosted glide bomb dropped from a Luftwaffe Heinkel He 177A heavy bomber. This sinking constituted the greatest loss of U.S. life at sea due to enemy action, even surpassing the tragedies of the USS *Arizona* and the USS *Indianapolis*. Details of the sinking were only released gradually over time; it was not until 1967 and the passage of the Freedom of Information Act that the U.S. Government revealed more details concerning the cause of the sinking, which makes Mr. Bushur's eyewitness account even more fascinating. Source: Naval History and Heritage Command, H-Gram 022: Loss of British Transport HMT Rohna, October 2018. www.history.navy.mil/about-us/leadership/director/directors-corner/h-grams/h-gram-022.html.

Picking Up The Dead

I better tell you also that when I left—when I left Pennsylvania, I did not have an officer, I had no company. I was by myself, and I was hand-carrying my orders—I hand-carried my orders. So when we went down, when the boat went down, I lost my orders! I had nothing. So I don't know what sent me off, but I ended up in Calcutta. And when I was in Calcutta, not having any company commander or anything like that, I was getting all the dirty details, and the dirtiest they had at that time was going into town and picking up the dead. See, the country was in a famine, and they were starving people, they were elderly people, but they came to Calcutta so they could bathe in the River Ganges. To their religion, they'd have to bathe in the River Ganges to be saved. Well, then they went into town. They'd unroll their little bamboo roll that they had, they'd lie down there and go to sleep and sometimes they didn't wake up. So every day there had to be a truck going through the entire city and picking up the dead. And then we would take them down to the river, put them on a big pile of wood, and burn them.

'One Day The Salvation Came'

That became very, very disheartening and very sad to see that happening. And I was catching that detail every day, every day! So that one day the salvation came. On a bulletin board they needed volunteers for a dangerous mission. They didn't promise anything except that you were going to be on a dangerous mission, but I think they did imply you might go home or something like that.

So there were three of us that volunteered. Lieutenant Dumpsha, Lieutenant Herne, and myself volunteered and we went into the hill country or the brush country where the Marauders were training. And I got the last two or three weeks of training before we went into Burma. So that's how I got into the combat.

Now in combat, I never did anything at all except be just a body count, you know. I did what I had to do. They told me to be a guard here and 'you're going to be in the right flank,' but I was in the Khaki Combat Team, Fourth Squad, the Fourth Platoon of I-Company of C-Battalion. Now, my battalion commander over there was Major Briggs. Some people called him colonel. I always called him colonel, but a lot of people, more people called him major rather than colonel.

'My Squad Leader Was A Convicted Felon'

My company commander was Major Lew, and my platoon commander was this lieutenant that I had volunteered with, Lieutenant Dumpsha, and I don't know why the Fourth Squad of the Fourth Platoon always gets called out for all the dirty work at the tail end, but here's an interesting thing. My squad leader was a convicted felon. His name was Tom Larson. He had been convicted of killing a man in Tennessee; it was his wife's lover. Tom was always quick to use a knife, he always kept a very sharp knife, and he killed a man with his knife. He was sentenced to life in prison.

And then that one time in the war—I think there was more than Tom in our unit who were felons, but there came a time when they would let them go into combat if they wouldn't take any training, just take them right from the prison and go right into combat. Well, Tom took it. He said, 'That's better than sitting here in the jail!' And he was the best man I knew. I would follow him into the hubs of hell. He was really a wonderful fellow.

My platoon leader was a fellow by the name of Rocky Curtain. Now Rocky was a very close friend of a Nisei interpreter by the name of Hank Gosho. The platoon guide was Whitney Dalmus. And that was the setup, more or less, of my unit.

'Poorest Goddamn Excuse For A Mule Skinner'

We, at that time, were not the Merrill's Marauders. We were just 5307 Provisional Composite Unit. Merrill's Marauders, everybody knows how that was just a media name, you might say. Some reporter used it, and it caught on and it became very famous. In combat, I don't know how to get to it, we had minor skirmishes [in the beginning], so I got the idea, you know, a guy could get killed out here. So I thought, well, I'm going to be a mule skinner, because I've seen these mule skinners bring the load up, deposit it, and then they go back to a safe area. So I thought, you know, 'That's for me. I want to be a mule skinner.' I got permission to go over and be a mule skinner. So the day I went over in that area, they gave me a mule and said, 'Now, this in your mule and this is your load. You're going to be responsible for this. So you are one of us now.'

So when morning came, I loaded that mule up, I got the pack all up on top of him. But the mule—and I think mules and horses do the same thing—they bloat themselves up a little bit with air. And like a horse now, if you put a saddle on them, you have to get that air out of them to get that cinch tight. I didn't realize that a mule would do that. So here I had this big load on top of the mule, and he was all bloated up and I didn't have no idea. So we take off. We go about seven steps, and he sucks in his air and that load just reversed from top to bottom. Here it had slid underneath his belly, you know. And he starts bucking and broke away from me! And everybody hollered, 'Loose mule, loose mule!' So here came the sergeant on his pony or horse. He goes down the trail after the mule and he gathers him in and brings him back to me and hands me the rein, and I'll never forget him looking down at me and he said,

'Poorest goddam excuse for a mule skinner I've ever seen!' At the end of the night, I was the BAR man—I said, 'Here, you can have your mule back. I'm going to get my BAR.' So I had one day as a mule skinner. It was just part of my life.

The Letter

In between fights, we would be dropped food and supplies, whatever we needed. And one day they dropped some mail along with the other things. So they were passing out the mail and said, 'Busher, who is that?' So I hollered and they sent it back to me. But it was an official letter, it had a little window in it. You know how they have the window? And it said, 'Private Kermit A. Busher.' So I thought, well, who in the heck could be sending me something, you know? So I opened that letter up and what had happened, when they refolded that letter, they folded it wrong so that the full address did not show up in the window. It was supposed to have gone to the commanding officer of Private Kermit A. Busher. Well, you know what that letter was? It was to hold my fifteen dollars. That letter is lost over in Burma somewhere. And I don't know if the government is going to come back on me now for my fifteen dollars. [*Laughs*] Well, that was just among some of the things that happened. You can look at it now and have a little chuckle out of it.

'We Can Disappear In The Jungle'

One thing I really thought that I would see was snakes. I did not see a snake! Now, I was amazed at the elephants. We would see an elephant herd ahead of us. And they would—you know how big an elephant is—and this is jungle that we could not go through ourselves unless we used a machete. That group of elephants can disappear into the jungle. It's streamlined, their trunk and everything like that, how they just slide everything over their back and every-thing like that and they're gone. But they're gone. You don't see them. And it was just—I was so—I was glad that I went into that area. First of all, when I was in Africa, I was afraid I'd be sent to Germany. And at the time they were having a lot of cold weather. The hedgerows, people were losing their fingers and toes and things like that, frostbite. And I thought, well, if I'm going to die, I want to be comfortable when I'm dying. So when I got into a warm climate, if you could be happy about it, I was comfortable with it, you know. What it also taught me, when we had Vietnam then, I could see—I could sympathize with the American troops that were in Vietnam because they were fighting guerillas. And we were gue-rillas; I could see what we could do. We could hit a base. We could shoot them up and we don't have to hold ground. We can disappear into the jungle. We'd be gone! That was the same situation in Vi-etnam. Those poor American boys, they had to stay there and hold the base. And the Viet Cong could attack at their discretion when they wanted to, fight as long as they want to and disappear. It was just reverse, what they were doing from what we had done. We were doing the same thing to the Japs that the Viet Cong was doing to the Americans. So I could fully sympathize with the American troops that were in Vietnam. That's one thing that my World War II experience did teach me on that.

Combat

We had one pretty heavy engagement called Walawbum. And I was not in the battle itself, I was on the right flank way out about three miles away from where the people were fighting in the com-munity in the town itself; there was a right flank out there and a left flank and I was way up on the right flank. Well, it was quiet where I was. So I thought, well, after I had my foxhole dug and I had my

302 | THE VOLUNTEER

BAR all set up and being quiet, I thought, this is a good time—there was a river right in front of me—this is a good time to just get in that river. And it was my birthday. It was March 22, 1944, and I was born March 22, 1924. I'm 20 years old today and I was in the river bathing and paddling around when all of a sudden right across from me, vroom! The Japanese had artillery right across the bank from me! And I know that they had me under the gunsight, but they wouldn't shoot because they didn't want to disclose their position or anything like that. And what they had done, they had a well over there that they had lured their artillery piece down into and had it camouflaged, and then they could bring it back up when they needed to, and they could shoot. So they were using the artillery to shoot into the town or where the battle was going on! Well, of course, I broke all records getting back to my foxhole and sat there or lay there for quite some while, and then finally, I saw how they got rid of that artillery piece, how they used our Air Force.

Major Briggs, he was my commanding officer who was with us at the time, and I've talked to him since then, he said he happened to have the Air Force liaison man with him in that combat time. And he had them bring in two fighter pilots. And I saw this one way off high and to the side so that the gun just kept on shooting because they didn't think they were in any danger from that plane way off far away. But what he didn't know was that that fellow way off high was giving the coordinates to his buddy, who came in at tree-top level and dropped an egg right on him, and just blew him right out of there, you know. It was just cooperation between the two, how they got rid of that. And Major Briggs said, 'Boy, was I ever glad that I had the liaison man with me at that point!', you know.

Well, the battle was somewhat a success, but my company was not the company that did the battle. We were only added as a little added support. So now it was Blue and Green Company of the Second Battalion who were doing the battle. They pulled back and then

we guarded their rear. They were going back, and they ended up—
it took us two days to get to Nhpum Ga. And at Nhpum Ga—I don't
know what you might know about the name or anything like that—
Nhpum Ga was one of our major battles. And when the boys pulled
through and they occupied the top of this hill or mountain or whatever you want to call it, that was Nhpum Ga.

The unit I was with then, we went through them and down into
the valley and we were expecting them to come on down the next
day, you know. But the Japanese were very angry because of the
devastation that had been brought on them at Walawbum. So they
were pursuing us; in the rear guard we had a few little battles with
them, to keep them from following us too close. They were shooting artillery at us. And we had a terrible time trying to hit their artillery, like you try to knock them out also. And we found out later
that they had mounted their artillery, they had mounted their mortars on an elephant, and they would shoot off of his back and then
kick it in the butt and he would move on, you know, off to another
side or something like that, so we couldn't pinpoint where they
were. They kept avoiding being hit. They were very spirited in
what they were doing on that, and we found this out later that that's
what they had done. So at Nhpum Ga then, that became a major
battle because the Japanese surrounded the boys [of the Second Bat-
talion] at Nhpum Ga. And they were surrounded there for like ten
days or something like that. And while we were down there in the
valley, that's when the decision was made by General Merrill and
another fella, Red Acker, that they needed artillery dropped to us.

General Merrill was on his way back for some reason and he
said, 'I'll have that here tomorrow.' So they did drop the artillery,
and he had two crew teams and there were two pieces dropped and
they were able to get the boys off of the hill eventually. It took about
two more days, but they broke the Japs up and they were able to get
them off.

Wounded

I got wounded in that action at that point because before they got the artillery, we had to fight kind of a delayed action, and we had gone around to the back side of the hill and we started up toward the summit and gave the Japs the idea that it was a force that they had to reckon with; we were trying to draw fighters away from the encirclement and fight us. We lost a few fellows, and I got hit. And then it was two days later that the artillery was dropped in and they did get the boys off on Easter Sunday, April the ninth of that year. I got hit on the 4th of April and they sent me back then to 20th General Hospital.

There was no airfield there, but the airplane [I was evacuated by], it was an L-5, had landed on a sandbar, a short sandbar. And what they had done, they tied the tail down to something that would hold it and then they let the engine rev up as much as possible and they chopped the rope holding the tail and it had a catapult action, you know. But still, we didn't get to rise that quickly because I remember looking off to the side and there were monkeys looking around before we got above the trees.

I was wounded in the right thigh. It was a light machine gun. And I must have got about 15 or 20 bullets in this area. [*Gestures to right thigh*] They blew out my leg completely. I lost the bone, and it was just hanging there. When they carried me down the hill, I weighed about 180 pounds at that time. I was actually heavier there than I was at any other time. I don't know why I was gaining weight. And I was a BAR man. I needed all that weight, but when they got me down to the aid station, the doctor was Dr. Hopkins. And he's the fellow that wrote the book, *Spearhead.* And he has documented what my [injury was]—I think I'm entry No. 67 or something in his book. And he used that when he disclosed what he knew about everybody, and he made the remark in there that I was back in the hospital in 33 hours, which was unusual in World War II. Nowadays with a helicopter and everything like that, it's just a matter of almost minutes or hours, you know, that the wounded are taken care of. But I was back in the hospital in 33 hours. And another thing, as I said before, I was hand-carrying my records. I had no records. Phil Piazza and Bob Passanisi, they've all tried to find orders of me joining the Marauders, and they cannot find them. I am a nobody. If it hadn't been for me being wounded and Dr. Hopkins including me in the book, [no one would have even known], but that's my proof that I was a Marauder. So it's just one of those things that has happened in my life.

Kermit Bushur (L) and other Marauders recovering from their wounds, Gaya, India. Library of Congress.

'I Can Save That Leg'

I was wounded on the fourth. The boys got out on the ninth. Well, the hospital knew there was going to be a lot of wounded and sick people coming off the hill, so they had to make room at the

20th General. So they made up a planeload of wounded; most of them were walking wounded. I happened to be one of the better patients, but this is God blessing my life, really what happened, because when they sent me back to there, I was the first person that the doctor looked at because I was the worst wounded. And he was a Southern gentleman, and he was from Hot Springs, Arkansas. He was an older fellow and he just smoked a pipe, and he took my records. He looked at the hospital records, then he uncovered my leg, and he looked at it. Then he read the record again. He looked at my leg and the first words he said to me were, 'They're just crazier than hell.'

I said, 'What's this, Doc?'

He said, 'They have suggested I remove the leg.' He said, 'I can save that leg; if you want to spend some time with me, I can save that leg.'

I said, 'I'll be your brother. I'll be right here, I'll be closer than anybody you ever know!'

So he worked with me, and he did save my leg. He fixed my bone, he fixed my muscles and everything. And it's just today in the past three weeks that I've had to use a cane because I broke my hip now, and I've haven't got my strength back yet. But I've had no pain, nothing bothered my leg at all in all these years. And the Veterans Administration have checked my leg and everything like that and they said, 'You're just perfect. You're in good shape.' But it was this old, Southern doctor from Hot Springs, Arkansas, that saved my leg. They were intending to have it removed; of course, the first hospital was at the edge of the jungle, hot, damp, and the flesh wasn't healing good, so that was their recommendation. Probably if I would have stayed there, I might have lost a leg.

The Nisei Interpreter

We were in a pretty heavy engagement, and we had pulled back that night and we dug in. And Hank Gosho, [one of our Nisei soldiers], was not my friend, he was a friend of Rocky Curtain, who was my platoon sergeant.[19] But Hank came through, I remember him coming through the area. We were all in foxholes, and he found Rocky, and he said, 'I'm going to go out and see what I can find out here in front of us.'

Rocky said, 'You know you're not supposed to go out.'

'I know it. I'm going to go out.'

So Rocky said, 'Okay, you're going out, then I'm going out.' So the two of them did go out; they were in no-man's land, we had no idea what was out there. But he did find a [Japanese] phone line, which he tapped into [to get information, learning our unit was about to be encircled]. All of that night while we were digging our foxholes, we were fairly close to that road and we could hear the Japanese trucks—which were Ford trucks, by the way—we could hear them coming up and the tailgate would drop down and then these Japanese were jumping off and the troops—maybe there would be eight or ten in the truck, they were bringing in a bunch of them. So I knew we were going to be in for a big engagement.

Well, through the knowledge that Hank found out, then we knew they were on the move. They knew we were there, even though it was night. They were trying to trap us. So he told us and got us to go, get out of there, get out of this area. And what the Japanese had done, they had made kind of a horseshoe-like [perimeter surrounding us] with an opening at the one end. We walked out through that end. They knew we were on the move, but they

---

[19] Hank Gosho-Sgt. Henry H. Gosho, Nisei interpreter with Lieutenant Weston's platoon, one of 14 Japanese-Americans who had volunteered for the Marauders.

didn't know where we were going, so they turned loose their little dogs on us. Now see, these are dogs that they use for food, like the American GIs will carry their food. The Japanese, they pull a little dog as he's walking, so they don't have no weight, you know. All they carry is a bag of rice. They have hard-boiled rice, which is just a sling over their shoulder, along with that dog, you know, they could live for months. Well, when the dogs got over among our feet, they would yipe. In the jungle you shoot at sounds more than anything else. When they heard a yipe, they would shoot at us. So we killed a bunch of dogs that day. We had to wring their necks, you know, and we were able to leave that area.

So now that's where Hank got me out of what I thought was almost certain death. I had dug my foxhole, and being a BAR man, I had a supporting rifle. And after we got that foxhole dug, I know I remember turning around and his name was—why do I have to even try and think of his name now, [and I can't bring it up]—but I turned to him, I said, 'It's been nice knowing you. I'm glad that we had this acquaintance.' And I said, 'I hope we can continue our friendship tomorrow morning.' And we really thought this was it. Well, that was the prelude to the battle at Nhpum Ga.

'The Men Who Altered My Life'

I have a letter here from General Merrill where he sent me home. Now this is almost unbelievable that he sent me home. What I had done—I'm working in the replacement depot now, and there were fellas being sent home, and I had fallen through the cracks. I was still there, [but remember, I had no papers]. So I wrote him a griping GI letter, just bitching, you know, about things. He didn't promise me nothing, as you can see in that letter, he just said that he was sorry. He said, 'Your time will come,' and everything like that. But look at the date of that letter, the fifth of May. Now here's the date on this, the sixth of May, general orders from his headquarters were cut to send me by myself, so on the ninth of May I'm on the road home. He gave me also number three priority; it was a 66-hour trip that I made in 55 hours. Other fellas came home by boat, things like that, you know. I made the trip in 55 hours.

Now I'm back home. I have my thirty-day leave. I get this letter that General Merrill wrote; that was my first inkling of why I was being sent home; I had no idea why I was going home. But the letter opened up avenues for me. At Illinois, after my thirty days, I was sent to Miami for another leave of R & R. One day I was eating at the cafeteria, which the army had taken over, and lo and behold, in the front door came two boys that I had taken basic training with! One of them had the bunk next to me. His name was—it had to be a B because things were alphabetical. But they were my first knowledge of what happened to them after they left—see, I went AWOL from these boys, and it turned out that they had gone to England without me. Now, this is Miami. This is a boy right here that I'm talking about now, who wound up in England. Both these boys got hit on D-Day! They were on the beaches, and they lost 95 percent of their personnel, of which I would have been one of. See, there's again the Lady Luck. They were taken prisoner, and he spent all of his time in a German prison camp. [The other] was taken prisoner, and he was in an Italian prison. So all of World War II in Germany, these two boys that I had trained with had spent it in the prison camp! And they were the only ones that ever were able to tell me what had happened to my unit, so I was mighty glad. Now see if General Merrill hadn't sent me home when he did, I would have never gotten to meet these fellas.

General Merrill sending me home when he did, I also ended up in Camp Shelby, Mississippi. And I met a WAC. Before that, I hated WACs, because we'd heard so many stories about, you know at that time, well, it said all the prostitutes in Pittsburgh enlisted en masse.

So we just assumed that they were all prostitutes. But this one WAC changed my mind. We had a courtship, got married, and had a very good life. Now if it hadn't been for General Merrill sending me when he did, I would never have met my wife and then had the family that I did have. So there's the two men [who altered my life], Hank Gosho and General Merrill.

Reconnecting With Truck

After I got out of the jungle, I wrote to Truckenbrote's parents. I had his address, they lived in Chicago, but I did not tell them anything except what I had said, 'I have lost track of Truck.' When the ship was going down, there was a lot of chaos, a lot of people running around, fire, all kinds of explosions, stuff like that. And it was an old English ship that had wooden planks for a stairway, and they burned out in no time, so there were people down in the hole that were trying to get out. You couldn't throw a rope down, because it would burn right away. I saw who I thought was Truck down there, and I did grab a hold of the fellow and he slipped out of my grip, and he fell down, and then I had to jump overboard myself. So in my mind I thought that Truck went down with the ship, and that's what I was more or less asking his parents, what they knew about where Truck was or anything like that, not saying anything.

Their answer back to me gave me a little glimmer of hope. They said, 'We don't know what happened to him, he was badly burned, but he was in India.' He was not far from where I was! In fact, if you look at the Merrill's Marauders directory, you will find his name in there. Now see, I told you he was a finagler; I don't know how he got listed in our directory, but he is in the directory. So when I had made membership badges for all the Marauders, and I sent them to everybody that I could find an address for, and when I was going through the book, I see Truck's name in there, I thought, Truck was never a Marauder, so I was not going to send him a membership badge or card. Instead, I sent him a personal letter. I never heard an answer. So I said, 'Uh-oh, he knows that I know that he was not a Marauder.'

That was in 1995. So then I forgot about trying to get a hold of Truck again, until about four years later I wrote another letter again, and I get an answer this time. It happened that the first letter came at about the same time his wife had died, and he may have seen the letter, he may not have seen the letter, but he was not at New York. He was now living in the Catskills in Upstate New York. So when I found that out, I went to see Ed. He didn't deny to me that he wasn't a Marauder, but he said he was wounded by a stray bullet at Shaduzup. Now whether he was or not, I don't know, but it was so good to see Truck, you know, after all these years. And he is the only guy that could testify that I was on the *Rohna*. I had nothing! So he and I depend on each other; I'm in contact with him right now. And it was just really, really good to see him and then to find out everything that I did find out about him.

'I Don't Know What A Hero Is'

Interviewer: Any parting thoughts that you have or last words, if you will?

I try to save those for birthday cards. I try to think up something wise, something that they'll remember you by. But no, now I'm just about out of last words and things like that. It's been a pleasure and again, I'd say I was not a hero. What is a hero? What's your definition of a hero? I don't know what a hero is. I think a hero might be someone—he's a normal person who saw a need, and did it. I know I was not a hero, because I never had to go into a position where I had to make daily decisions like that, you know. You knew we needed ten men here; we needed a hundred men there. I was just part of that body count, and I was just following orders, something like that. [But] I remember one time lying on the hillside. We were pinned down and we couldn't move. And all of a sudden, I heard the darndest thing—I call it a roar. And I don't know why I called it a roar, but I turned around just momentarily and a guy by the name of Boshart rushed past me and I got to see his eyes, and I swear they were glazed. But whether his temperament had broken or what it was, he went up and he wiped out a machine gun right in front of us! What caused him to do that, see? He might have been a farm boy. He might have been a city boy. He might have been anybody, but all of sudden there for a moment he was acting on an impulse and he did something wonderful.

So what is a hero? I don't know.

Kermit Bushur passed away on July 11, 2009, at the age of 85.

David L. Quaid standing next to his motion picture camera,
World War II. Library of Congress.

CHAPTER SIXTEEN

The Combat Cameraman
II

David's boyhood interest in newsreel photography brought him to India in the Army, where he wound up on General Stilwell's staff and somehow got away with going AWOL to continue on the missions with Merrill's Marauders. In his assignment as a member of the 164th Signal Photo Company, he had to carry a heavy 35mm Bell & Howell motion picture film camera and still cameras along with his regular infantry gear, documenting their travails and exploits, suffering from the same tropical diseases and severe weight loss, and even survived being hit by a sack of mule feed during an air supply drop. He told an interviewer later that his survival was partly a matter of will. 'I've been shot at so much I just can't tell you. Sooner or later, a good combat cameraman will be a dead one. You just have to feel a little lucky.'

His military decorations included two Bronze Stars and the Legion of Merit.

David Quaid

Getting To India

We landed at Cape Town, South Africa, and we were given a 24-hour pass. And so, the guys I hung out with were an interesting bunch and we knew right away we want to get out of town, be all these GIs all over the place. So we went up into the hills and we found a pub run by an old lady, and she told us her son had been killed in North Africa, but he got mentioned in dispatches, which is very important, and it's like getting a decoration. So anyhow, Bill Safran and myself decided we should do something nice for this lady who was very nice to us, and we found a flower shop, bought some flowers for her, and then we went back into town. We were having a dance. And so, I'm paired off with a very beautiful young girl, and I said, 'What's your name?'

'Well,' she said, my name is such and such, 'but all my friends call me Chippy.' Well, I almost broke up because when I was a kid, a Chippy was a young woman of some doubt about her; anyhow, I almost died. And here's something, again, no one will tell you. You know what they did at these dances? The whole idea was to encourage white American guys to come back to South Africa and settle, to redress the balance.

And so, we get back on the boat and we head for Bombay. And halfway over, our ship goes up in flames, torpedoed. And then we took a train right across India to Calcutta, which I found very interesting, looking out at what was going on. We came to a place called Bilaspur, and as my train came in, another train came in. I opened the compartment door, the guy on this other side opened the compartment door, and there's Joe Rottenberg, my friend Warren's brother. It's amazing. I was on my way in, he was on his way out. And so, we get to Camp Kendrapara, which was a huge staging area for troops. And it was actually, in peacetime, it was some industrialist who had set that up as a retirement place for sacred cows, see, to get them off the streets, if you want the truth.

Getting To Stilwell's Headquarters

When we were still at Camp Crowder, they had sent three units of the 164th overseas. One of them went to China; none of us knew where they went. One went to Stilwell's headquarters, and one went with Merrill's Marauders. So, a guy from Stilwell's headquarters had been accepted for OCS and was on his way home and they needed a volunteer to go up and find General Stilwell's headquarters. Well, that's a pushover for me, old Eagle Scout, so I volunteered. And I must say, I don't think Hatfield, Cochrane, and Beeler ever forgave me for leaving them. They ended up in Karachi, 2,500 miles away from the front, but I couldn't accept that [kind of posting].

So they cut orders for me, and I took off. I got in a C-47, and two Red Cross girls loaded on when I did. And we were airborne for a while, and the pilot invited the two girls [into the nose] to see how you fly a plane. Then two pilots came out and said, 'Oh yeah, we left one of them in, and we put the plane on automatic pilot, and she thinks she's flying it.'

I said, 'You two, get your asses back in there! She could panic and grab something, and we're all going to buy the farm, come on!'

'Oops.' These Air Corps guys were, what, 20, 21 years of age?

I ended up landing at Chaba intact, but then, I had to find my own way down. As I remember, we used to get, when you're traveling, three bucks. It was a lot of money then. In fact, a great deal of money. And we get three bucks to handle our own food and things like that, when it couldn't be handled by some outfit that we would end up. So, at Ledo, they said, 'Don't go anyplace else but this Chinese restaurant. It's terrific.'

Well, it was terrific, but these guys were deserters from the Chinese Army from when Stilwell had to walk out. This was some of the 38th Division that decided to go into business at Ledo, but they were so damn good, nobody bothered them. You follow me? I mean, they should have been picked up instantly. Nobody bothered them.

So I put in for a flight into Burma on an L-5, [a small liaison transport aircraft]. Before that, I had to get jungle equipment and stuff like that. So, I go into the supply office and the supply sergeant says, 'Okay, give me your gas mask.'

I said, 'No, why should I give you my gas mask?'

He says, 'You're going to look like some horse's ass, the only GI in North Burma with a gas mask.' Well, it turns out they figured that Japs were not going to use gas. But they weren't as well read as I was, because I know the Japs did use gas on the Chinese. They flew over them, but anyhow, he won. He got my gas mask.

We fly into a place called Minh Quang in North Burma that had a small strip, and there's nobody there, just the pilot and myself in the L-5. And then another L-5 comes in, and we notice that the landing gear is [pitched on one side], it should be at 45 degrees, and one leg of it is, but the other is hanging this way, rocking back and forth. Well, that was because wherever he picked up this wounded Chinese man, the plane must have [clipped] a tree on the way up. Well, we started watching him as he came in, and the guy was terrific. What he did, after he made a turn, took a look at the strip, he came in like this [motions with hands in a tilting motion] and he angled the broken strut back at 45, and then it looked like he was going to crash. At the last minute, he [maneuvered] it over and the two wheels hit the ground. And, of course, it collapsed finally, and the plane spun around, and the pilot and I ran forward and helped him and the wounded man out. And nobody's hurt! It was a great performance. And then, finally, an ambulance came from the Seagraves Hospital Unit, which was beyond the trees, which I couldn't see, and picked him up.

I put my pack on and grabbed my rifle, and I know I have to go south on what was called the combat trace, which was just a jeep track; it's still over somewhere down there, no one seemed to know its exact location at the time. So I shot off.

Now, another L-5 circles the field and comes in. And at that point, a jeep comes from the south and goes to this L-5, and I see them unloading foot lockers and stuff like that into the jeep. And they get finished, they come by me and the jeep stops and Major Arnold turned up. His name was Major Arnold, one of Stilwell's staff, and he said, 'Hey, Sergeant, where are you going?'

I was all by myself. He said, 'Where are you going?'

I said, 'I'm supposed to go down to Stilwell's headquarters.' I said, 'I understand it's that way.'

He said, 'It is, but it's a long way.'

He said, 'Get in, we're going there.' And so, we get to Stilwell's headquarters, and they put me in a basha hut with his bodyguard, which was just about twenty feet from his tent. I think I'm going to have to get a glass of water. I was given the last bunk in front of the door where the rain blows in, naturally; I was the last man there. So, the driver and Major Arnold take this one footlocker and put it on what is now my bunk, and hook it up. And see, these guys had been up there for three months, had never gotten a PX ration of any kind, and Arnold was coming back from Calcutta, where he picked up a few things, like he picked up a whole bunch of corn cob pipes, some Prince Albert tobacco, oh God, what else? I mean, crazy stuff. Oh yeah, I remember a couple of Baby Ruths [candy bars], man. That's what they had. So, they parceled it out for the bodyguard, and there's two left, one for Major Arnold and one for

General Stilwell. So, he said, 'Gee, Sergeant, I'm awfully sorry. We didn't know you were coming.'

I said, 'Come on, I've been living [high on the hog]. You guys don't worry about it.'

So anyhow, he goes into Stilwell's tent, and he comes back, and he lays out the corn cob pipe, Prince Albert tobacco, two Baby Ruths on my bunk. I said, 'I thought he said that there's nothing for me.'

He said, 'The general would like you to have it.' It's a fact. He mentioned that there was a new man in, and he laid it all out. So then, later, and this is off the continuity of the story, but after going through the Marauders and all that sort of business, I ended up with typhus and malaria in 20th General Hospital. And you're not allowed to go back, but I had this wonderful pass, it had my picture on it, signed by Lieutenant General Joseph Stilwell, and it said, 'You are hereby directed to provide this man with any rations and assistance of any kind necessary to carry out his photographic mission.' Now I could have taken that pass and flown home, I mean that's how powerful that card was. I'd just have to show it and zingo, I'd be on my way to the States. So anyhow, even though I was ordered not to, I could never go back into Burma, I went down to the L-5 strip.

'Where do you want to go, Sergeant?'

I said, 'I want to go back to Stilwell's headquarters.'

So I get there, and I'm very weak—and I didn't get into how I bribed my way out of the hospital, that was interesting—but I decided to take a walk down the combat trace, I had a pistol with me, I had a 45. I was always a curious person, and I'm walking, looking down, and it's always muddy, and there was this huge paw print in the mud. As I looked at it in fascination, a single pearl of water came up in the middle of it, so then I thought, you know, 'this is fresh,' and I went up this tiny little game trail, so I knew it had to be a tiger.

I decided to track it, to see how close I could get, I wanted to see it, so I'm tracking it, and I'm getting closer and closer, I think. Then I noticed it veered to the right, and it actually had to break some stuff to do that, so then my Boy Scout manual came back to me—the tracker becomes the tracked, where they circle around behind!

So I went to the left, see, and I came to a chong, which is a river, and I immediately went into that, and went upstream toward where Stilwell's headquarters was. I figured that at least he couldn't track me in the water, but actually, they're not that worried about water themselves. I finally get on the other bank, and there's another trail following the river, so I'm going down this trail fast, and suddenly I stopped cold. I said to myself, 'What the hell's the matter with you?', and I started to look, and I saw a thin brown vine at eye level, coming down, and there it was, and against all this green, it was a little shocking, when you finally realize that in the crotch of the tree in front of you, there's a British hand grenade that this line is hooked to. Now, the British hand grenade was a wonderful weapon, because with the American grenade, where you pulled the pin, throw it, five seconds later, it exploded. Well, the British grenade had two screw-in fuses; one would give you a four-second delay, the other was instantaneous, so it made a marvelous booby trap, the instantaneous setting, and these had been all captured by the Japs at Rangoon.

So I just ducked under it, and I figured I'd leave that for the engineers to handle, and then I ran into what was a recent Jap encampment—I could tell it was a Nip encampment, and it was only, God, less than a mile from Stilwell's headquarters, and so I reported all that when I got back, and they sent some MPs in, and they shot the grenade out of the tree, and that was the end of that.

The Chinese

So I was with this Chinese outfit after I came back out of the hospital, after the campaign to Myitkyina. They had a weird sense of humor. By the way, I'm going to get editorial now, just really editorial. Now, the Marauders lived on K-rations and nothing but that for five months. The Chinese wouldn't eat it, so the Chinese were dropped corned beef, cucumbers, peanut oil, to cook all the vegetables we dropped to them, all this sort of business, but they couldn't seem to do that for us, I mean, that just seems dumb, and by the way, I went in 178 pounds, and I would come out in the 130s, and so did everybody else.

I was sitting on a big teakwood log that was lying on the ground, and the Chinese captain was sitting next to me. Now, we used to always joke with the Chinese and all that sort of business, we'd say, [foreign language] meaning American women are the greatest, and they would say, [foreign language] and would do these little monosyllabic things. Well, it was lunchtime, and I refused to use chopsticks, because I could always say that this bent spoon I had was much more efficient in eating than those damn chopsticks. This is part of the little competition, see, and so I was sitting next to this Chinese captain on a log, and he had his bowl of rice, and they just pour it in their mouth like this, and I was like a patrician eating my chow with my spoon, and I nudged this guy, and I said, 'fun tong,' well 'fun' is rice, 'tong' is dog, 'chowhound,' right?

He put down this bowl of rice, and he had a little bit of rice stuck here on his chin, and he picked up his carbine, and made a 180 degree turn for me, and went bang, now his men are falling down, because he's enraged, and finally, he ends up pointing it between my eyes, and there's a little bit of smoke coming out of the barrel, and my eyes are focused on the rice on his chin, but I was with the Chinese long enough, there's no way I'd lose face. I just looked at him, and maybe my eyes crossed, I don't know, but there it was, and then finally he put the carbine down, that was the end of it, but that's the kind of thing you run into.

Then, and then there was another time, though I was not present, but it was in my group, some of us had been issued what's called jungle hammocks then, which were excellent pieces of equipment, they were terrific, you hung them between two trees, and there was mosquito netting, zipped up, and then where your head is, there was a strap where you could put a .45, see, and the Chinese for some reason really treasured .45s.

One night, this Chinese soldier carefully unzipped the zipper and reached in, grabbed the .45, and the guy in there grabbed the Chinese and started to yell and the Americans got the Chinese. They notified his commanding officer, who came and ordered the soldier to dig his grave, and then he knelt in it and the Chinese officer took his pistol, killed him, but we all knew it was the Chinese officer that sent him to get the pistol, see. And that's what they did, and that's sort of typical.

These are vignettes. In the Battle of Myitkyina, I was with Bob Ray, who was a cameraman with the 101 Detachment OSS. The two of us were up with the 88th Chinese Regiment, as I remember it, and we were in the process of taking cover in a bomb crater. There were some Japs occupying a building up ahead, and the Chinese were wheeling a 37mm cannon. It had the wheel that came out of the arsenal on one side, and the other side was a wheel that came off a yak cart, one of the ancient wooden wheels. It was such a funny sight, but they were firing at the Japs, and the Japs were firing back, and also firing at Bob and myself. I hear something behind me, and I turn and look, and there's this little Chinese soldier, with a little pair of blue shorts made of parachute silk, and a white T-shirt made of parachute silk. And he's got a carrying stick, and on each side he had wooden boxes of British grenades he was bringing forward, and he came running forward, and I was yelling, 'Xiàng xià,' 'Down, down,' 'bad, it's bad, down!' and he came right to the edge of our bomb crater, and he looked down, and I grabbed for his leg to pull him in, and bango, he got it right dead center, he slid down and he looked at me, and he said, 'Méiguānxì,' that means, 'it doesn't matter,' and he died. That was the end of it, but you know, the Chinese, in those days, lived a day and a half away from salvation, all their lives, and they had a different point of view.

Newsreel Wong

So, now we get back to Merrill's Marauders—there's a lot of digression, but I'm either blessed or cursed with total recall, but I have it, take my word. So I would go out, for instance, with Newsreel Wong, you ever hear of him? Very famous, he was on the *Panay*, the gunboat that the Japs shot up, but he was a very famous cameraman, the reason he was called 'Newsreel' was so *News of the Day*, who he worked for, could reach him in China, because there's a million Wongs, see, so the Newsreel separated him from a million other Wongs. He is famous for making that shot of the little baby crying at the railroad station in Shanghai when the Japs bombed the railroad station, and this probably did more to hurt the Japanese than almost any action prior to that shot, I mean, everybody related to that baby.

Original caption: 'This terrified baby was one of the only human beings left alive in Shanghai's South Station after the brutal Japanese bombing in China.' H. S. Wong (1900–1981), Public Domain.

But Wong could travel anywhere, he could go to the Communists [or the Nationalists] in China, he was welcome anywhere, because I guess he probably did a rather disinterested job in a way, he didn't editorialize. So he shows up here, and he and I become friendly. And so I said, 'Let's get down to the front, let's see what's happening,' so I borrow a jeep from headquarters, and we get down, but we're stopped down the combat trace and there's all these tanks in line. This was Colonel Roswell Brown's Chinese American tank group. In those days they had the light tanks, and the Japs had climbed these trees, and they had picric acid, an explosive, about 10 inches square block, about 2 inches thick, with a hole drilled in it, that you had to put a fuse. But as these tanks came under these trees, these Japs jumped down on top of the tanks, lit the fuse, and tamped it with their bodies, and right into these five tanks, knocked them out. I see Newsreel chattering with this Chinese officer, and pretty soon I see Newsreel Wong lining up Chinese soldiers and directing them. So I said, 'The hell with that!'

There was a mopping-up platoon going into the mountain pass that separated the Hukawng Valley from another. The Japs were dug in there, and their line of defense there had been ruptured, so I went up with this platoon, and we were going to mop up there. Their defenses were dug under banyan trees. Now, banyan trees are at least fifteen feet in diameter, huge trees, and they dug in their machine guns underneath the roots of these trees, so even our artillery did nothing. Those are huge trees. When my back was turned while I was shooting film, a Nip threw a grenade at me, and he was killed immediately, so I went up, I got some very good footage. I sent it in with Newsreel Wong's footage, and when I tried to get it after the war, *News of the Day* owned it, see, I couldn't even get it, but in any event, it was amazing.

Anyhow, I finish up with my job, I get down, and Newsreel's done with his, and now we're driving back to headquarters, and I'm not saying anything.

And so we finally get to the basha hut, and he says, 'Dave,' in his Chinese, English accent, he said, 'You are upset with me, Dave.'

I said, 'Of course I am, what you did is phony.' I said, 'We don't direct action, we photograph action, we don't direct it!

He said, 'Dave, a dead cameraman is good to no one,' and he said, 'The Japanese have $50,000 gold on my head!' When you think of 1942, that's a lot of money. And that's because of the baby shot, that wounded them terribly, worldwide, but I wouldn't let up, I told him it was not right. I did see a review from a British BBC researcher. I met her later, by the way, she gave me all her notes, and she said it was obvious that this is all directed action, because there's no movement. [Now, when she looked at my work, she said that] obviously the camera was on a tripod, the greatest compliment I've ever had, but I'd lean against trees and steady it.

Going AWOL

I am now Stilwell's motion picture cameraman, but I rarely had a chance to photograph him—he was a busy guy, mostly in his tent, actually. I went up north up the Hukawng River and photographed the aftermath of a tank battle, and I was getting short of film. I was near Meng Kwan, which was an airstrip, so I went back there, and at that point, they were evacuating Marauders, and we had a unit of four or five men in there, so I happened to look up as an L-5 came in, and there was Marvin Kirsten, one of the cameramen, so I went up to him, and I said, 'What's going on, Marvin?'

He told me that Anderson had died of cerebral malaria, and he had malaria and other digestive problems, and that Lieutenant Lubin was still in there, but when I got up there, Lubin was on a mule, and the mule bucked, and he broke his leg, and so there's nobody there. So I drove back to Stilwell's headquarters, and Clancy Topp, who was a captain, gave me an official document and I opened it.

S. Sgt. Signal Corps cameraman David L. Quaid peers out from the door of the ruined American Mission School at Myitkyina after the battle, August 1, 1944. Photographer T/4 Shearer. U.S. Signal Corps, Public domain.

It said, 'To Sergeant David L. Quaid, serial number 32355750, you are hereby directed to proceed without delay to Ledo, Assam, India, to become NCO in charge of the photographic unit documenting the construction of the Ledo Road. Sign by endorsement.'

So I told Clancy, 'Clancy, I'm leaving, I'm going in with the Marauders.' I said, 'There's nobody in there,' and I was a professional, you gotta understand, even though I was a young kid, I was a pro. 'It's an intolerable situation,' I said. 'I'm going in!'

'No, you're supposed to be here!'

'I'm going in.'

'What about this letter?'

I said, 'Send it back through channels.'

I was AWOL by my own signature, okay, I figured, you know, they'll catch up to me someday, and I'll go to Leavenworth, what the hell, but I'll be damned if I was gonna just not take care of what I thought was my problem, my responsibility. So I show my little badge to the guy that ran the L-5s, and then I started out.

Traversing the Mountains

I started to photograph the march over the mountains; I got some fantastic footage of General Merrill and General Stilwell, in the middle. He flew in right after me, and we're getting the last air drop of the camp, of the move down the mountains to Myitkyina. I got these fantastic shots of the two of them talking, and with a plane just going right over their heads, you know, all this beautiful stuff, but I kept following them, you know, with my camera, and when you look at the footage, you wonder what the hell they're doing, because they're walking this way, they're walking this way, they're walking that way, they're walking this way, and the whole thing is that they're discussing these final marching orders, secret. Here I am stuffing the camera in their noses, and they're trying to avoid me, and then finally they walk to his hut. And so I go trotting my way up to him and his big MP [grabs me] by the chest and says, 'Out.' But you understand, those two guys, you know, they were lieutenant general and major general. They could have done anything to me, but they knew I was doing my job. You know, it was amazing. I think kindly of them.[20] So then finally, when Stilwell

---

[20] General Stilwell remains a controversial figure in Marauder veteran circles. General Merrill and Colonel Hunter promised the men much needed

left, I spoke to Merrill and I said, 'Hey, General, I'm going to come along with you. Any objections?'

Brig. General Frank Merrill and Lt. General Joseph Stilwell. Burma, 1944. U.S. Signal Corps (Photographer David Quaid?) Public domain.

---

rest following the airfield fight; instead, Stilwell insisted that the exhausted men continue the fight for the city of Myitkyina in support of the Chinese in the weeks that followed, as long as they could walk and hold a rifle. Men were falling asleep under fire; one disgruntled soldier was overheard to have said, "I had him in my rifle sights. No one would have known it wasn't a Jap that got the son-of-a-bitch." In later conflicts with Chiang Kai-shek, he was relieved of command and returned to the United States, where he died in 1946 at the age of 63 after surgery for stomach cancer.

"I had him in my rifle sights"- Source: Tuchman, Barbara. *Stilwell and the American Experience in China, 1911-45*. New York: Macmillan, 1971. Page 539.

'Not a one; come on along.'

So after that, it was over the mountains, which was very difficult because the monsoons started that day, and we lost 18 miles off the trail. The Kachins said that the trail had not been used in ten years to begin with, and mules absolutely could never make it. Well, Merrill sent a platoon with Kachins and some of our men up, and we actually had to cut steps, to get the sure-footed mules up the cliff, but finally, eighteen of them fell and went over. When I heard the rifle fire, they were putting them out of their misery, but I thought, 'My God, already, and we've hit the enemy!' Actually, in the footage, if you ever see it, you can see where we would have to take the saddles off the mules. The saddles weighed 96 pounds. And then we'd have to put the saddles on men and have them climb up until you hit a place where the mules could handle it. It was pretty rugged, then I know they said, 'From now on, according to the maps, it's sort of all downhill.' It was worse than before, and it was terrible.

'I'm No Damned Volunteer'

So we finally hit a place called Ritpong. The Japanese had a full company there. The Chinese 88th Regiment was following us, and as the British term it, they were unbloodied, they'd never been in a fight, but it was determined that they would attack there. There were a lot of men doing it. They used to actually blow a bugle, and attack on a bugle. But anyhow, they did that. And before it was all over, myself and another photographer by the name of Warren Bucklin, who was with the *St. Louis Post-Dispatch* in peacetime, went up. Now, the Kachins used to, in the mountains, they would find a grove of large bamboo, eight or ten inches in diameter. And they would dig a trench around that. In the rainy season, all the rain would settle in and then suck up into the bamboo, and then when they had to travel through in dry season, they could cut into that and have water. So we saw a young soldier taking protection in one of these circles, and we jumped in with him and started to talk to him. His name was Page, P-A-G-E. He was telling me he came from Anniston, Alabama, and it was his birthday. I asked him why he volunteered for this.

'I'm no damn volunteer!'

I don't know how he got involved, but he was no damn volunteer. But at that point, the sergeant went by. An order had come to this platoon to move forward toward Ritpong, and the sergeant left to get more detailed orders. When he came back, I'll never forget Page saying, 'Sarge, did you talk him out of it? Sarge, did you talk him out of it?' Apparently, they didn't, because we started to move forward, and I lost track of Page. Suddenly, I heard this loud bang, like an M1, and this whimper-like cry.

I said, 'Well, we got one of them.'

We got some Chinese stretcher bearers in. They rolled this person on the stretcher, and who was it but young Page, on his birthday.

We had a guy of Swedish descent who was a medic and a conscientious objector. He volunteered for the Marauders, even though he carried no weapon. He said, 'Well, the volunteers are gonna need medical help.' And so he was a conscientious objector who did it through real conviction. He got Page out and we took a parachute and made a little aid station out of it. Captain Armstrong, one of our surgeons, was taking care of Page; I photographed Page, and Tony Colombo, Colonel Beach's runner, stayed with Page all night, kidding him along.

PFC Anthony Columbo

We had just gotten back from having about 20 or 30 wounded Chinese soldiers. They were all chewed up, and we got a call that

Page had been hurt, and hurt badly. I went out with Dr. Armstrong, we set up a makeshift operation. I was no medic, but I just helped him. He was talking. He was coherent for the earlier part of the evening, and then he started to fade and fade away. He was afraid, and we knew he was going. He was going to die. I don't know. It's hard to explain. I was nineteen years old. He was eighteen. From what I understand, that was his birthday. I just sat there and held his hand. He lay there until I don't know what time in the morning, and then just expired.

David Quaid

Page died that night on his 18th birthday. [*Pauses*] Nice kid.

'The Most Important Thing In This Outfit'

Then, the whole idea, tactically, was for us to handle the Ritpong situation and let A Battalion slide through unnoticed and go down a trail to Myitkyina. We were a diversion. So we were sent again over the mountains to a place where we ran into this reinforced Jap battalion, and our first scout was killed, but we held there for two days, and I photographed real jungle combat. You could actually see the bullets flying through the trees and all that sort of business. But then, let's say there's a lull, so I wanted to see what had happened with our guys. One guy next to me was firing rifle grenades that killed a Japanese warrant officer and two privates. I wanted to find out what had happened, and I slid off this area down to a trail. It was a high bank that I came down, and then I found a place where I could reload the camera. And now I started up the trail, right down the middle of it, and Bill Toomey, a machine gunner, was setting his heavy machine gun into the tripod. He saw me, and he said, 'Dave, Dave, what are you doing?'

I suddenly realized that I was walking right up the middle of the trail, which no one does. And at that point a Jap machine gun opened up, and the guy was very good. He walked it right down, and he expected me to fall; he walked the bullets right up the trail. Only I went to the right, where the trail fell off, and the Jap followed me, and I heard this 'sock,' like a meat cleaver hitting a side of beef. I rolled down, and I ended up behind about an eight-inch tree. And I'll never forget I heard this tinkle, tinkle, tinkle. And I sort of looked up without lifting my head; it was his machine gun bullets going right through the tree, and stuff was hitting my helmet. Father Barrett and Captain Armstrong had a theory that if you got to a man right away with plasma, and a friendly word, chances are he would not go into shock. So they would follow the skirmish line right up and do this. I heard Colonel Meade say, 'Damn it, you're my chaplain, and you're my medic. I order you to stop that. Lie back. We'll get the men to you!' They wouldn't do it. So suddenly, I saw Armstrong and Barrett come in. And I thought what I saw was that I photographed all of it, and Barrett was giving Toomey the last rites.

The Chinese stretcher bearers took him out. At the time, you see, you were not allowed to shoot, to photograph, American casualties during the war. I made up my mind—I was going to photograph Toomey. I mean, here's this guy, if it wasn't for him, I would have been dead, and the least I'd do is memorialize him. And so I photographed him being wrapped in his poncho and buried.

The guys were furious at me. They thought it was terrible. And Father Barrett gave a lecture, saying Dave was probably doing the most important thing in this outfit, showing people what war is really like, and so the guys laid off after that.

After the war, my young daughter was registered into a little parochial school in New York. And it was only six classes; they were building [the infrastructure] as they got money. So I came home one night from the studio, and there was this request for money, there's a few memorials left. And one of them were the bells that would be rung when the school was to change classes. So I said to my wife, I said, 'We're going to buy that bell for Toomey.' I said, 'He's buried in Buddhist country, but I think he may be a Catholic boy, and every time those bells ring, it will also call the attention of the Buddhist spirits where he's buried.'

So that's what we did. And his family has gotten in touch with me, and I actually sent them the footage. I told them, you got to understand you're going to see your brother get killed, better know what you're looking at.

*

After two days, we felt we had held up. We had allowed A Battalion to go for the airstrip. So then we started south, to get on the main trail south, and what I do remember vividly, of course, is it was a night march, and we were almost to Myitkyina, and I heard this sigh, and then something fell.

The next thing I knew, I tripped over a dead horse and fell. The horse had worked himself to death. Mules will not do that. A mule will stop and get its breath, but you can work a horse to that, and this one just died on its feet.

We come out on this Jap road, and what I remember is most of us are aghast when we look at the footage. We just walked down this road without flankers out or anything. A little strange, so, anyhow, they needed us at the airstrip. So Dave Richardson of *Yank Magazine* and myself went across with A.B. Weingarten's platoon to get to the airstrip. [Now, to get film out], I would send footage out with wounded men on a litter, I'd get plasma boxes from the medics, and I sent out two boxes of film. They went with the wounded until they hit Arang, which was a clandestine OSS airstrip. The plane took off again with a wounded man and my film and crashed into a tree; it was too short, but nobody was hurt, strangely enough. But they took my film and everything else they could on the plane and threw it into a drainage ditch. Dave Richardson of *Yank Magazine*, who was with the Marauders all the way from beginning to end, would have to leave after a portion of each campaign to go back and write up his stuff. So he flew into Arang to join up with us again. And he got out of the plane and saw two boxes of film. One is still up in the L-5 in a tree, but one box of film had my name on it. And he redirected it to the chief signal officer, New Delhi, India, before his pilot, who was flying back empty, could take off, he got it into the plane. Yeah, otherwise it wouldn't exist. [They made newsreel footage out of it]; oh yeah, it's very famous. It's really the only combat film that exists in the Marauders. There are plenty of very, very good stills.

Hit By a C-47 Air Drop

I'm the only human being that ever got hit from a free drop from a C-47 and survived. Yeah, I did. In fact, just in June, I've had this leg fixed from that. Unfortunately, I was opening a window at home, and I fell, and I'm afraid they were going to have to do it all over again. Terrible. I could go on and on and on forever. [But my war ended], and I can tell you that exactly. So, this was a Thanksgiving airdrop. And the president said, 'Wherever your sons or daughters are, on land or sea or in the air, they will have a turkey dinner.' And I was photographing this airdrop, to prove that the whole thing was a lie. [*Laughs*] And so I got hit with... now see, the trouble was that the first- and second-string troop carriers had been rotated home. They were great. We used to say they didn't drop to us, they stacked it, because if it went into the trees, it was gone. So these guys were special.

Now, they brought an outfit in from the ETO surplus unit, and they were dropping right on our trail, and they didn't have their radio on. One of our officers said, 'Get me two BAR men up here, and if this son of a doesn't turn on the radio, shoot him down!' And then they started the free drop of mule feed, well, that goes off in about thirty to forty 70-pound bags at a time. I heard them coming, and I was a good swimmer as a kid, and so I made a racing dive, but it caught me in the air. And if I had my feet planted, I would have been Jello. The force is so unbelievable. In fact, Captain Worley, a medic, came up to me. I mean, while this is still going on. Brave man. He says, 'Sergeant, how does it feel to jump off the Empire State Building?' And then there was a long pause. He said, 'And live?'

Then they started to drop the heavy stuff on parachutes, and there was one coming down directly on me, and I yelled to my buddy, I said, 'Bill, Bill, it's going to hit me!' And he stood up, and he said, 'Don't worry about it!' Oh, he tried to catch it; he would have been mud. But it just missed my feet, and so he didn't have to commit himself.

They put me on a plane. The morphine wouldn't work, they kept giving me syrette after syrette of morphine. Finally, I went out. I was at the 14th Evacuation Hospital.

I woke up, and there was an orderly with a flashlight.

'Hey, can you do something about that guy? He's moaning all the time. I can't sleep.'

The [orderly shrugged]. He says, 'Sergeant, you're the only one in here!'

So finally, they finally flew me back to 20th General Hospital. They hung me up in traction for five months; in fact, I have an eight-by-ten shot of Lady Mountbatten visiting me, and here I am with all these wires. I looked like a Wright biplane, you know? And so anyhow, then it came time to go home.

'I Had Never Cried In My Life'

This is what you really want. And they were packing me into a...
[*pauses*] —I'll tell you something—I cried, and I never had cried in
my life. When they were going to ship me home, I wanted to go
back. I wanted to, I told myself and my friends that we weren't going to quit until we hit Shanghai. And I felt terrible. And so anyhow,
a captain comes in and gives me wads of postal money orders, wads
of them, because I never took any pay, I was always gone. And then
he says, 'Raise your right hand, Sergeant.'

'Why?'

He said, 'Well, you got a field commission, but you've never been
sworn in. So you've got to be sworn in.'

I said, 'Wait a minute.'

I said, 'Captain, can I do duty in the rank of a second lieutenant?'

He looked at me now—I was in a cast from here to the bottom
with a stick across the legs, and he said, 'Sergeant, I don't see a
chance.'

I said, 'Well, I'm not going to take any rank that I can't do duty
in, period,' and I turned it down. So then they put me on an airplane, and they fly me to Casablanca. Now, by this time, I got kidney
stones from lying on my back for five months and them pouring in
calcium because bones don't knit in the tropics. They give me
enough morphine to handle the kidneys, and now they're going to
take me to this airplane. They put me in a forklift truck and stuffed
me in the door. And there's these two big white-clad orderlies, and
they grab me, and [they can't get me in the doorway].

'Okay. Turn him over.'

'Try it this way.'

'Try it that way.' Then, finally, they get me in by breaking the
cast in many places. Now, we take off, and out came one of the officers, and the flight nurse. She goes down to the ambulatory guy,

the first ambulatory guy. 'In the event of ditching, you put this over your neck, your thighs, by here, blah, blah, blah.' Yeah. Then she goes to the next guy, and the next guy, and the next guy, and then the last of the ambulatory guys. The two of them turn around and look at me, then they look at each other. She pats me on the forehead and says, 'Sergeant, don't be concerned. Regulations say, in case of ditching, the litter patients are offloaded first.' Oh God. [*Laughs*]

Then we landed in Florida, and they took me to Coral Gables Hotel Hospital, which was an Air Force hospital. They wheel me in on a gurney, and there's everybody crying.

I said, 'What the hell's going on here?' Somebody had passed. 'What's the matter with you people?'

'What's the matter with you? The president died!' That was when President Roosevelt died at Warm Springs.

"You're The Guy I've Been Looking For'

I had a long way to go. I'll give you one more. We set off to Rhodes General Hospital, which was for bones and stuff. I was a motion picture cameraman, so obviously I'm a projectionist. When I could get around, one of the things I had to do was wheel a projector around and show these combat films, including a lot of my own stuff, to these guys, because the war was still on and they're going to go to the Pacific. They didn't want them to lose their edge. But I would leave some of these wards afterwards with these guys [bouncing] off the ceiling, you know? So much for psychiatry. [*Laughs*]

So, I was supposed to help a captain on some photographic problem they had. He came in, and he was incoherent. He was trying to describe how one bomb could blow up a city, and he couldn't do it, because there wasn't much information at that point. I do remember when we heard that the war was finally over. We heard at night, and someone started to sing Christmas carols. That's what we sang all night.

Every Saturday, the board would come through. That's all these doctors, and they would go over your case, then they would board you in or out. Either you'd stay for treatment, or you would be boarded or discharged out to a veterans hospital. They kept saying, 'You're going to be sent to a veterans hospital.'

I said, 'Cut it out! You guys didn't give me the proper PT treatments,' which they didn't. I said, 'You guys get it fixed. I'm not leaving.' Well, I held them off. Then they finally say, 'This Saturday, you're out.' So, I was supposed to go down to the MP shack, like, you know, at the gate and everything where there'll be a bus to take me to the train to take me to some other place. Now, this one leg was at right angles, frozen like this. But I was on crutches, and I was good at crutches. So finally, the bus comes in, and some guys get on it. I get on it, and I'm up about two steps. A jeep comes around the corner. This black, curly-haired guy said, 'Sergeant! Sergeant! You get out. Get down there.'

I said, 'Who the hell are you?' and it was a major. 'What do you want?'

He said, 'This bus is for discharge. You're not ready for that.' I said, 'Who are you?' He said, 'I'm Major Perlman. I'm in charge of orthopedics. Get off there, come with me.'

He brought me into the MP shack, measured me. Laid me out on the desk, and he said, 'Now look, Sergeant, get in the jeep. You're going back. First of all, I want to know who boarded you out. Second, yeah, we can probably help you.'

He said, 'We can put you in what's called a turnbuckle cast that has a hinge here, and has a lead screw. You're going to have to take up two turns a day in that screw to break this loose.'

He said, 'It's going to hurt like hell for three months. But I guarantee you that you'll walk with a cane, or you'll walk without any. But you won't be on crutches.'

I said, 'Man, you're the guy I've been looking for!'

We did just that, and I ended up walking for six years on this leg. We needed more treatment, but yeah. Now, it's 1948. I always swore if I ever got into Cincinnati, where he was a big shot at George Hospital in Cincinnati, I said I had to go in and thank Major Perlman. So, it was a Saturday, and Truman was just about to be elected. So I went in and spoke to his receptionist, and she said, 'Just wait till we get rid of this load. I know the major is going to want to talk to you.' So he comes out, he recognized me right away. Well, we spent three months together. Then he bullied me because I wasn't exercising my thigh, and, you know, he said, 'Now look, how long are you going to be here?'

I said, 'I'm making a picture for Proctor & Gamble.' I said, 'I'll be here, you know, probably a couple more weeks at least. More than that maybe.'

He said, 'My wife's a great cook. I'm off on Wednesdays. How about you come to my house on Wednesday? My wife, I'm sure she's going to want to meet you.'

I said, 'Sure. Fine.'

So, Tuesday afternoon, somebody kicked a light, and I jumped off the camera crane and caught my heel in a camera cable. I went down on a deck, and I broke my arm. So, everybody wants to get me to the hospital and all the sort. I said, 'No way. No one touches me but Major Perlman.'

So, I went back to the Netherland Plaza Hotel. I had a copy of the *Weekend New York Times*, I got the magazine section. I wrapped it around the arm, and we have what we call camera tape, which is white tape. I wrap the whole thing in it. I went to sleep this way, up to my chest. Next morning, I grab a cab. Before that, I called them up. I said, 'Major, Dave Quaid.'

'My wife is very happy, we got everything set. It's going to be a wonderful evening.'

I said, 'Wait a minute. Hey, Major, we have to talk business.'

'What do you mean by that?'

I said, 'I broke my arm.'

'Please, meet me at George Hospital. I'll meet you over there.'

So I get to George Hospital. I identified myself, and the receptionist breaks up. 'Ha ha ha ha. So you're Mr. Quaid, who he has to fix up all the time. Ha ha ha ha.' You know? Finally, he got me repaired, and then it was time to go home. So he said, 'I don't want you to go home. I want to handle your recovery myself.' Then he said, 'But who's your doctor?'

I said, 'Dr. Rosenthal, in Richmond Hill.'

He said, 'Abner Rosenthal?'

I said, 'Yeah!'

He said, 'He was my roommate for four years in medical school!' See, it never stops. All right, that's enough.

John Easterbrook, retired U.S. Army colonel and grandson of General Joseph W. Stilwell, noted about Quaid's work and the estimated 23,000 pictures in total taken by the 250 men of the 164th Signal Photo Company: 'They made a significant contribution to the knowledge of Chinese history during the Allies-Japanese war. In some small way, these photographs also provided recognition of the American assistance to the Chinese people during those hard and difficult days.'[20]

David Quaid featured in a 1952 camera advertisement.

After the war, David Quaid went into commercial cinematography and direction, filming the very first television commercial (for Ipana toothpaste) and working in Hollywood feature films. He passed on August 19, 2010, at the age of 90.

*Surrender ceremonies, 2,000 plane flyover,
USS MISSOURI left foreground.
National Archives. Public domain.*

Afterword

"It is my earnest hope, and indeed the hope of all mankind, that from this solemn occasion a better world shall emerge out of the blood and carnage of the past—a world founded upon faith and understanding, a world dedicated to the dignity of man and the fulfillment of his most cherished wish for freedom, tolerance, and justice."

—Remarks By General Douglas MacArthur, Surrender Ceremony Ending The War With Japan And World War II, September 2, 1945

"Can't we just let go of this war? My father spent four years in, [and] my uncles four years; they NEVER talked about it! Long dead soldiers, long ago war!"

-Adult American commenter on one of the author's social media posts, highlighting the series, *The Things Our Fathers Saw*, September 2024

*

Was it really that long ago?

Seventy-nine years ago this month, Admiral 'Bull' Halsey's flagship USS *Missouri* was in Tokyo Bay awaiting the arrival of the Japanese delegation with General MacArthur and Admiral Nimitz aboard, positioned near the spot where Commodore Matthew C. Perry had anchored his 'Black Ships' on his first visit to Japan in 1853. On display aboard the battleship that morning was the flag that flew on December 7, 1941 over Hickam Field at Pearl Harbor, and the 31-starred Old Glory standard of Perry's flagship from nearly a century before, now accompanied by hundreds of American warships. The Japanese delegation was escorted promptly aboard at 9:00 a.m., and at MacArthur's invitation, signed the terms of surrender. As if on cue, four hundred gleaming B-29 bombers roared slowly by in the skies overhead, escorted by fifteen hundred fighters.[21]

In the United States and Europe, it was six years to the day that the bloodiest conflict in human history had begun; after those six years of savage fighting, the devastation was unprecedented and incalculable. Between sixty and eighty-five million people—the exact figure will never be known—would be dead. Overseas, the victors would be forced to deal with rubble-choked cities and tens of millions of people on the move, their every step dogged with desperation, famine, and moral confusion. American servicemen, battle-hardened but weary, would be forced to deal with the collapse of civilization and brutally confronted with the evidence of industrial-scale genocide. Old empires were torn asunder, new ones were on the ascent. The Chinese Communists were victorious in China before the end of the decade; the British and other colonial powers began shedding their colonies in South Asia and elsewhere. In 1952, American occupation ended, lasting nearly twice as long as the war with America itself.

Now, the 'American Century' was well underway. American power and leadership of the free world was unparalleled and unprecedented. The Marshall Plan literally saved Europe. Enemies became allies. Former allies became adversaries. The Atomic Age began. And the United States of America rebuilt, reconstructed, and remodeled Japan. Of course, this 'American Century' was not free from hubris, error, and tragic mistakes, but all of this is part of the legacy that shapes us to this day.

*

In regards to the end of World War II, I can recall, in the early 1980s as a young history teacher in training, observing a veteran teacher describing the end of the war with Japan by making an analogy to his eighth graders:

'It's like two brothers who had a fight. The winner picks up the loser, dusts him off, and they go on as brothers and friends.'

Overlooked, perhaps, were the eight million Chinese civilians and millions of others in Asia slaughtered by Japanese troops in their imperial lust for conquest, the Allied prisoners of war brutalized and worked to death or executed in slave labor camps, the Allied seamen shot while foundering in the water at the explicit orders of the Japanese Imperial Navy, to say nothing of the deceitfulness of Pearl Harbor. I'm sure my twenty minutes observing the teacher in action left out what he hopefully covered in class; he must have known World War II veterans, just as I did. And these are things I suppose you learn later in life, as I did—but only because I wanted to know as much as I could learn. I was born sixteen years after the killing stopped, but ripples of that war have never ended.

If you are a reader of this series, you know how I got our veterans involved once I found my footing in my own classroom. My fascination with World War II began with the comic books of my 1970s pre-teen days, Sgt. Rock and Easy Company bursting off the pages in the bedroom I shared with my younger brothers at 2 Main Street. As a newly minted college grad a decade later, I was drawn to the spectacle of our veterans returning to the beaches of Normandy on the black-and-white TV in my apartment for the fortieth anniversary of D-Day. I was reading the only oral history compilation I was aware of, Studs Terkel's euphemistically titled 1984 release, *The Good War: An Oral History of World War II*, over and over. I studied that book, planting the seed for my own debut in the classroom. And in retrospect, I think I reached out to my students asking them if they knew anyone in World War II, yes, as a way to engage them in the lessons at hand, but also to satisfy my own selfish curiosity: just what 'resources'—really national treasures—did we have in our own backyard, surrounding our high school? I was going to find out. Man, was I going to find out!

Of course they 'never talked' about it! Why would they bring 'The War' up with their wives, their sons, their daughters? And frankly, most of the civilians they returned home to and surrounded themselves with at work, in the community, and even in their own families, weren't really all that interested in hearing about it. It was time to get on with life.

But then those guys headed back to the Normandy beachheads, now approaching retirement age, most in their early sixties, if that (about my age right now) ...

Somebody was now listening! Somebody gave a damn! And maybe the old soldier could talk about that kid who was shot and lingered on for a while in the far-off jungles of Burma, the country boy far from home who was proud to be a soldier, the eighteen-year-old who wondered now if he was going to die. The combat photographer David Quaid spoke to his interviewers until he was too exhausted to go on. But somebody was interested, and he had things to say—things to get off his chest—before he would no longer be able to say them; like David, a lot of the guys I knew opened up like a pressurized firehose after all those years of silence. It was frankly cathartic, and maybe now they could 'let go of this war.'

Should we?

*

I didn't respond to the commenter in the thread, but another person added,

"I understand, but if there is no conversation, nothing gets shared— nothing gets learned! May your family all rest in peace!"

I know in my heart that opening up to others, even complete strangers, but especially to the young, finally brought our veterans peace.

*

A Final Thought

"I don't want to see [that] we are in a history book, and a page is turned, and we are forgotten." 9/11 FDNY firefighter, 2024, in tears, called off at the last moment by a friend who took her place. Three hundred forty-three of her brothers and sisters died that day.

I finished this 10th volume on the 23rd anniversary of the 9/11 attacks; watching CBS's *60 Minutes* that Sunday before, I was struck profoundly by that firefighter's tears.

Which brings me to my final thoughts. Over the past nine years, I've strung together over a million words out of the mouths of our World War II veterans and Holocaust survivors. People will ask me now, are you going to continue to tell their stories of World War II? Are you going to do books involving oral histories of other American wars? The answer is, maybe; I just don't know. When I was actively collecting stories, the priority was on the oldest veterans still with us, and frankly many of the veterans of following wars and conflicts were just not ready yet; I know some of them felt in some degree intimidated by the World War II generation, and we know, of course, that many of our Vietnam veterans were mistreated when they returned home. What I think I really would like to do with the time I have left is help other teachers bring them into the classroom, connecting with our young people, keeping our history alive. School leaders need to recognize the importance of strengthening their community by encouraging the type of oral history projects that, in our case, have literally helped to heal the world; in fact, look for the four-part miniseries on my book *A Train Near Magdeburg* in 2025, in time for the eightieth anniversary of liberation and the end of World War II. I hope our work will inspire our teachers and school and community and political leaders to see the value of our veterans and this type of history education with our young people as a national resource for learning about our past.

I also plan on working on a much-needed sequel to *A Train Near Magdeburg*, having learned so much more, meeting and interviewing so many more soldiers, survivors, and second-generation survivors since that book's 2016 debut, not to mention all of the subsequent visits to the authentic sites of persecution and liberation, and connecting with the German schoolkids who are bravely keeping the history alive in their own backyard.

So, rest assured, I do have a few more books in me. I'll keep looking through my notebooks, getting ideas, keeping the history alive. With you and others reading, listening to, and embracing their stories, maybe our veterans and their friends won't be long dead. In the meantime, as always, thank you for your investment of time with us, and please keep sharing our *raison d'être*:

Dying for freedom isn't the worst that could happen.
Being forgotten is.

IF YOU LIKED THIS BOOK, you'll love hearing more from the World War II generation in my other books. I can let you know as soon as the new books are out, give you film updates, and offer you exclusive discounts on some material. Just sign up at matthewrozellbooks.com

Some of my readers may like to know that all of my books are **directly available from the author, with collector's sets which can be autographed** in paperback and hardcover. They are popular gifts for that 'hard-to-buy-for' guy or gal on your list.

Visit my shop at matthewrozellbooks.com for details.

THE THINGS OUR FATHERS SAW® SERIES:

VOICES OF THE PACIFIC THEATER

WAR IN THE AIR: GREAT DEPRESSION TO COMBAT

WAR IN THE AIR: COMBAT, CAPTIVITY, REUNION

UP THE BLOODY BOOT-THE WAR IN ITALY

D-DAY AND BEYOND

THE BULGE AND BEYOND

ACROSS THE RHINE

ON TO TOKYO

HOMEFRONT/WOMEN AT WAR

CHINA, BURMA, INDIA

ALSO: A TRAIN NEAR MAGDEBURG

ABOUT THE AUTHOR

Photo Credit: Joan K. Lentini; May 2017.

Matthew Rozell is an award-winning history teacher, author, speaker, and blogger on the topic of the most cataclysmic events in the history of mankind—World War II and the Holocaust. Rozell has been featured as the 'ABC World News Person of the Week' and has had his work as a teacher filmed for the CBS Evening News, NBC Learn, the Israeli Broadcast Authority, the United States Holocaust Memorial Museum, and the New York State United Teachers. He writes on the power of teaching and the importance of the study of history at TeachingHistoryMatters.com, and you can 'Like' his Facebook author page at MatthewRozellBooks for updates.

Mr. Rozell is a sought-after speaker on World War II, the Holocaust, and history education, motivating and inspiring his audiences with the lessons of the past. Visit MatthewRozell.com for availability/details.

About this Book/
Acknowledgements

*

A note on historiographical style and convention: to enhance accuracy, consistency, and readability, I corrected punctuation and spelling and sometimes even place names, but only after extensive research. I did take the liberty of occasionally condensing the speaker's voice, eliminating side tangents or incidental information not relevant to the matter at hand. Sometimes two or more interviews with the same person were combined for readability and narrative flow. All of the words of the subjects, however, are essentially their own.

Additionally, I chose to utilize footnotes and endnotes where I deemed them appropriate, directing readers who wish to learn more to my sources, notes, and side commentary. I hope that they do not detract from the flow of the narrative.

First, I wish to acknowledge the hundreds of students who passed through my classes and who forged the bonds with the World War II generation. I promised you these books someday, and now that many of you are yourselves parents, you can tell your children this book is for them. Who says young people are indifferent to the past? Here is evidence to the contrary.

The Hudson Falls Central School District and my former colleagues have my deep appreciation for supporting this endeavor and recognizing its significance throughout the years.

Cara Quinlan's sharp proofing and suggestions helped to clean up the original manuscript.

Naturally this work would not have been possible had it not been for the willingness of the veterans to share their stories for posterity, with the New York State Military Museum's Veterans Oral History Project and the Library of Congress Veterans Oral History Project. Please see the 'Source Notes.'

I would be remiss if I did not recall the profound influence of my late mother and father, Mary and Tony Rozell, both cutting-edge educators and proud early supporters of my career. To my younger siblings Mary, Ned, Nora, and Drew, all accomplished writers and authors, thank you for your encouragement as well. Final and deepest appreciations go to my wife Laura and our children, Emma, Ned, and Mary. Thank you for indulging the old man as he attempted to bring to life the stories he collected as a young one.

NOTES

Source Notes: **Morgan Vaux.** Interviewed by Mark D. Doud. Undated. Deposited at the Veterans History Project, American Folklife Center, Library of Congress.

Source Notes: **Emma Jane Hanks.** Interviewed by Erica Sugar. Undated. Deposited at the Library of Congress Veterans History Project.

Source Notes: **Patrick Scarano.** Interviewed by Robert von Hasseln and Michael Aikey, January 23, 2001, Syracuse, NY. Deposited at NYS Military Museum.

Source Notes: **Norman Handelman.** Interviewed by Michael Russert and Wayne Clarke, January 11, 2005. New York, NY. Deposited at NYS Military Museum.

Source Notes: **Robert D. O'Brien.** Interviewed by Michael Russert and Wayne Clarke, July 30, 2002. Latham, NY. Deposited at NYS Military Museum.

Source Notes: **Leonard R. Reeves.** Interviewed by Sharon House. May 26, 2005. Deposited at the Veterans History Project, American Folklife Center, Library of Congress.

Source Notes: **Kenneth Wilbur Thomas.** Interviewed by Tony P. Lupo. Undated. Deposited at the Veterans History Project, American Folklife Center, Library of Congress.

Source Notes: **Samuel V Wilson.** Interviewed by Mark R. Franklin. May 15, 2014. Deposited at the Veterans History Project, American Folklife Center, Library of Congress.

Source Notes: **Philip B. Piazza.** Interviewed by Christy Chason. 2005. Deposited at the Veterans History Project, American Folklife Center, Library of Congress.

Source Notes: **Morris H. Factor.** Interviewed by Gunnar Gunnarsson. October 26, 2012. Deposited at the Veterans History Project, American Folklife Center, Library of Congress.

Source Notes: **Herbert Clofine.** Interviewed by Christy Chason. 2005. Deposited at the Veterans History Project, American Folklife Center, Library of Congress.

Source Notes: **Roy Matsumoto.** Deposited at the Veterans History Project, American Folklife Center, Library of Congress.

Source Notes: **Robert E. Passanisi.** Interviewed by Carrie Schneider. 2005. Deposited at the Veterans History Project, American Folklife Center, Library of Congress.

Source Notes: **Warner Katz.** Interviewed by Sheila Dyer. 2005. Deposited at the Veterans History Project, American Folklife Center, Library of Congress.

Source Notes: **David L. Quaid.** Interviewed by Aaron Swan. 2005. Deposited at the Veterans History Project, American Folklife Center, Library of Congress.

---

[1] Hagerty, James R. Russell Hamler, Last Surviving Member of a World War II 'Marauders' Unit, Dies at 99. *The Wall Street Journal*, January 26, 2024. Page A-9.

[2] *Three quarters of a million Filipinos died*- Bamford, Tyler. The Global Impact of the Spanish-American War. Aug. 14, 2023.https://usnhistory.navylive.dodlive.mil/Recent/Article-

View/Article/3491710/the-global-impact-of-the-spanish-american-war/

[3] *half the population already had a life expectancy rate of just thirty years*-Tuchman, Barbara. *Stilwell and the American Experience in China, 1911-45*. New York: Macmillan, 1971. Page 181.

[4] *third posting to China/several staff officer positions*-Stilwell, Joseph Warren Sr. American War Memorials Overseas, Inc. https://www.uswarmemorials.org/html/people_details.php?PeopleID=1644.

[5] *drew a caricature/vinegar bottle*-Tuchman, Barbara. *Stilwell and the American Experience in China, 1911-45*. New York: Macmillan, 1971. Page 125.

[6] *Japanese government ordered the British to close the Hong Kong frontier and the Burma Road*- Tuchman, Barbara. *Stilwell and the American Experience in China, 1911-45*. New York: Macmillan, 1971. Page 257.

[7] *agreed in theory to follow a 'Europe First' policy*- Tuchman, Barbara. *Stilwell and the American Experience in China, 1911-45*. New York: Macmillan, 1971. Page 290.

[8] Tuchman, Barbara. *Stilwell and the American Experience in China, 1911-45*. New York: Macmillan, 1971. Page 261.

[9] Haight, Jr., John McVickar. *FDR's "Big Stick"*. Proceedings of the U.S. Naval Institute, Vol. 106/7/929. July 1980. www.usni.org/magazines/proceedings/1980/july/fdrs-big-stick

[10] *you have 24 hours to think up a better candidate*- Tuchman, Barbara. *Stilwell and the American Experience in China, 1911-45*. New York: Macmillan, 1971. Page 295.

[11] *I claim we got a hell of a beating*-Tuchman, Barbara. *Stilwell and the American Experience in China, 1911-45*. New York: Macmillan, 1971. Page 362.

[12] Ford, Daniel. *Flying Tigers: Claire Chennault and His American Volunteers, 1941-1942*. Smithsonian Institution Press, 1991. pp. 30–34.

[13] *'Circus Day'*- Lendon, Brad. *These American Mercenaries were the Heroes of China,* CNN, July 24, 2020.
[14] Belden, Jack. *Chennault Fights to Hold the China Front.* August 10, 1942. Life. Time Inc. p. 70.
[15] *Chennault debriefed his pilots*- Eisel, Braxton. *The Flying Tigers: Chennault's American Volunteer Group in China.* Air Force Sixtieth Anniversary Commemorative Editon, Air Force History Museums Program. United States Department of Defense. Undated, likely 2007.
[16] Norton, Thomas. *Flying Tigers Nurse Jane Hanks Dies.* General Aviation News, November 16, 2009.
[17] *aluminum plated mountain/650,000 tons were airlifted-* World War II: Time-Life Books History of the Second World War. Morristown, New Jersey: Silver Burdett, 1978. Pages 64, 80.
[18] Brooks, Drew. Warrior, diplomat and academic: Lt. Gen. Samuel V. Wilson dies at age 93. *Fayetteville Observer*, June 12, 2017. www.fayobserver.com/story/news/military/2017/06/12/warrior-diplomat-and-academic-lt-gen-samuel-v-wilson-dies-at-age-93/20606511007/
[19] Slotnik, Daniel. Samuel V. Wilson, Ex-Director of Defense Intelligence Agency, Dies at 93. *The New York Times*, June 26, 2017. www.nytimes.com/2017/06/26/us/samuel-v-wilson-dead-general-headed-defense-intelligence-agency.html
[20] Xu, Zhao. Cameras and carbines capture life during wartime. *China Daily*, August 14, 2018. www.chinadaily.com.cn/a/201508/14/WS5a2b40f7a310eefe3e99f257.html
[21] Dower, John W. *Embracing Defeat: Japan in the Wake of World War II.* New York, W. W. Norton & Company. 1999. P. 43.